Irish Migrants in Britain 1815–1914

Erskine Nicol, RSA (1825–1904) *Irish Immigrant Landing at Liverpool*,
reproduced by permission of the National Gallery of Scotland.

Irish Migrants in Britain
1815–1914
A Documentary History

edited by

ROGER SWIFT

CORK UNIVERSITY PRESS

First published in 2002 by
Cork University Press
University College
Cork
Ireland

British Library Cataloguing in Publication Data
A CIP catalogue record for this book is available from the British Library.

Library of Congress Cataloguing-in-Publication Data
Irish migrants in Britain, 1815–1914 : a documentary history / edited by
Roger Swift.
  p. cm.
 Includes bibliographical references and index.
 ISBN 1–85918–236–4 (alk. paper)
  1. Irish—Great Britain—History—19th century. 2.
Ireland—Emigration and immigration—History—19th century. 3.
Ireland—Emigration and immigration—History—20th century. 4.
Irish—Great Britain—History—20th century. I. Swift, Roger
 DA125.I7 I76 2002
 941'.0049162—dc21

                              2001042515

ISBN 1 85918 236 4 hardback

Typeset by Tower Books, Ballincollig, Co. Cork
Printed by MPG Books Ltd, Cornwall

For Sheridan Gilley

Contents

DEPARTURE AND ARRIVAL

PART 2. SETTLEMENT

INTRODUCTION   27

DISTRIBUTION IN BRITAIN

DESCRIPTIONS OF THE IRISH

LIVING CONDITIONS

PART 3. EMPLOYMENT

PART 4. SOCIAL CONDITIONS:
POVERTY, HEALTH AND CRIME

SICKNESS AND HEALTH

HOUSING

CRIMINAL ACTIVITY

PART 5. CATHOLICISM, PROTESTANTISM AND SECTARIANISM

CATHOLIC DEVOTIONS

ANTI-POPERY

ORANGEISM

SECTARIAN RIVALRIES

PART 6. RADICAL AND LABOUR MOVEMENTS

INTRODUCTION   149

RADICALISM

CHARTISM

SOCIALISM AND LABOUR

PART 7. NATIONALISM

UNION AND REPEAL

FENIANISM

HOME RULE

PART 8. UNIONISM

INTRODUCTION   197

RESISTANCE TO HOME RULE

CARSON AND COVENANT

List of Illustrations

Acknowledgements

This book has been many years in the making and its contents emanate in part from a range of materials which I assembled and utilised in the teaching of undergraduate and postgraduate courses on the Irish in Britain at the Institute of Irish Studies, University of Liverpool, between 1988 and 1990 and, subsequently, at the Centre for Victorian Studies at Chester College. A work of this kind inevitably incurs a debt of gratitude to other scholars whose work has in various ways helped to provide a contextual framework within which the sources contained in this volume can be understood, and I trust that this debt is acknowledged in the notes and select bibliography. This said, I am particularly grateful for the advice and encouragement provided by close academic friends and colleagues, including Don Akenson, Owen Ashton, John Belchem, D. George Boyce, Patrick Buckland, Nessan Danaher, Graham Davis, Marianne Elliott, Clive Emsley, Eric Evans, David Fitzpatrick, John Herson, Christine Kinealy, Elizabeth Malcolm, Mark McLaughlin, Hugh McLeod, Donald MacRaild, Frank Neal, Alan O'Day, Paul O'Leary, Patrick O'Sullivan and Dorothy Thompson. I wish to thank the National Gallery of Scotland, the National Portrait Gallery, the Tate Gallery, London, Tyne and Wear Museums Service, Wolverhampton Library and Museums Service, the Ulster Historical Foundation and Routledge for permission to reproduce copyright material. I should also like to acknowledge the support provided by Chester College, who granted me a three-month sabbatical in 1996 in which some sections of the book were completed, and by Peter Francis and the staff of St Deiniol's Library, Hawarden. My greatest debt, however, is to Sheridan Gilley, to whom this volume is dedicated.

Roger Swift
Chester, 2001

General Introduction

The past twenty years have witnessed a veritable renaissance in the historiography of the Irish in Britain, notably in the context of the Irish migrant experience during the nineteenth century, when Irish migration to Britain was most pronounced. This burgeoning historiography – in part a reflection of the development of the Irish studies movement in Britain during the 1980s – has made possible the development of a range of undergraduate and postgraduate courses devoted to the study of the history of the Irish in Britain, not merely in specialist centres such as the Institute of Irish Studies at the University of Liverpool and the Irish Studies Centres at the University of North London and Bath Spa University College but also in several other British colleges and universities. Moreover, with the advent in 1990 of the Joint Matriculation Board's new history syllabus, *Modern Irish History*, sixth-form students were provided with the opportunity to follow Advanced Supplementary and Advanced level courses on the history of the Irish in Britain between 1815 and 1914.

These developments are all the more significant in view of the fact that until the 1970s the study of the experience of Irish migrants in Britain had comprised a relatively dormant theme in modern British social history. There were, of course, some exceptions to this. Arthur Redford's *Labour Migration in England, 1800–1850*, published in 1926,[1] was the first academic study of the social and economic consequences of Irish immigration in nineteenth-century Britain. However, Redford's work, based as it was on the selective use of a limited range of primary sources, most notably Parliamentary Papers, echoed the more negative and stereotyped anti-Irish perceptions of some early nineteenth-century British commentators by depicting Irish immigration as little short of a social disaster. This thesis was subsequently challenged by the pioneering research of James Handley, whose *The Irish in Scotland, 1789–1845* (1943) and its sequel, *The Irish in Modern Scotland* (1947), presented the Irish experience in more detailed and sympathetic terms, highlighting the range of problems with which the Irish in Scotland had to contend, including popular prejudice, and exploring their contribution to the development of modern Scottish society. Handley's greatest achievement, however, was in demonstrating that the study of the Irish immigrant experience was worthy of academic enquiry, and historians of the Irish in Britain are greatly in his debt. Sadly,

---

[1] Full references to each work cited will be found in the select bibliography.

however, both studies are now out of print. A much broader, if equally sympathetic, study of the Irish experience in Britain was provided by J.A. Jackson in 1963. Following in the footsteps of Handley, but with a British focus within a broader time-span, Jackson's *The Irish in Britain* – also now out of print – emphasized both the difficulties which Irish migrants encountered in adapting to their new homeland and the positive contribution they made towards the development of British society. However, apart from the work of Redford, Handley and Jackson, E.P. Thompson's succinct revisionary essay in *The Making of the English Working Class* (1963), and a subordinate body of literature on the history of Roman Catholicism, by the mid-1960s the Irish in Britain occupied a very marginal place in modern British historiography.

However, the 1970s witnessed a gradual revival of interest in the academic study of the history of the Irish in Britain. This revival was stimulated by several contemporary British political and social issues, notably the resurgence of 'The Troubles' in Northern Ireland, and the public debate on the place of immigrants and minorities in an increasingly multicultural society. In the context of these issues, the study of the historical experience of the Irish in Britain assumed a contemporary relevance which had hitherto been lacking. In 1979, Lynn Hollen Lees produced *Exiles of Erin: Irish Migrants in Victorian London*, the first systematic analysis of the experience of the Irish in a British city, soon to be followed by Francis Finnegan's *Poverty and Prejudice: A Study of Irish Immigrants in York, 1840–75* (1982), and by the early 1980s a considerable body of secondary material, largely in the form of scholarly monographs on aspects of the local and regional dimensions of the Irish emigrant experience in nineteenth-century Britain, was in being.[2] Thus Sheridan Gilley and I attempted to take stock of the historical debate in our edited collection of essays, *The Irish in the Victorian City* (1985), which sought to reflect the consensus on the subject by describing both the degree of demoralisation and disadvantage experienced by Irish migrants in Victorian Britain, and the positive aspect of the Irish Catholic achievement in creating enduring religious and political communities by the end of the nineteenth century. Four years later, in a companion volume of essays, *The Irish in Britain 1815–1939* (1989), we sought to explore the extent to which some of these more traditional emphases in the historiography of Irish migration required modification and reinterpretation, most notably the idea that the Irish consistently comprised an 'outcast' element in modern British society. We also identified some of the gaps in the scholarly knowledge of the subject, noting, in particular, the need for further local and regional studies.

The 1990s have witnessed not only a substantial increase in the pace and scale of research and an extension of the parameters of scholarly study, but

---

[2] See, for example, M. Hartigan and M.J. Hickman (eds), *The History of the Irish in Britain: A Bibliography* (London, 1986).

also the deployment of more refined and sophisticated methodologies in the examination of what is, in essence, a complex subject, and several developments are particularly worthy of note, albeit briefly.[3]

First, the publication of Graham Davis's *The Irish in Britain, 1815–1914* (1991), with its emphasis on the themes of emigration, 'Little Irelands', Irish labour, Catholics and Protestants, Chartism, and Nationalism, and the publication of Donald MacRaild's, *Irish Migrants in Modern Britain, 1750–1922* (1999), with its stress upon the tensions created within British society by Irish migration, not only represent significant attempts to place the experiences of Irish migrants in a national context but also establish important baselines for further research. Shorter but equally incisive overviews have also been provided in essays by David Fitzpatrick, Brenda Collins, and Donald Akenson.[4]

Second, the local and regional study of Irish migration and settlement has continued unabated, with the result that the geographical boundaries within which research is being conducted have been extended substantially. Thus W.J. Lowe's important study, *The Irish in Mid-Victorian Lancashire* (1989), examined the process of community formation among the Irish in Liverpool, Manchester, Oldham, Preston, St Helens, Salford and Widnes, towns located within a region where the largest concentration of Irish immigrants in mid-Victorian England lay. South Lancashire also provided the focus for Steven Fielding's *Class and Ethnicity: Irish Catholics in England, 1880–1939* (1993), which provided a micro-study of communal dynamics by examining the social, cultural, religious and political experiences of the Irish Catholic working class in Manchester, set within the broader context of Irish settlement in England. By contrast, Cumbria provided the setting for Donald MacRaild's *Culture, Conflict and Migration: The Irish in Victorian Cumbria* (1998), a case-study of the relationship between Irish migration and communal tension in a region which had hitherto received little attention from historians of the subject.

Moreover, the work of Fielding and MacRaild, with its focus on the later

---

[3] For the historiography of the subject, see especially R. Swift, *The Irish in Britain 1815–1914: Perspectives and Sources* (London, 1990); R. Swift, 'The Historiography of the Irish in Nineteenth-Century Britain', in P. O'Sullivan (ed.), *The Irish World Wide* (Leicester, 1992), 52–81; R. Swift, 'Historians and the Irish: Recent Writings on the Irish in Nineteenth-Century Britain', in D.M. MacRaild (ed.), *The Great Famine and Beyond* (Dublin, 2000), 14–39.

[4] D. Fitzpatrick, 'A Curious Middle Place: The Irish in Britain, 1871–1921', in R. Swift and S. Gilley (eds), *The Irish in Britain, 1815–1939* (London, 1989), 10–59; D. Fitzpatrick, '"A Peculiar Tramping People": The Irish in Britain, 1801–70', in W.E. Vaughan (ed.), *A New History of Ireland*, vol. 5, *Ireland Under the Union, I, 1801–70* (Oxford, 1989), 623–60; D. Fitzpatrick, 'The Irish in Britain: Settlers or Transients?', in P. Buckland and J.C. Belchem (eds), *The Irish in British Labour History* (Liverpool, 1993), 1–10; B. Collins, 'The Irish in Britain, 1780–1921', in B.J. Graham and L.J. Proudfoot (eds), *An Historical Geography of Ireland* (London, 1993), 366–98; D.H. Akenson, *The Irish Diaspora: A Primer* (Belfast, 1996), 189–216.

decades of the nineteenth century, redressed an imbalance evident in the local study of Irish migration and settlement in nineteenth-century Britain, which had for too long been confined largely to the immediate pre- and post-Famine periods. Our knowledge and understanding of the Irish experience in Scotland has been enhanced substantially by a collection of essays edited by Tom Devine, *Irish Immigrants and Scottish Society in the Nineteenth and Twentieth Centuries* (1991), which, by examining the identities and values of Irish immigrant communities and by exploring the processes whereby Irish people were assimilated into Scottish society during the period, presented the first major reassessment of the Irish presence in modern Scotland since the pioneering research of James Handley. More recently, Sheridan Gilley and I have complemented our earlier studies with a further collection of essays, *The Irish in Victorian Britain: The Local Dimension* (1999), which illustrates the diversity of the Irish experience in specific towns, including Birmingham, Camborne, Hull, Liverpool, London and Stafford, and regions, including South Wales, Lancashire and the North-East. Finally, the pioneering research of J.V. Hickey during the 1960s on the Irish in South Wales[5] has been extended substantially by Paul O'Leary's *Immigration and Integration: The Irish in Wales, 1798–1922* (2000), the first monograph on the subject.

Inevitably, perhaps, Liverpool has continued to loom large in studies of the Irish in Britain, and Frank Neal's *Sectarian Violence: The Liverpool Experience, 1819–1914* (1988) and the volume of essays edited by John Belchem, *Popular Politics, Riot and Labour: Essays in Liverpool History, 1790–1940* (1992), illustrate effectively the ways in which the Irish migrant experience in one city can be examined and understood in its local social, economic and political setting. In addition to these major studies, it is also important to acknowledge the significance of the numerous local studies, published in journals and periodicals (see bibliography), which have extended our understanding of the Irish presence in other Victorian towns.

Third, there have been some notable single-volume studies of discrete themes associated with Irish migration and settlement in nineteenth-century Britain. These include Ruth-Ann Harris, *The Nearest Place That Wasn't Ireland* (1994), which examined the dynamics of Irish emigration between 1800 and 1845; Anne O'Dowd, *Spalpeens and Tattie Hokers* (1991), which traced the history of the seasonal and migratory movements of Irish farm workers in the British Isles from 1650 to 1915; Frank Neal, *Black '47: Britain and the Famine Irish* (1997), which explored the experiences of the tens of thousands of destitute Irish men, women, and children who sought refuge in British towns and cities, and responses to them, in 1847, the worst year of the Famine; Elaine McFarland, *Protestants First: Orangeism in*

---

[5] J.V. Hickey, *Urban Catholics: Urban Catholicism in England and Wales from 1829 to the Present Day* (London, 1967); see also J.V. Hickey, 'The Origin and Growth of the Irish Community in Cardiff' (University of Wales MA thesis, 1959).

Nineteenth-Century Scotland (1990), which emphasized the remarkable survival and longevity of Orangeism in Scotland; and Mary Hickman, *Religion, Class and Identity: The State, the Catholic Church and the Education of the Irish in Britain* (1995), which argued that the experience of Irish Catholic immigrants was conditioned by the policies of the British state, and that the Catholic Church, the chief institution involved with the immigrants, was to a remarkable degree a government instrument in both controlling the immigrants' conception of their own identity and 'incorporating' them into British life.

Finally, and at long last, the historical study of the Irish in Britain has been placed more firmly in the wider context of Irish diaspora studies. *The Irish World Wide*, a multi-volume series of collected essays edited by Patrick O'Sullivan between 1992 and 1996, explored, within a multi-disciplinary framework, a range of themes common to the diaspora and promises to provide a much-needed boon to the broader historiography of the Irish emigrant experience. Much the same might also be said of Donald Akenson's *The Irish Diaspora: A Primer*, which offered discrete studies of the Irish in Canada, Australia, South Africa, New Zealand, the United States and Great Britain, and the volume of essays edited recently by Andy Bielenberg, *The Irish Diaspora* (2000). When placed alongside Alan O'Day's seminal historiographical essay, 'Revising the Diaspora' (1996), the pioneering work of O'Sullivan and Akenson, emphasising as it does the themes of time and place, of similarity and difference, of change and continuity, and of connections, in Irish migration studies, clearly offers new opportunities to historians of the Irish in Britain, most notably in regard to comparative studies.

Thus, as the reductionism of some earlier studies has been challenged by the greater emphasis that historians have placed on the inter-related issues of identity, diversity and accommodation, the historical debate on the Irish in nineteenth-century Britain has become more refined and complex. Nevertheless, three broad questions have continued to dominate the historical debate. First, why did Irish people leave their homeland and settle in particular districts in Britain, and what were the consequences of this process? Second, how were these migrants variously perceived by British society and how far, and why, did attitudes towards them change? Third, to what extent did Irish emigrants integrate into British society or preserve a distinctive identity? This collection of original source materials seeks to provide teachers and students of modern British social history and Irish studies with access to some of the main primary sources that will help them to address these questions. This said, the extracts contained in this collection merely offer a way in; needless to say, there is no substitute for work on the original documents in their entirety, whenever possible.

The volume comprises eight sections which correspond with the major themes identified within the historiography of the subject. The divisions are inevitably arbitrary and are by no means mutually exclusive. Nevertheless,

Part 1, 'Migration', illustrates some of the causes of Irish migration and the complexities of migration. Part 2, 'Settlement', examines the nature and distribution of Irish settlement in Britain, contemporary attitudes towards Irish migration, and the diversity of Irish settlement patterns. Part 3, 'Employment', illustrates the variety of occupations, both urban and rural, which Irish men and women undertook, often at the margins, yet also offers evidence for upward mobility by the end of the nineteenth century. Part 4, 'Social Conditions', illustrates, by reference to the themes of poverty, health and crime, the range of social problems encountered by Irish migrants in what was, for many, an alien urban environment. This section not only illustrates the experience of poverty in the round but also highlights contemporary responses to the Irish dimension of the 'Condition of England Question'. Migration from Ireland during the abnormal conditions of the Famine period played a crucial role in shaping contemporary attitudes towards the Irish in Britain, and for this reason the selection of documents in this section is weighted towards this period. Part 5, 'Catholicism, Protestantism and Sectarianism', explores the nature and significance of Irish Catholic identity within Irish communities and examines some of the causes and features of anti-Catholicism, with particular reference to Orangeism and sectarian violence. Part 6, 'Radical and Labour Movements', explores aspects of Irish involvement in trade unionism and radical political movements, including Chartism, during the nineteenth century. Part 7, 'Nationalism', illustrates the extent to which the Irish in Britain sympathised with, and sought to advance, the Home Rule cause, while Part 8, 'Unionism', examines Irish Unionist activity in Britain, with particular reference to developments in Liverpool and Glasgow during the period 1885–1914.

Each section comprises a short contextual commentary, a selection of primary sources, and notes which include suggestions for further reading. This collection is illustrative of the broad range of primary source materials – qualitative, quantitative, and visual – available for the study of the Irish in Britain during the nineteenth century, and a more detailed analysis and evaluation of these original materials is provided in the concluding 'Note on Primary Sources'. While every effort has been made to achieve balance in the selection of documents, this has not always been possible; some themes, such as the Irish Catholic experience and Irish Nationalism, are more accessible and have received much greater attention from historians than, say, the Irish Protestant experience and Irish Unionism in Britain. Readers should also note that some of the gaps in our knowledge of the experiences of Irish migrants in Britain during the period are in part conditioned by the nature and limitations of the available evidence, with a paucity of material before 1830. Thereafter, and certainly up to about 1870 – when, in the broader context of the Famine exodus, the 'Condition of England Question', the revival of Roman Catholicism and renewed Irish

Nationalist agitation, the Irish in Britain were perceived to be 'a problem' – there is a relative wealth of material, not only in the form of Parliamentary Papers and local newspapers, but also in a whole range of local archives. After 1870 the volume of this material diminishes substantially and 'the Irish' are, once again, more difficult to trace, as this volume to some extent illustrates.

Moreover, much of the qualitative material is often impressionistic and emanates largely from 'non-Irish' sources, providing external (usually middle-class) and at times partial perceptions of the Irish poor. And although *The Nation* survey of 1872 and John Denvir's *The Irish in Britain* of 1892 offer alternative perceptions from Irish Nationalist and Catholic perspectives, these too are no less partial and impressionistic. Nevertheless, my prime intention is to allow the sources to speak for themselves and for readers to interpret the witting and unwitting testimony of the documents accordingly. In so doing they will also identify within many of the extracts evidence of a range of contemporary perceptions of Irish migrants, including some which are far from sympathetic. Of course, it would have been possible to have devoted a section solely to negative stereotypical representations of Irish migrants, but to have done so would have run counter to the reality of their experience. While some Irish men and women undoubtedly encountered hostility and prejudice from the host society, others did not, and just as the experiences of Irish migrants varied in time and place, so too did attitudes towards them.[6]

---

[6] The study of this subject appears to have become somewhat *passé* in recent years, although the longevity of negative portrayals of the Irish remains a subject worthy of further study. The publication of a revised edition of L.P. Curtis Jr., *Apes and Angels: The Irishman in Victorian Caricature* (Newton Abbot, 1971; rev. ed., Washington and London, 1997), especially chap. 9, 'Historical Revisionism and Constructions of Paddy and Pat', 109–47, with its attack on S. Gilley's seminal study, 'English Attitudes to the Irish in England, 1780–1900' in C. Holmes (ed.), *Immigrants and Minorities in British Society* (London, 1978), 81–110, and on other writers like Roy Foster, may well engender this. See also Roy Foster, *Paddy and Mr Punch: Connections in Irish and English History* (London, 1993), chap. 9, 'Paddy and Mr Punch', 171–94, and chap. 14, 'Marginal Men and Micks on the Make: The Uses of Irish Exile, c.1840–1922'. For a useful contextual essay see D.M. MacRaild, 'Irish Immigration and the "Condition of England" Question: The Roots of an Historiographical Tradition', *Immigrants and Minorities*, 14 (1995), 67–85, and D.M. MacRaild, '"Principle, Party and Protest": The Language of Victorian Orangeism in the North of England', in S. West (ed.), *The Victorians and Race* (Aldershot, 1996), 128–40.

Part 1

Migration

Erskine Nicol, RSA (1825–1904) *The Emigrant's Departure*,
reproduced by permission of the Tate Gallery, London.

INTRODUCTION

Emigration was perhaps the most notable feature of Irish social history during the nineteenth century. Admittedly, it is almost impossible to enumerate the actual number of Irish men, women and children who emigrated during this period, in part due to the inaccuracy of official emigration statistics (which invariably represent an undercount), but it has been suggested that at least eight million people migrated from Ireland between 1801 and 1921.[1] Moreover, the pace of Irish emigration increased during the nineteenth century, despite short-term and cyclical fluctuations: approximately one million people left Ireland between 1815 and 1845; emigration peaked between 1845 and 1851, during the Great Famine, when at least one and a half million people left Ireland; and a further four million emigrated between 1851 and 1914. The prime destinations of those who emigrated beyond the British Isles between 1851 and 1921 were Canada, Australia, New Zealand and, overwhelmingly, the United States of America (**Doc. 1.1**). Nevertheless, Great Britain provided an important focus for Irish migrants: between 1851 and 1921 the number of Irish-born in Great Britain was never less than at least one-quarter of all Irish emigrants world-wide (**Doc. 1.2**). Yet even in the immediate post-Famine period Irish migrants in Britain never represented more than 3.5 per cent of the total population (**Doc. 1.3**), although there were differences in settlement patterns in Scotland, England and Wales during the period.

Of course, nineteenth-century Irish emigration needs also to be placed in the broader context of emigration from the British Isles. Between 1815 and 1914 some seventeen million people left these islands to seek a new life abroad, thus Irish emigrants comprised about forty per cent of all emigrants during the period. Nevertheless, it was this massive emigration from Ireland which by the end of the nineteenth century led Irish nationalists to lament that there were more Irish men and women living abroad than there were in Ireland. But who emigrated from Ireland during the period and why did they leave? Why did some Irish men and women choose to migrate to Great Britain and others to migrate to North America or Australasia? Why was emigration sometimes represented as 'exile' by Irish men and women? These are just some of the questions which have spawned an extensive historiography and which continue to provide the focus for a lively debate among historians.[2]

---

[1] For a discussion of the statistics of Irish emigration, see especially Akenson, *The Irish Diaspora: A Primer*, chap. 2, 'The Homeland and the Outflow', 15–58.

[2] The extent of the historiography is well illustrated by the numerous essays and bibliographies contained in P. O'Sullivan's monumental series, *The Irish World Wide* (6 vols., London, 1992–7). See also A. O'Day's seminal essay, 'Revising the Diaspora', in D.G. George Boyce and A. O'Day (eds), *The Making of Modern Irish History: Revisionism and the Revisionist Controversy* (London, 1996), 188–215.

Explanations for emigration from Ireland during the nineteenth century were many and varied. The classic explanation, voiced by many British commentators during the early nineteenth century and epitomized in the *Third Report of the Royal Commission on the Condition of the Poorer Classes in Ireland* of 1836 (**Doc. 2.1**), held that Irish emigration was largely the consequence of a mounting Irish economic crisis of Malthusian dimensions, whereby a backward Irish agrarian economy was increasingly unable to support an impoverished rural population which had increased from four million to just over eight million between 1785 and 1841. As the *Devon Report* of 1845 illustrated (**Docs. 2.2, 2.3**), central to this argument was the belief that Ireland's agrarian problems were the product of feudal tenurial arrangements and an abundance of discontented labourers and petty farmers, who kept wages low and prevented Irish landlords and British investors from modernising agriculture and making it profitable. Similarly, over-population was regarded as the product of Catholic improvidence. Hence poverty, dearth and distress, which reached their peak during the Great Famine of 1845–51, were regarded as the inevitable outcome of Ireland's backwardness and mass emigration as the only escape from famine and destitution.[3]

This classic Malthusian explanation appears increasingly inadequate in the light of recent research which has shed doubt on the whole concept of a mounting Irish economic crisis.[4] In general, whilst most historians, and particularly Irish historians, accept that British domination and exploitation lay at the root of Ireland's problems, they have also conceded that the complex causes of Irish emigration are perhaps best explained in terms of the interaction of a combination of social and economic factors, some 'pushing' the Irish out of Ireland, others 'pulling' them from Ireland. Indeed, both 'push' and 'pull' factors were prerequisite to every individual decision to leave Ireland, and there is some evidence to suggest that 'push' factors tended to predominate in the pre-Famine period, and 'pull' factors thereafter.[5]

Clearly, several major strains put pressure on Ireland's economy during the early nineteenth century, pushing some sectors of Irish society towards emigration. These included the growth of population, the decline of domestic industry, the commercialisation of agriculture, and proto-indus-trialisation. In particular, the commercialisation of agriculture witnessed the increasing conversion of arable land to pasturage, which led to growing dependence on the potato for subsistence; an increased rate of farm

---

[3] See, for example, J.A. Jackson, *The Irish in Britain* (London, 1963), 1–5.

[4] See especially J. Mokyr, *Why Ireland Starved: A Quantitative and Analytical History of the Irish Economy, 1800–1850* (London, 1983); C. Ó Gráda, 'Some Aspects of Nineteenth-Century Irish Emigration', in L.M. Cullen and T.C. Smout (eds), *Comparative Aspects of Scottish and Irish Economic and Social History, 1600–1900* (Edinburgh, 1977), 65–73.

[5] D. Fitzpatrick, *Irish Emigration, 1801–1921* (Dubliln, 1984), 226–9.

consolidation, which added many smallholders and cottiers to the ranks of landless labourers; and the application of new farming techniques, which made agriculture less labour intensive and contributed to underemployment and unemployment. Poverty thus became the norm for many smallholders and labourers, largely Roman Catholic and some Gaelic-speaking, particularly in the rural West of Ireland. For many, faced with growing inequality between rich and poor, and prospects of a marginal existence at home, there was little choice other than to emigrate, provided they had the human and material resources to do so.

Thus emigration was an increasingly rational alternative to the hardships of life in pre-Famine Ireland. Indeed, there was a well-established pattern of emigration from Ireland by the early nineteenth century, particularly to North America.[6] These pre-Famine migrants included Ulster Protestants and Anglo-Catholics who were increasingly defining their goals in materialist terms by seeking 'independence' and upward social mobility in the free market economy. For these Irish men and women, life in Ireland offered limited rewards, whereas emigration to Britain or the British colonies provided them with the opportunity to achieve levels of expectation and standards of living which were far higher than the actual possibilities at home.[7]

Moreover, emigration was also an increasingly feasible proposition during the pre-Famine period, due largely to the improvement in communications between Ireland and Britain and between Britain and North America. In 1818 the first steam packet, the *Rob Roy*, linked Belfast with Glasgow, and by the 1820s ferry services were also operating from Dublin and Cork, principally to Liverpool, the main port for trans-Atlantic embarkation and the focus for English trade with Ireland.[8] Thereafter, competition between ferry companies reduced fares for the Irish Sea routes to as low as 10d. in steerage, and 3d. on deck, whilst the trans-Atlantic passage offered lucrative rewards for those shipping companies who competed for the emigrant trade. This, by mid-century, had become big business and, for those who could afford it, emigration was becoming relatively easy and inexpensive.

However, there was also a range of 'pull' factors which made emigration from Ireland an increasingly attractive proposition. Much Irish emigration resulted from the prospect of relatively well-paid employment in the industrialised economies of Britain and North America, the latter having the additional attraction of being free from British rule. Moreover, the material

---

[6] G. Davis, 'The Historiography of the Irish Famine', in O'Sullivan, *The Irish World Wide*, vol. 6, 21–5.

[7] K. Miller, *Emigrants and Exiles: Ireland and the Irish Exodus to North America* (Oxford, 1985), 267–80.

[8] For an interesting discussion of the centrality of Liverpool's role in Irish emigration, see R. Scally, 'External Forces in the Famine Emigration from Ireland', in E.M. Crawford (ed.), *The Hungry Stream: Essays on Emigration and Famine* (Belfast, 1997), 17–24.

aspirations of many Irish people were further fuelled by letters from Irish emigrants[9] which (as well as providing the historian with fascinating insights into some of the personal motives of Irish emigrants) presented attractive images of the prospects of a new life in America and Australia (**Doc. 3.1**), and by the incessant propaganda of shipping companies. Of course, in the last resort, people had to want to leave Ireland and during the pre-Famine period it was essentially those with the resources, the will, the information and the aspiration to move who sought a new life abroad.[10]

In many respects, the Great Famine of 1845–51 (**Doc. 4.1**) served as a catalyst for these processes. First, although estimates vary, at least one million Irish men, women and children died during the Famine and one and a half million emigrated; this population loss, coupled with the evictions which accompanied the Famine, greatly accelerated the commercialisation of Irish agriculture, the decline of domestic industry, and the Anglicisation of Irish culture.[11] Second, there is some evidence that the Famine confirmed the already-established patterns of pre-Famine emigration. The highest rates of emigration, as before, were from South Ulster, East Connaught, and mid-Leinster: here people were poor but not absolutely destitute, since they had the means to leave. In contrast, emigration was least in areas where pauperism was either negligible, in which case people lacked the incentive to leave, or very high, in which case they lacked the means. The abject poor and destitute, who suffered the kind of appalling hardships described by Inspector Caffin in Schull and Skibbereen (**Doc. 4.2**), died during the Famine. The highest mortality rates were in West Connaught and Munster, where the scale of the catastrophe was such that local communities could not even guarantee famine victims a proper burial, as *The Times* observed in March 1847 (**Doc. 4.3**). Third, the Famine affected different groups in different ways, and this was reflected in the nature of the Famine exodus. Indeed, it was the largely Catholic, Gaelic-speaking smallholders, cottiers and labourers, dependent as they were on the potato crop, who were driven from Ireland by the imminent threat of destitution, death or eviction.[12]

Of these, the majority fled to America, via Liverpool, some bitterly blaming Britain for what they perceived to be forced exile, as epitomized in the verse 'Poor Pat *Must* Emigrate'. In contrast, the poorest emigrants, who could not afford the passage to America, tended to migrate to England,

---

[9] See especially D. Fitzpatrick, *Oceans of Consolation: Personal Accounts of Irish Migration to Australia*; P. O'Farrell, *Letters from Irish Australia, 1825–1929* (Sydney, 1984). The collection of letters edited by C. Erikson, *Invisible Immigrants: The Adaptation of English and Scottish Immigrants in Nineteenth-Century America* (Ithaca, NY, 1972), also contains passing references to Irish migrants.

[10] C. Holmes, *John Bull's Island: Immigration and British Society, 1871–1971* (London, 1988), 22.

[11] Miller, *Emigrants and Exiles*, 131–2.

[12] For a recent analysis, see J.S. Donnelly, Jr., 'Mass Eviction and the Great Famine: The Clearances Revisited', in C. Póirtéir (ed.), *The Great Irish Famine* (Dublin, 1995), 155–73.

Scotland and Wales, unless they could take advantage of a limited number of inititiatives promoting programmes of assisted emigration.[13] Yet the Famine exodus also included formerly wealthy farmers who saw the Famine as proof of the futility of living in Ireland and who decided to cut their losses and emigrate to Britain or America. Finally, the Famine rein-forced the process of 'chain-migration', whereby the selection of future emigrants lay with their predecessors. Thus familial and communal ties were re-forged abroad.

Most Irish emigrants, whether Catholic or Protestant, left Ireland of their own free will and improved their material conditions by doing so. By and large, they also settled in places in the English-speaking world where the British had gone before them, hence there is a considerable geographical overlap between the British and the Irish diasporas.[14] Yet some historians have argued that many Irish Catholic emigrants clung to the view that they had been driven out of Ireland by political, economic and religious forces beyond their control, forces which were the reflection of 'British tyranny' (**Doc. 5.1**). For these Irish men and women, emigration was nothing less than 'exile', an involuntary banishment from 'Mother Ireland'. The culture of 'exile' was reflected in the emigrants' leave-taking ceremonies in Ireland. The form of these ceremonies was much the same throughout Ireland and they were generically known as 'American wakes', although the name varied from one county to another: in Galway it was called the 'farewell supper', in Donegal it was known as 'American bottle night', in Meath it was called the 'parting spree', whilst in parts of Ulster it was known as a 'convoy'. Prior to his or her departure, the emigrant informed relatives and neighbours of the decision to leave and invited them to attend an 'American wake' at the parents' home on the eve of departure. The basic elements of the wake were neighbourliness, friendship, and the shared sense of loss at the impending departure of a loved one. As such, they combined gaiety and grief. The evening was characterised by singing, dancing, smoking and drinking. Reminiscences were exchanged, stories were told, letters from America were read and advice was given. Early in the morning the emigrant took leave of his or her parents and was escorted by a convoy of brothers, sisters and friends to the edge of the village, if not to the port itself, where final goodbyes were said.

The culture of 'exile' was further epitomized in, and reinforced by, romantic

---

[13] See, for example, R.A. Harris, '"Where the poor man is not crushed down to exalt the aristocrat": Vere Forster's Porgramme of Assisted Emigration in the Aftermath of the Irish Famine', in P. O'Sullivan, *The Meaning of the Famine*, 172–94; P.J. Duffy, 'Emigrants and the Estate Office in the mid-Nineteenth Century: A Compassionate Relationship?', in E.M. Crawford (ed.), *The Hungry Stream: Essays on Emigration and Famine* (Belfast, 1997), 71–86; T. Parkhill, '"Permanent Deadweight": Emigration from Ulster Workhouses during the Famine', in Crawford, *The Hungry Stream*, 87–100; C. Kinealy, *This Great Calamity: The Irish Famine, 1845–52* (Dublin, 1994), 297–341.

[14] Akenson, *The Irish Diaspora*, 39.

and melodramatic imagery, including the well-known sketch depicting a priest blessing emigrants as they left Ireland, paintings such as Erskine Nichol's *The Emigrant's Departure*, or Irish emigrant songs and ballads (**Doc. 5.2**). Many of these emphasized, in nationalistic terms, the sorrow and guilt of having to leave Ireland, the involuntary nature of emigration, and the desire to return. The 'American wake' and emigrant ballads also served to keep Irish-American nationalists, in particular, emotionally oriented to their childhood homes and committed to redressing Ireland's grievances. Indeed, although large-scale Irish emigration to the United States was essentially a nineteenth-century phenomenon, the culture of 'exile' has continued to inform the sentimental and romantic attachments of some Irish-Americans to 'Mother Ireland' during the twentieth century. Yet the whole concept of a 'culture of exile' is in many respects open to question; at best, it is unrepresentative of the experiences of all Irish migrants.

Britain provided a significant focus for Irish migration and settlement throughout the period and beyond, although the nature and pattern of Irish migration to Britain differed in several respects from the migrations to North America and Australasia.[15] First, migration to Britain never quite had the permanent qualities of migration to the New World due to the short distances involved and the social, economic, political and cultural links between Britain and Ireland. It should also be noted that during the period of the Union, the Irish were internal migrants rather than immigrants *per se* (although they were often perceived as such) and that although Britain might be perceived as one discrete destination for Irish migrants there were some differences in Irish migration and settlement patterns between Scotland, England and Wales (see Part 2).

Second, there was a long-standing tradition of migration from Ireland to Britain which can be traced back to the Middle Ages, and even by the early eighteenth century there were notable Irish settlements in several English towns, including London, Bristol, Canterbury and Norwich, and in garrison towns such as York. Indeed, many Irish soldiers in the British army took up permanent residence in Britain following their discharge from military duties, notably after the conclusion of the Napoleonic Wars in 1815. Moreover, the demand for Irish labour during the Industrial Revolution witnessed the emergence of significant Irish enclaves in the industrial districts of South Lancashire and the Central Lowlands of Scotland, notably in Liverpool, Manchester and Glasgow, by the end of the eighteenth century.

Third, as the *Report on the State of the Irish Poor in Great Britain* noted in 1836 (**Doc. 5.3**), there was a long-standing tradition of seasonal migration

---

[15] See, for example, the introductions to the three volumes edited by Swift and Gilley, *The Irish in the Victorian City, The Irish in Britain, 1815–1939,* and *The Irish in Victorian Britain: The Local Dimension*; G. Davis, *The Irish in Britain, 1815–1914* (Dublin, 1991); B. Collins, 'The Irish in Britain, 1780–1921', in Graham and Proudfoot, *An Historical Geography of Ireland*, 366–98.

from Ireland to Britain whereby smallholders, principally from the counties of western Ulster and Connaught, sought casual employment on British farms during the harvest season in order to supplement the family income and support their domestic holdings in Ireland. The scale of Irish seasonal migration increased substantially during the early nineteenth century, reaching a peak of almost 100,000 by the 1860s.[16] Seasonal employment also encompassed casual work in mines, docks, and construction industries.[17] Fourth, although some seasonal migration led ultimately to permanent residence in Britain it was not until the nineteenth century that large-scale Irish settlement became a permanent feature of urban life in Britain and, even then, Irish communities contained a well-recognized transient population.

Finally, a large but unknown proportion of Irish migrants only settled in Britain temporarily until they had the means to emigrate elsewhere, hence 'step-wise' migration often characterised their experience in Britain as they found employment and accommodation in different localities until they could afford their passage to America or Australasia. Remittances from expatriate friends and relatives also played an important part in this process, as *The Illustrated London News* observed in 1850 (**Doc. 5.4**), and it has been estimated that £34 million was sent back from America to the United Kingdom between 1848 and 1867 alone.[18] Much of this went to Ireland, frequently in the form of pre-paid tickets or the 'American Money'. Preparations for the passage to America were not without their hardships for some emigrants, including the frequently hazardous passage across the Irish Sea (**Doc. 5.5**) and exploitation at the Liverpool quays and lodging-houses (**Doc. 5.6**).

By the end of the nineteenth century, Irish communities were well established throughout urban Britain, although sojourning migrants, like the harvesters from Mayo described by the special correspondent of the *Birmingham Daily Gazette* in 1893, at the height of the debate over Gladstone's Third Home Rule Bill (**Doc. 5.7**), were not an unfamiliar sight in the British countryside, even if their numbers were now declining. Moreover, as the portrait of the London Irish painted by C. O'Conor Eccles in 1902 illustrates (**Doc. 5.8**), the Irish who settled in Britain were by no means an homogeneous group, for their ranks contained both rich and poor, middle class and working class, skilled and unskilled, Catholics and Protestants (and unbelievers), Nationalists and Loyalists, and people from a variety of distinctive provincial rural and urban cultures in Ireland. Nevertheless, in their search for better economic opportunities, most of these men and women shared a common bond with their compatriots in the wider Irish diaspora: they accepted that to leave Ireland was a necessary fact of life.

---

[16] D.M. MacRaild, *Irish Migrants in Modern Britain 1750–1922* (London, 1999), 22–3.

[17] See especially A. O'Dowd, *Spalpeens and Tattie Hokers: History and Folklore of the Irish Migratory Agricultural Worker in Ireland and Britain* (Dublin, 1991).

[18] R.F. Foster, *Modern Ireland, 1600–1972* (London, 1988), 350.

DISTRIBUTION OF EMIGRANTS

Doc. 1.1: Destinations of Irish Emigrants outside Britain, 1851–1921

Based on Reports of the Colonial Land and Emigration Commissioners, 1851–72, and on Board of Trade Returns, 1873–1921, cited by Miller, *Emigrants and Exiles: Ireland and the Irish Exodus to North America*, 569.

Year	Numbers (Thousands) and Destinations				Total
	USA	Canada	Australasia	Others	
1851–55	740.2	104.8	53.8	2.2	901.1
1856–60	249.6	13.2	47.7	4.4	315.0
1861–70	690.8	40.1	82.9	4.7	818.6
1871–80	449.5	25.8	61.9	5.4	542.7
1881–90	626.6	44.5	55.5	7.9	734.5
1891–1900	427.3	10.7	11.5	11.8	461.3
1901–10	418.9	38.2	11.9	16.3	485.4
1911–21	191.7	36.2	17.6	9.7	255.3
Total	3,794.8	313.6	342.8	62.7	4,514.0
As %	84%	6.9%	7.5%	1.4%	100%

Doc. 1.2: Percentage Distribution of Permanent Irish-Born Residents Living outside Ireland, 1851–1921

Commission on Emigration and Other Population Problems, 1948–54 (Dublin, 1954), Table 95, from Collins, 'The Irish in Britain, 1780–1921', in Graham and Proudfoot, *An Historical Geography of Ireland*, 367.

Year	England & Wales	Scotland	Total GB	USA	Canada	Aust
1851	27	11	38	50	12	N/A
1861	22	7	29	60	11	N/A
1871	20	7	27	65	8	N/A
1881	19	7	26	61	6	7
1891	16	7	23	65	5	8
1901	17	8	25	64	4	7
1911	18	8	26	63	4	7
1921	21	9	30	59	5	6

Doc. 1.3: Distribution of the Irish-Born outside their Native Counties, 1851–71

Based on information in Fitzpatrick, 'Emigration, 1801–70', in Vaughan, *A New History of Ireland*, vol. 5, 609.

[i] Numbers [in thousands]						
Year	Ireland	Britain	USA	Canada	Aust	Total
1851	549.6	727.3	961.7	227.0	70.2	2535.8
1861	459.9	805.7	1611.3	286.0	177.4	5260.7
1871	489.2	774.3	1855.8	223.3	213.8	3556.3

[ii] As a Percentage of the Local Population						
Year	Ireland	Britain	USA	Canada	Aust	Total
1851	8.4	3.5	4.1	9.2	17.4	4.7
1861	7.9	3.5	5.1	8.7	15.4	5.2
1871	9.0	3.0	4.8	6.0	12.9	4.7

AGRICULTURE

Doc. 2.1: The Condition of Agricultural Labourers in Ireland, 1836

Third Report of the Royal Commission on the Condition of the Poorer Classes in Ireland, Parliamentary Papers, XXX (1836).

There is not in Ireland the division of labour that exists in Great Britain; the body of the labouring class look to agricultural employment, and to it only, for support; the supply of agricultural labour is thus so considerable as greatly to exceed the demand for it; hence come small earnings and widespread misery. In Great Britain the agricultural families constitute little more than a fourth, while in Ireland they constitute about two-thirds of the whole population. There were in Great Britain in 1831, 1,055,982 agricultural labourers, in Ireland 1,131,715, although the cultivated land of Great Britain amounts to about 34,250,000 acres and that of Ireland only to about 14,600,000. It further appears that the agricultural produce of Great Britain is more than four times that of Ireland; that agricultural wages vary from 6d. to 1s. a day; that the average of the country in general is about 8d.; and that the earnings of the labourers come, on an average of the whole class, to from 2s. to 2s. 6d. a week, or thereabouts, for the year round.

Thus circumstanced, it is impossible for the able-bodied, in general, to provide against sickness or the temporary absence of employment, or against old age or the destitution of their widows and children in the contingent event of their own premature decease. A great proportion of them are insufficiently provided at any time with the commonest necessaries of life. Their habitations are wretched hovels, several of a family sleep together upon straw or upon the bare ground, sometimes with a blanket, sometimes without even so much to cover them; their food commonly consists of dry potatoes, and with these they are sometimes so scantily supplied as to be obliged to stint themselves to one spare meal in the day. There are even instances of persons being driven by hunger to seek sustenance in wild herbs. They sometimes get a herring, or a little milk, but they never get meat, except at Christmas, Easter and Shrovetide. Some go in search of employment to Great Britain during the harvest, others wander through Ireland with the same view. The wives and children of many are occasionally obliged to beg; they do so reluctantly, and with shame, and in general go to a distance from home that they may not be known. Mendicancy too is the sole resource of the aged and impotent of the poorer classes in general, when children or relatives are unable to support them. To it, therefore, crowds are driven for the means of existence, and the knowledge that such is the fact leads to an indiscriminate giving of alms, which encourages idleness, imposture and general crime.

With these facts before us, we cannot hesitate to state that we consider remedial measures requisite to ameliorate the condition of the Irish poor. What these measures should be is a question complicated, and involving considerations of the deepest importance to the whole body of the people both in Ireland and Great Britain. Society is so constructed, its various parts are so connected, the interests of all who compose it are so interwoven, the rich are so dependent on the labour of the poor, and the poor upon the wealth of the rich, that any attempt to legislate partially, or with a view to the good of a portion only, without a due regard to the whole of the community, must prove in the end fallacious, fatal to its object, and injurious in general to a ruinous degree.

Doc. 2.2: Tenurial Arrangements in Ireland, 1845

Royal Commission on the Occupation of Land in Ireland, Parliamentary Papers, XIX (1845), 16–17 (Devon Report).

It is well known that in England and Scotland, before a landlord offers a farm for letting, he finds it necessary to provide a suitable farmhouse, with necessary farm buildings for the proper management of the farm. He puts the gates and fences into good order and he also takes upon himself a great part of the burden of keeping the buildings in repair during the term; and the rent is fixed with reference to this state of things.

In Ireland the case is wholly different. The smallness of the farms, as they are usually let . . . render the introduction of the English system extremely difficult, and in many cases impracticable. It is admitted on all hands, that according to the general practice in Ireland, the landlord builds neither dwelling house nor farm offices, nor puts fences, gates, etc. into good order, before he lets his land to a tenant. In most cases, whatever is done in the way of building and fencing is done by the tenant, and in the ordinary language of the country, dwelling houses, farm buildings, and even the making of fences are described by the general word 'improvements', which is thus employed to denote the necessary adjuncts to a farm, without which, in England and Scotland, no tenant would be found to rent it.

Many witnesses of various classes have spoken of the discouragement to improvement that arises from the want of some certain tenure in the land. Some of these refer to the necessity of enforcing the grant of leases as a remedy for this evil . . . while others, again, seem to think that the same end will be effectually obtained by some legislative provision, securing to the tenant, under certain circumstances, a fair remuneration for any expenditure made by him of labour or capital, in permanent improvements on the farm.

On the other hand, it not infrequently occurs that the only capital which the occupier of the soil possesses is to be found in the labour of himself and his family; if you show to him in what manner the application of that labour may be rendered most conducive to his own comfort and permanent benefit, and assist him with money or materials which his labour cannot supply, you will generally find the Irish peasant ready to co-operate with you in effecting improvements beneficial alike to himself and to the country.

It is because we believe that the attainment of these desirable objects is impeded by the feelings of distress and insecurity that too often prevail amongst the tenant class in Ireland, that we venture to recommend some legislative interference upon this point.

Doc. 2.3: Sub-tenancy in Ireland, 1845

Royal Commission on the Occupation of Land in Ireland, Parliamentary Papers, XIX (1845), 105 (Devon Report). Minutes of Evidence.

156. [Question] To what particular class do you apply the term 'middle-man'; do you apply it to a person who takes a considerable tract of land, and occupies and farms a portion of it and lets off the remainder, or to a man who is never absent from the land?
     [Answer] To both. To the tenant who takes fifty or sixty acres of land, and sets twenty of it; but the persecution of this class of middleman to his tenant is the most barbarous and cruel I have ever heard of or could imagine.

157. [Q] Will you state the various ways in which they carry that persecution into effect?
     [A] A man holds of me at £1 the Irish acre; he sets the worst part of the land at £2 or £3 an acre. I call on him for a year's rent, due 1 May last;

he has the rent of his tenant, due 1 November last, in his pocket, and about the 10th he will drive his pig to the pound and take the bed from under him to enforce it. Instances of this kind come under my eye every day in the year.

160. [Q] Is it common for the middleman to raise the rent of the sub-tenants?

[A] He will.

161. [Q] If he wishes to get rid of a sub-tenant, what means does he take usually?

[A] He will turn him out by an ejectment.

162. [Q] Do they frequently turn them out without any compensation?

[A] There is no feeling of that kind at all amongst them.

174. [Q] Do the middlemen, to whom you allude, make use of any other mode except distress to recover their rents?

[A] They drive them, and sell everything. They will put them out by ejectment or by process, and send them to gaol; that is a very common thing. They get a decree against their body, and send them to gaol, and worry them out by that means.

LETTERS FROM IRISH EMIGRANTS

Doc. 3.1: Extract from a Letter Written by James Halloran, an Irish Convict in Australia, to his Wife in 1840

Patrick O'Farrell, *Letters from Irish Australia, 1825–1929* (Belfast, 1984), 18. Reproduced by kind permission of the Ulster Historical Foundation.

We sailed on the 6th of July and landed on the 29th of January eighteen hundred and forty and Dr. Catherine if you can in the world get one pound for yourself and the children, and come to the immigrant office in Dublin and come to this country and if you can bring my brother John with you and he will get out for the same, this is the best country under the sun, for any well behaved person labourer man will get from thirty to forty pounds per year and a servant maid will get twenty pounds p. year and get your certificate bring it to the Rev. Doctor McCabe and he will sign it for you and then there can be nothing to prevent you . . . I am very thankful to my prosecutors for sending me here to the land of liberty and freedom . . . you may let my friends know that in course of six months I expect to have as much as any of my friends at home.

Doc. 3.2: Extract from a Letter Written by Mary Jane Adams of Geelong to her Brother in Portglenone, Co. Antrim, 27 December 1847

Patrick O'Farrell, *Letters from Irish Australia, 1825–1929* (Belfast, 1984), 40. Reproduced by kind permission of the Ulster Historical Foundation.

I humbly trust the famine and distress is quite over now. We cannot understand why Government don't send them out here, as there is plenty of room and plenty of food and to spare. We are giving from £28 to £30 a year to all our men, hut keepers and shepherds; our married couple get £36 a year and all our neighbours are giving from £40 to £50 a year, and cannot even get them at that. We require 13 and 14 men constantly and a man and his wife . . . You would be delighted with this climate. Everything can be grown in the open air, although the winters are generally wet and cold, yet few ever get colds or fevers. Since I last wrote you we have got a very good comfortable house built which has cost £200 . . . I still have plenty of fowls 24 turkeys 12 ducks and a large flock of geese. I take the credit of having the best poultry in the country. We have plenty of eggs and lots for killing. We can also kill our own beef, pork etc. and a sheep every day, and Muirhead brings up every little thing from town that I require, so we live most comfortably. We have plenty of potatoes, vegetables, cheese and milk and butter, so that I have every comfort that this country can afford. You would be delighted with our place. We are surrounded by the fine Grampians and Mount William.

FAMINE

Doc. 4.1: Disease in the Potato Crop, 1845

Freeman's Journal, 11 September 1845.

We regret to have to state that we have had communications from more than one well-informed correspondent announcing the fact of what is called 'cholera' in potatoes in Ireland, especially in the north. In one instance the party had been digging potatoes – the finest he had ever seen – from a particular field, and a particular ridge of that field, up to Monday last; and on digging in the same ridge on Tuesday he found the tubers all blasted, and unfit for the use of man or beast.

Doc. 4.2: Conditions in Scull and Skibbereen

Famine Reports, Parliamentary Papers (1847), LI, 452–5; LII, 162–6 (Caffin's Report).

31 DECEMBER 1846: The Parish of Scull is very extensive, lying between Roaring Water Bay and Dunmaus, and contains about 18,000 inhabitants; and of these about 16,000 are in a state of utter destitution, and most of the remainder will be similarly situated as soon as the little stores they have are

consumed . . . A great number of people must inevitably be swept off by starvation, and by diseases arising from starvation, such as bowel complaints, scurvy, dropsy and fever. Food is daily becoming scarcer, and much dearer, and where are future supplies to come from? Hitherto, Skibbereen, with its immediate neighbourhood, has been the peculiar object of solicitude, but Scull, as well as Kilmore, the neighbourhood of Dunmaus Bay, Carigboy, and the promontory of Sheepshead are equally badly off . . . I am quite positive that unless something be speedily done by throwing in supplies at a moderate price, by affording gratuitous relief, or by affording immediate means of emigration for the most destitute, the bulk of the population must be swept off. The desolation is indeed complete; the people seem harmless and inoffensive; political agitation has hardly reached them, and the inhabitants of these remote south-western parts are fit objects for the especial protection of government.

15 FEBRUARY 1847: Having in the course of my late duty at Scull being brought into direct contact with the distress that prevails there and in its neighbourhood, I venture to lay before you that which I had ocular demonstration of . . . Having a great desire to see with my own eyes some of the misery which was said to exist, Dr. Traill, the Rector of Scull, offered to drive me to a portion of his parish. I found there was no need to take me beyond the village to show me the horrors of famine in its worst features. I had read in the papers accounts of this state of things, but I thought they must be highly coloured to attract sympathy; but there I saw the reality of the whole – no exaggeration, for it does not admit of it – famine exists to a fearful degree, with all its horrors! Fever has sprung up, consequent upon the wretchedness; and swellings of limbs and body, and diarrhoea, from the want of nourishment, are everywhere to be found. Dr. Traill's parish is twenty-one miles in extent, containing about eighteen thousand souls, with not more than half a dozen gentlemen in the whole of it. He drove me about five or six miles; but we commenced our visits before leaving the village, and in no house that I entered was there not to be found the dead or dying. Never in my life have I seen such wholesale misery, nor could I have thought it so complete. I am convinced in that district it is not in human power to stay the evil; it may be to alleviate it; but this must be by a good organized system, and the supply chiefly gratuitous. A board of health is now also wanted, as it cannot be expected but a pestilence will rage when the mass of these bodies decompose. They have ceased to put them into coffins, or have the funeral service performed, and they merely lay them a few inches under the soil.

Doc. 4.3: Famine Victims: Neglect of Burial, 1847

The Times, 9 March 1847.

There is one feature of the Famine in Ireland which has forcibly impressed itself on the English public. So shockingly prominent is it, that we venture to say, it will ever be recorded as distinguishing the present from similar calamities. The astounding apathy of the Irish themselves to the most horrible scenes immediately under their eyes and capable of relief by the smallest exertion is something absolutely without a parallel in the history of civilised nations . . . We are told by eye witnesses of scores and hundreds of poor creatures actually dying for want of a meal; families perishing a member a day; an old woman found half-starved on Monday, dying on Tuesday, dead on Wednesday, unburied on Saturday, half-devoured by rats on Monday, dragged along the ground by a dying brother or roughly carted to the burial ground and there laid with not even a sufficient covering of soil. We are told of whole families found dead at a time in populous neigh-bourhoods. Churchyards are scarcely deeper than the soil usually is for planting potatoes, and the coffins – coffins there are – laid three deep on the surface. But the naivete with which these horrors are related by persons perfectly competent to prevent them is what utterly passes an English apprehension. Informants of all kinds – laymen able at least to write a letter to a newspaper and make a speech to a meeting – and clergymen living in castles and parsonage houses with horses, servants and carriages – tell us these things with as much composure as they would of a murrain in a rookery or the destruction of a colony of rats.

DEPARTURE AND ARRIVAL

Doc. 5.1: Exodus of the Celtic Races, 1852

The Illustrated London News, 3 April 1852.

What has been called the 'Exodus of the Celtic races' continues. The return of spring has witnessed once more the flux of the emigrational tide towards the shore of the New World. The quays of Dublin, Cork, and Liverpool are crowded with Irish emigrants, departing to other lands, and carrying with them, in too many instances, we are afraid, a feeling of bitter hatred to this country. They blame England for the evils that have befallen them in their own land, instead of blaming, as they ought to do, their own landlords, their own indolence, their own religious and party feuds, and their own listless reliance upon the easily raised but miserable root, the potato. Year after year the efflux continues. Strong men that are the very life-blood of a nation, and that will become so to that great kindred nation of America, which is destined in due time to overshadow the world with its power and glory, leave our shores in countless multitudes. The greater the numbers who emigrate in any one year, the larger the amount of funds received in Ireland in the next, to enable friends and relatives to follow to the land of plenty and independence. The potato failure is thus working a mighty revolution. It has caused the property of the Irish landlords to change hands; it has converted proprietors into paupers; it has caused England to spend ten millions of money for the relief of the people with as little real benefit as if the sum had been sunk into the sea; it has consigned upwards of one million of human beings – some accounts say upwards of two millions – to a premature death by famine and fever; and it has driven the very flower of the Celtic race across the Atlantic, to subdue and to cultivate the forests and prairies of the almost illimitable regions of the far West, and thus to open up the long-buried East, and to menace Japan and China with a European invasion. This mighty emigration pays for itself. It seeks no aid from the public purse, but it should be remembered that it establishes itself in regions that owe no fealty to the Crown of England.

Doc. 5.2: The Emigrant's Farewell to Donegal

A New Song Called the Emigrant's Farewell to Donegal, Copy of broadside in Clarke Collection, National Library of Australia, Canberra, cited by D. Fitzpatrick, 'Flight from Famine', in Póirtéir, *The Great Irish Famine*, 183–4.

> So now my dear you need not fear
> The dangers of the rageing sea,
> If your mind is bent I am content
> So now prepare and come away.
> She says my dear if you'll agree
> To marry me, I'll quick prepare.
> We'll join our hands in wedlock's bands
> And we will stay no longer here.
> It was in the year of '46
> I was forced to leave my native land,
> To old Ireland I bid a long adieu
> And to my fond relations all.
> But now I'm in America
> No rents or taxes wee pay at all,
> So now I bid a long farewell
> To my native land old Donegal.

Doc. 5.3: The Passage from Dublin to Liverpool, 1833

Report on the State of the Irish Poor in Great Britain (Cornewall Lewis Report), *Parliamentary Papers* (1836) Appendix II, *State of the Irish Poor in Liverpool*, 8–9. Evidence of Mr. Samuel Perry, Agent to the City of Dublin Steam Packet Company.

The steamers of this Company carry a great deal of poor Irish between Dublin and Liverpool, and Belfast and Liverpool, both ways; the chief part are carried to and from Dublin; about one-tenth more go to Belfast. The regular charge for deck passengers is 5s. per head, both ways, both to Dublin and Belfast. During an opposition the rates vary, and sometimes have been 6d., but only for a few days. We never vary our charges either way from any other motive than opposition. If the Irish have come at a low rate, and gone back at a high rate, this has been mere accident and not design. During the whole of last summer our fares both ways were 3s.6d. All the poor Irish who come to Liverpool from Dublin come in our packets.

The government boats bring none, so that, with the exception of a few who come in sailing vessels, we bring all that come through Dublin. Sometimes, in May and June, preparatory to the hay and corn harvests, they come over in the number of two to five hundred in a vessel. We are forced to exercise great vigilance, in order to prevent being defrauded of the fare; they practise all kinds of tricks to evade payment. But in general they are well-behaved and perfectly sober on board, both going and coming; whenever a disturbance arises, it is to avoid the payment of their passage money. The drovers, who have charge of the cattle which are brought over in the packets, are uniformly drunken, and are very troublesome when on board. They are quite a different class from the harvest-men. The harvest-men in general do not bring over their wives and families; when they do, they are paid for by the head, except children in arms. Scarcely a day passes but I send over gratis half a dozen poor Irish, either males or females, who, being destitute in this country, are desirous of returning.

Doc. 5.4: Emigration to North America and the British Colonies, 1850

The Illustrated London News, 6 July 1850.

The great tide of emigration flows steadily westward. The principal emigrants are Irish peasants and labourers. It is calculated that at least four out of every five persons who leave the shores of the old country to try their fortunes in the new are Irish. Since the fatal years of the potato famine and the cholera, the annual numbers of emigrants have become so great as to suggest the idea, and almost justify the belief, of a gradual depopulation of Ireland. The colonies of Great Britain offer powerful attractions to the great bulk of the English and Scottish emigrants who forsake their native land to make homes in the wilderness. But the Irish emigration flows with full force upon the United States. Though many of the Irish emigrants are, doubtless, persons of small means, the great bulk appear to be people of the most destitute class, who go to join their friends and relatives, previously established in America.

The emigration of the present year (1850) bids fair to exceed even the unprecedentedly large emigration of 1849. This human stream flows principally through the ports of London and Liverpool; as there is but little direct emigration from Scotland or Ireland. In the year 1849, out of the total number of 299,498 emigrants, more than one half left from the port of Liverpool. We learn from a statement in a Liverpool newspaper that in the months of January, February, March and April of the present year the total emigration was 50,683 persons; and as these four months include two of the least busy months of the year, it is probable that the numbers during the months of May, June, July and August, the full emigrational season, will be much more considerable, and that the emigration for the year will exceed that for 1849.

It would appear that very few out of the vast army of Irish and other emigrants that proceed to the United States or the British Colonies go out as mere adventurers, without some knowledge of the country, or their chances of doing well, when they get there. The sums received by them before they leave this country are sufficient proofs that they have prosperous friends upon the other side: and it is to be presumed that the friends who send them the money do not avoid sending them advice, and giving them full information, to the best of the means, as to their movements upon arrival.

No passenger ship is allowed to proceed until a medical practitioner appointed by the emigration office of the port shall have inspected the medicine chest and passengers, as shown in our first engraving, and certified medicine etc. are sufficient, and the passengers are free from contagious disease.

There are usually a large number of spectators at the dock gates to witness the final departure of the noble ship, with its large freight of human beings. It is an interesting and impressive sight and the most callous and indifferent can scarcely fail, at such a moment, to form cordial wishes for the pleasant voyage and safe arrival of the emigrants, and for their future prosperity in their new home. As the ship is towed, hats are raised, handkerchiefs are waved, and a loud and long-continued shout of farewell is raised from the shore, and cordially responded to from the ship. May all prosperity attend her living freight!

Doc. 5.5: Crossing the Irish Sea, 1854

First Report of the Select Committee on Emigrant Ships, Parliamentary Papers (1854). Minutes of Evidence, S. Redmond, 88–9.

[Q] On board the 'Prince', what did you see?
[A] I must speak generally. I will first mention the names of the ships I have travelled in, and then I will state generally what I saw, not on board any particular ship, but a general statement of the circumstances. I have travelled by the 'Prince', the 'Trafalgar', the 'Princess', and the 'Times', in which I have travelled oftener than the others.
[Q] What did you see?
[A] I saw the passengers exposed on the deck without any covering belonging to the ship, and the covering they had of their own was very scanty.

[Q] On board of these steamers carrying a large number of passengers, were cattle carried?

[A] I have never travelled from Dublin to Liverpool, but they always carried a large number of cattle.

[Q] Is it your opinion that the sufferings arise from carrying more on board of these vessels than they are authorised to do by the Act [Certification Act, 1851]?

[A] The sufferings of course are greater amongst a crowd of people than they would be amongst a smaller number; they are generally crowded round the funnel of the steamer, or huddled together in a most disgraceful manner; and as they have not been used to sea passages, they get sick, and perfectly helpless, and covered with the dirt and filth of each other. I have seen the sea washing over the deck of a steamer that I came over in one night, completely drenching the unfortunate people, so much so that several of them got perfectly senseless. There were 250 deck passengers on board, and they were in a most dreadful state; it was an extremely stormy night, and the vessel heaved about in a very awful manner; the sea washed over her tremendously, and it was only by great exertions that some of these people were not carried overboard. I could not get further than the head of the stairs, but very early in the morning, when it became light, I went up and saw 50 or 60 of these people, including some four or five children, perfectly stiff and cold. The captain was a very humane man, and although it was blowing a stiff gale of wind, I suggested to him to have these people taken into the cabin, and he did so, bringing the worst in first; they were all perfectly wet, and whatever clothes they had on were obliged to be taken off. There was a very fine boy, apparently dead, but by a great deal of exertion, and rubbing him in hot water, and laying him before the fire, he was revived. A very interesting looking young woman, about 20 years of age, was so bad from the effects of cold and the wetting, that she remained in a state of insensibility from between about five o'clock in the morning until we got into Liverpool about seven o'clock in the evening; the captain brought the people down in the cabin, caused a great fire to be made, and hot water to be got, and did everything that humanity and kindness could do to revive them again.

[Q] Were many of them in a state of great destitution and poverty?

[A] No; there were some who were not emigrants who were.

[Q] Were some of them emigrants?

[A] A great portion of them were emigrants, but some of them were not, and they were in a state of greater destitution than the emigrants.

[Q] What is the passage-money?

[A] It varies according to the opposition; it is sometimes 1s., sometimes 1s.6d., sometimes 2s., and sometimes 2s.6d.

[Q] You have known it as low as 1s. per head for deck passengers?

[A] Yes, that is the general price, except at harvest time, when the agricultural labourers come over from distant parts of Ireland to this country to reap the harvest; the great bulk of the passengers, that is 90 per cent, are emigrants.

Doc. 5.6: Exploitation of Irish Emigrants in Liverpool, 1850

The Morning Chronicle, 15 July 1850.

As soon as a party of emigrants arrive in Liverpool they are beset by a tribe of people, both male and female, who are known by the name of 'mancatcher', and 'runner'. The business of these people is, in common parlance, to 'fleece' the emigrant, and to draw from his pocket, by fair means or foul, as much of his cash as he can be persuaded, inveigled, or bullied into parting with. The first division of the man-catching fraternity are those who trade in commissions on the passage money, and call themselves the 'runners' or agents of the passenger broker . . . These man-catchers procure whatever sums they can from emigrants as passage money – perhaps £5 or £6, or even more – and pay as little as they can to the passenger-broker, whose business they thus assume – often as little as £3 or £3.5s . . . . It is obviously the interest of the brokers as well as of the emigrants that this system of plunder should be stopped; and the active and intelligent government agent for emigration at Liverpool, without whose approval no licence can be obtained, has done his best to extirpate this particular class of man-catchers.

But these are not the only class of the man-catching fraternity, nor do they confine their operations to an exorbitant profit upon passage money. The man-catchers keep lodging-houses for emigrants – wretched cellars and rooms, destitute of comfort and convenience, in which they cram them as thickly as the places can hold. The extra profits they draw from this source cannot be inferior in amount to their previously-mentioned gains . . . In addition to this trade, some of them deal in the various articles composing the outfit of emigrants, such as bedding, clothes, food, cooking utensils, and the knick-knacks of all kinds which they can persuade them to purchase. Some of the storekeepers in this line of business pay their 'runners' or man-catchers as much as ten per cent commission on the purchases effected by the emigrants; from which the reader may form some estimate of the enormous plunder that must be drained from the poor ignorant people. As every emigrant must provide his own bedding, the sale of mattresses, blankets, and counterpanes enters largely into this trade. After the bedding is provided, the 'man-catchers', who are principally Irishmen themselves, and know both the strength and weakness of the Irish character, fasten upon their countrymen – many of whom, poor and miserable as they look, have sovereigns securely stitched amid the patches of their tattered garments – and persuade them into the purchase of various articles, both useful and useless. The 'man-catching' business in all its departments has been reduced to a regular system, and no London sharper can be more sharp than the Liverpool runners.

It is in the neighbourhood of the Waterloo and northwards to the Clarence Dock that the principal lodging-houses for poor emigrants are to be found, most of them of the filthiest kind externally and internally. The wretched accommodation provided for the multitudes of emigrants that daily pass into Liverpool, to await the departure of the vessels by which they have secured their passage, and the robberies of all kinds to which they are subjected during their stay, are evils that the philanthropic citizens of Liverpool, who feel for the misery of their fellow-creatures, might well hasten to remedy.

Doc. 5.7: Seasonal Migration from Mayo, 1893

Letter from the Special Correspondent of the *Birmingham Daily Gazette*, Castlebar, 8 June 1893.

The Mayo folks are great temporary migrants. From the County Mayo and its neighbour Roscommon come the bands of Irish harvesters which annually invade England. Latterly they are going more than ever, and the women also are joining in large numbers. The unsettled state of the country and the threat of a College Green Parliament have made work scarcer and scarcer, and the prevailing belief among the better classes that the Bill is too absurd to become law, is not sufficient to counteract the chronic want of confidence inspired by the presence of Mr Gladstone at the helm of state. Five hundred workers went from Westport Quay to Glasgow the other evening. More than two-thirds were women from Achil [sic] Island, sturdy and sun-burnt, quaintly dressed in short red kirtle, brilliant striped shawl, and enormous lace-up boots, of fearful crushing power. Though not forbidding, the women were very plain, ethnologically of low type, with small turn-up noses, small eyes, large jaws, and large flat cheekbones. The men were ugly as sin and coarse as young bulls, of which their movements were remindful. A piper struck up a jig and couples of men danced wildly about, the women looking on. Five shillings only for forty hours' sea-sickness, with permission to stand about the deck all the time. Berths were, of course, out of the question. And the boat moved slowly into the Atlantic with hundreds of bare-headed women leaning over the sides. Another boat-load will land at Liverpool, to return in September and October. The best-informed people of these parts think that under the proposed change the young female population of Mayo would be compelled to stay in England altogether, and that their competition in the English labour market would materially lower the rate of factory wage. 'They live hard and work like slaves when away from Ireland,' said an experienced sergeant of the Royal Irish Constabulary. 'And yet they are lazy, for on their return they will live somehow on the money they bring back until the time comes to go again, and during the interval they will hardly wash themselves. They will not work in their own districts, nor for their friends, the small farmers. Partly pride, partly laziness; you cannot understand them. The man who attempts to explain the inconsistencies of the Irish character will have all his work before him.'

Doc. 5.8: Irish Migrants in Edwardian London

C. O'Conor Eccles, 'Scottish, Irish and Welsh London', in G.R. Sims (ed.), *Living London* (London, 1902; reprinted as *Edwardian London*, 4 vols., London, 1990), vol. 3, 98–9.

Every year from Scotland, from Ireland, and from Wales young men flock in hundreds to London. They are of all classes, all degrees of education, united in one common aim, that, namely, of making a living. The newcomers find employment in many different ways. Scotland and Ireland largely recruit the ranks of the police force. The Civil Service, too, in all its branches employs many Irishmen, whose brilliant talents often enable them to rise from small posts to places of high emolument and power. Scottish and Irish doctors, too, abound, from men who have made a name and dwell in fashionable squares to struggling practitioners in Whitechapel and Southwark. Irish barristers are numerous, and, thanks to the eloquence which is their birthright, win fame and fortune in their profession. Journalism likewise attracts large numbers of Scotsmen and Irishmen so that it is a saying in Fleet Street that English editors are kept simply to correct the 'shalls' and 'wills' of their colleagues . . . Very many Irishmen of the poorest class likewise drift to London in search of employment. Debarred by lack of means from lodgings where the rate of payment is high, and yet compelled to be near the great industrial centres where chance jobs may be most easily picked up, they and their families are automatically forced into slum dwellings in such neighbourhoods as Poplar, Islington, and Southwark, where they form colonies of people wonderfully good and helpful to each other, but over-crowded, deprived of all that brightens and beautifies existence, and compelled to bring up their children under circumstances that give the little ones but a slender chance of developing their highest possibilities.

Part 2

Settlement

Caribee Island, Wolverhampton
This narrow cul-de-sac off Stafford Street housed some of Wolverhampton's
poorest Irish families during the 1840s and 1850s; reproduced by permission
of Wolverhampton Library and Museums Service.

INTRODUCTION

The early decades of the nineteenth century witnessed a substantial increase in the pace and scale of Irish migration to Britain. The 1841 census enumerated the Irish-born population of England, Wales and Scotland at 419,000 and by 1851, in consequence of the massive Famine exodus, this figure had risen to 727,000. In 1861 the Irish-born population peaked at 806,000, when it comprised 3.5% of the total population. Thereafter, as migration from Ireland to Britain declined, the number of Irish-born immigrants in Britain also progressively fell, declining to 550,000 in 1911 (or 1.3% of the population), reviving only later in the twentieth century (**Doc. 6.1**).

Census returns do not, however, provide an entirely accurate enumeration of the number of Irish migrants and their dependents in nineteenth-century Britain. First, by providing merely decennial 'snapshots' of the Irish-born in specific places at particular points in time, they ignored intercensal patterns of migration, settlement, and re-emigration. Second, they excluded the vast army of seasonal migrants who travelled between Ireland and Britain. Third, and most important, they did not include the children of Irish migrants born in Britain, who were variously described in the census registers as English, Scottish or Welsh. Thus the actual size of ethnic Irish communities was undoubtedly much higher than contemporary census records suggest and in 1872 *The Nation*, a Dublin newspaper, argued that the number of Irish-born indicated in official statistics should be doubled in order to obtain a more realistic enumeration of the true size of the ethnic Irish community in Britain.[1]

In general, the vast majority of these migrants travelled from Ireland to Britain by one of three well-established emigrant routes, each distinguished by place of origin and destination. Thus migrants from Ulster and North Connaught took the northern route from Derry, Newry and Belfast to Scotland, via Glasgow, and to Cumbria; emigrants from Connaught and most of Leinster took the midland route from Dublin to Holyhead and Liverpool; whilst migrants from South Leinster and Munster took the southern route from Cork to Bristol, South Wales and London.[2] However, the extent to which the ultimate destinations of Irish migrants in British towns and cities were determined by economic and cultural criteria related to their regional origins in Ireland, or by the ports of embarkation and arrival, is still a matter for academic enquiry. The census enumerators only recorded the country, and not the county of birth where it lay outside

---

[1] See H. Heinrick, *A Survey of the Irish in England in 1872* (Dublin, 1872; edited with an introduction by Alan O'Day, London, 1990).

[2] A. Redford, *Labour Migration in England, 1800–1850* (London, 1926; rev. ed. Manchester, 1964), 132–49.

England and Wales, thus the regional origins of the urban Irish in nineteenth-century Britain sometimes remain as opaque as their motives for settling in one town as opposed to another. Moreover, there is some evidence to suggest that migrants from specific localities in Ireland clustered within British towns rather than in specific towns, thereby establishing differentiated 'Irish' communities on a local level.[3]

The majority of Irish immigrants were young, single people. Males slightly outnumbered females in both England and Scotland until the end of the century when, in England at least, the ratio was reversed. Once disembarked, most of these newcomers settled in the ports of entry, notably Glasgow and Liverpool, in London, in the industrial towns of South Wales, the Midlands, South Lancashire and the North-East, and in Scotland, where there were notable concentrations in Edinburgh and Dundee. These settlement patterns pre-dated the Irish Famine and were confirmed by the 1841 census (**Doc. 6.2**), which indicated that Irish settlement was most pronounced in the Scottish counties of Renfrew (14.8%), Lanark (14.6%) and Wigtown (12.3%) and in the English counties of Lancashire (8.9%), Cheshire (5.7%), Durham (5.4%) and Cumberland (5.1%). Similarly, the four towns with the largest Irish-born populations were London (108,548 or 4.6% of the population), Liverpool (83,813 or 22.3%), Glasgow (59,801 or 18.1%) and Manchester (52,504 or 13.1%), although almost two-thirds of all Irish-born immigrants were scattered in towns and cities outside these four great centres. By 1861 the Irish-born were more widely distributed throughout Britain, with developing communities in the North-East, South Wales and the Midlands which reflected the expanding industrial economies of, and associated opportunities for employment in, these districts (**Doc. 6.3**). However, by 1891 the pattern of Irish settlement in Britain was remarkably similar to that of 1841 and mirrored the overall decline in the size (both numerically and proportionately) of the Irish-born population (**Doc. 6.4**).[4]

Clearly, Irish settlement in nineteenth-century Britain was an overwhelmingly urban phenomenon and some towns and cities contained substantial Irish communities, although a comparison of the 'top twenty' towns with Irish-born inhabitants in 1851 and 1871 shows that Irish migrants headed for those towns where there was a demand for labour, thereby reflecting broader changes in the mid-Victorian economy (**Doc. 6.5**).

Nevertheless, during the first half of the nineteenth century, Irish

---

[3] C. Pooley, 'Segregation or Integration?: The Residential Experience of the Irish in Mid-Victorian Britain', in Swift and Gilley, *The Irish in Britain, 1815–1939*, 71–110. For a useful overview of Irish migration and settlement during the period, see MacRaild, *Irish Migrants in Modern Britain*, especially chap. 2, 'Concentration and Dispersal: Irish Labour Migration to Britain', 42–74.

[4] Fitzpatrick, 'A Curious Middle Place?: The Irish in Britain, 1871–1921', in Swift and Gilley, *The Irish in Britain, 1815–1939*, 19–70.

migration to British urban-industrial districts was generally unpopular, despite the occasional expression of sympathetic sentiments (**Doc. 7.1**). Indeed, even before the massive influx of poor Irish men, women and children during the Great Famine, some social investigators and commentators, including James Phillips Kay (**Doc. 7.2**), Thomas Carlyle (**Doc. 7.3**) and Frederick Engels (**Doc. 7.4**) variously perceived Irish immigration as little short of a social disaster which, it was argued, exacerbated urban squalor, constituted a health hazard, increased the burden on the poor rates, and lowered the living standards of the non-Irish, whilst Irish fertility rates aroused fears of racial deterioration. These fears, rooted as they were in the poverty of Irish migrants, were endorsed by the economist J.R. McCulloch (**Doc. 7.5**) after the Famine (by which time the Irish-born population of England, Scotland and Wales had virtually doubled), and need to be understood in the context of the many contemporary issues – urban squalor, disease, disorder, vagrancy and unemployment – with which they became entangled. In a sense, it was a tragic coincidence that the growing awareness of acute urban problems during the 1830s and 1840s, reflected in the 'Condition of England' question, occurred at the same time as the rising tide of Irish immigration.[5]

This said, it is difficult to strike a proper mean between the lighter and darker sides of the Irish urban experience, which differed from one settlement to another. Much contemporary qualitative evidence, which referred specifically to 'the lowest Irish' – the very poorest Irish – rather than to all Irish migrants, suggested that during the 1830s and 1840s in particular the newcomers were located in socially immobile and unintegrated ghettos or 'Little Irelands', isolated in particular streets and courts from the surrounding populations. The image of these districts, including St Giles, graphically described by Flora Tristan and Montague Gore in 1840 and 1851 respectively (**Doc. 8.1**), or Manchester's 'Little Ireland', observed by Frederick Engels in 1844 (**Doc. 8.2**), was popularly perceived to be a reality of Irish urban settlement, and many towns possessed so-called 'Irish quarters' populated by extended families, including Goit Side in Bradford, Rock Row in Stockport, Sandygate in Newcastle, Bedern in York, and Caribee Island in Wolverhampton (**Doc. 8.3**).[6] The tendency of the Irish poor to cluster in

---

[5] For a full discussion of attitudes to Irish immigration during this period, see especially S. Gilley, 'English Attitudes to the Irish in England, 1780–1900', in C. Holmes, *Immigrants and Minorities in British Society*, 81–110; G. Davis, 'Little Irelands', in Swift and Gilley, *The Irish in Britain, 1815–1939*, 104–33; MacRaild, 'Irish Immigration and the "Condition of England" Question', 67–85.

[6] See C. Richardson, 'The Irish in Victorian Bradford', *The Bradford Antiquary*, 9 (1976), 294–316; P. Millward, 'The Stockport Riots of 1852: A Study of Anti-Catholic and Anti-Irish sentiment', in Swift and Gilley, *The Irish in the Victorian City*, 207–24; F. Finnegan, 'The Irish in York', in Swift and Gilley, *The Irish in the Victorian City*, 59–84; R. Swift, 'Crime and Ethnicity: The Irish in Early Victorian Wolverhampton', *West Midlands Studies*, 13 (1980), 1–5.

such districts was influenced by the availability of cheap accommodation, including lodging-houses (**Doc. 8.5**), the existence of familial and kinship networks, proximity to available employment, and the development of Irish social, cultural and religious organizations.

Yet the whole question of Irish 'ghettoisation' requires the most careful consideration, for the Irish did not congregate in 'ghettos' to the exclusion of other ethnic groups. For example, St Giles was not inhabited exclusively by the Irish poor and was, as a criminal rookery, atypical of Irish districts in London. Similarly, while there were areas of concentrated Irish settlement in Liverpool, Blackburn and Bolton, they were not wholly isolated from the host community, and even where Irish immigrants dominated particular streets, courts and squares they were seldom shut off from the native population.[7] Indeed, in Liverpool almost half the Irish lived in enumeration districts with low or medium concentrations of Irish people (**Doc. 8.4**),[8] and this also appears to have been the case in London and York, where the Irish lived cheek by jowl beside natives of the same social class.[9] This was also true of Irish settlement in smaller English towns such as Stafford and Chester, where the Irish-born population was geographically dispersed and where the formation of an identifiable Irish community was inhibited by a high level of out-migration.[10] In short, the poor Irish lived among the English poor, and the upwardly mobile among the English upper-working or middle class.

This said, 'Little Irelands' were far from being static communities, for these districts, inhabited as they were by a notoriously transient populace which moved both within and between towns, experienced continual in-migration and out-migration, with only a relatively small number of migrants establishing permanent settlements.[11] Moreover, Victorian slum

---

[7] Pooley 'Segregation or Integration', 71–110.

[8] For further details, see J.D. Papworth, 'The Irish in Liverpool, 1835–71: Family Structure and Residential Mobility' (University of Liverpool PhD thesis, 1982).

[9] For London, see L.H. Lees, *Exiles of Erin: Irish Migrants in Victorian London* (Manchester, 1979), 55–87; For York, see F. Finnegan, *Poverty and Prejudice: Irish Immigrants in York, 1840–75* (Cork, 1982), 16–68.

[10] For Stafford, see especially John Herson's two essays, 'Irish Migration and Settlement in Victorian England: A Small-Town Perspective', in Swift and Gilley, *The Irish in Britain, 1815–1939*, 84–103, and 'Migration, "Community" or Integration?: Irish Families in Victorian Stafford', in Swift and Gilley, *The Irish in Victorian Britain: The Local Dimension*, 156–89; For Chester, see K.T. Jeffes, 'The Irish in Early Victorian Chester: An Outcast Community?', in R. Swift (ed.), *Victorian Chester: Essays in Social History, 1830–1900* (Liverpool, 1996), 85–118.

[11] For a useful micro-study, see Mervyn Busteed's recent work on the Irish in Manchester: M.A. Busteed, R.I. Hodgson and T.F. Kennedy, 'The Myth and Reality of Irish Migrants in Mid-Nineteenth Century Manchester: A Preliminary Study', in O'Sullivan, *The Irish World Wide*, vol. 2., *The Irish in the New Communities*, 26–51; M.A. Busteed, '"The Most Horrible Spot"?: The Legend of Manchester's Little Ireland', in S. Briggs, P. Hyland and N. Sammells (eds), *Reviewing Ireland: Essays and Interviews from Irish Studies Review* (Bath, 1998), 74–89.

zones and their occupants were themselves constantly shifting, and by the 1880s many of the slums depicted in the 1830s and 1840s, including Manchester's 'Little Ireland' and Wolverhampton's Caribee Island, had disappeared in the wake of the Artisans Dwellings Act of 1875 and their populations had been dispersed elsewhere. In some towns, districts once inhabited by the Irish were populated by later immigrants, as in Stepney, which became a focus for Eastern European, and largely Jewish, settlement by the end of the century.[12]

Thus the pattern of Irish settlement was determined largely by economic considerations, and if there was an 'Irish community' it did not rest on a pattern of rigid residential segregation. Clearly, this whole question warrants further study, in part through the continued application of quantitative analysis to the diachronic study of census returns on a local level. Of course, this does not altogether dispose of the ghetto, for there were clusters of predominantly poor and relatively immobile Irish households in specific streets and courts which lay at the heart of so-called 'Little Irelands'. In 1872, for example, *The Nation* testified to the existence of Irish Catholic communities like that of Birmingham (**Doc. 8.6**) which were largely working class and poor. But the ghetto at its strictest was not completely sealed, and the term may well be inappropriate to describe the living conditions of most of the Irish in Britain, particularly during the second half of the nineteenth century.

DISTRIBUTION IN BRITAIN

Doc. 6.1: The Irish-Born Population of Britain, 1841–1911

Census abstracts, 1841–1911.

YEAR	POPULATION (THOUSANDS)						
	England & Wales		Scotland			Britain	
	Number of Irish-born	As % whole	Number of Irish-born	As % whole	Total pop.	Total Irish-born	Irish-born as % whole
1841	291,000	1.8	128,000	4.9	18,534,000	19,000	2.3
1851	520,000	2.9	207,000	7.2	20,816,000	727,000	3.5
1861	602,000	3.0	204,000	6.7	23,128,000	806,000	3.5
1871	566,000	2.5	208,000	6.2	26,072,000	774,000	2.9
1881	562,000	2.2	219,000	5.8	29,710,000	781,000	2.6
1891	458,000	1.6	195,000	4.8	33,028,000	653,000	1.9
1901	426,000	1.3	205,000	4.6	36,999,000	631,000	1.7
1911	375,000	1.0	175,000	3.7	40,831,000	550,000	1.3

[12] See A. Bartlett, 'The Churches in Bermondsey, 1880–1939' (University of Birmingham PhD thesis, 1987).

Doc. 6.2: The Distribution of the Irish-Born in Britain in 1841

J.A. Jackson, *The Irish in Britain* (1963), 8.

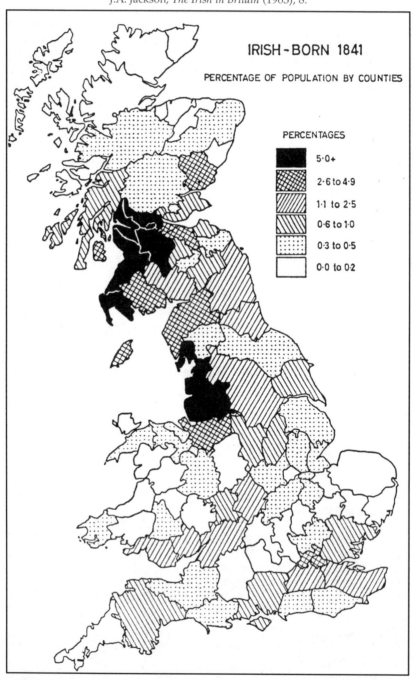

Doc. 6.3: The Distribution of the Irish-Born in Britain in 1861

J.A. Jackson, *The Irish in Britain* (1963), 12.

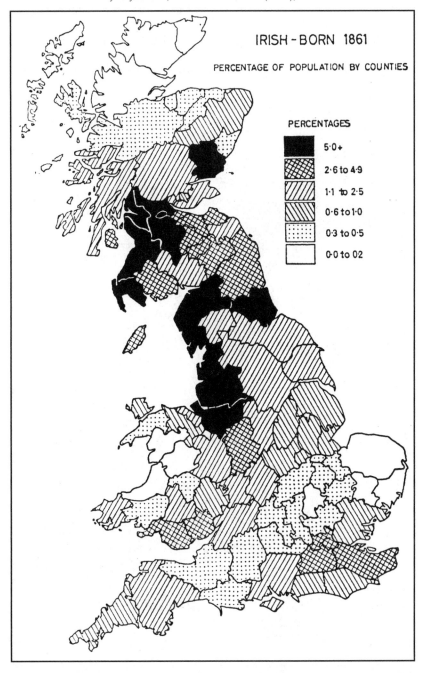

Doc. 6.4: The Distribution of the Irish-Born in Britain in 1891

J.A. Jackson, *The Irish in Britain* (1963), 16.

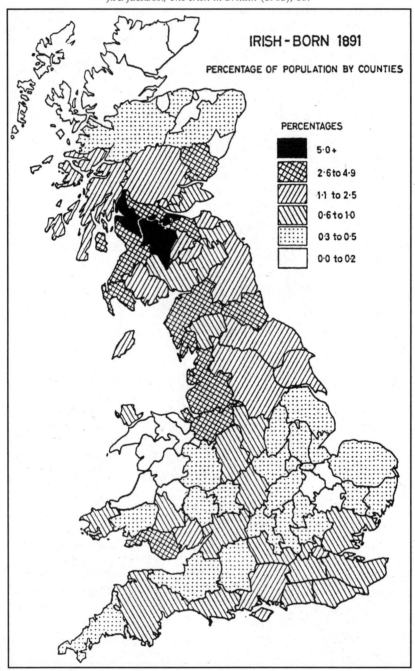

IRISH - BORN 1891

PERCENTAGE OF POPULATION BY COUNTIES

PERCENTAGES

5·0+

2·6 to 4·9

1·1 to 2·5

0·6 to 1·0

0·3 to 0·5

0·0 to 0·2

Doc. 6.5: The 'Top Twenty' Irish Towns in Britain, 1851–1871.

From C. Pooley, 'Segregation or Integration? The Residential Experience of the Irish in Mid-Victorian Britain' in R. Swift and S. Gilley (eds.), *The Irish in Britain, 1815–1939*, 66–7.

Town	1851 Number Irish-born	As % total	Town	1871 Number Irish-born	As % total
London	108,548	4.6	London	91,171	2.8
Liverpool	83,813	22.3	Liverpool	76,761	15.6
Glasgow	59,801	18.2	Glasgow	68,330	14.3
Manchester	52,504	13.1	Manchester	34,066	9.0
Dundee	14,889	18.9	Dundee	14,195	11.9
Edinburgh	12,514	6.5	Leeds	10,128	3.9
Birmingham	9,341	4.0	Greenock	9,462	16.6
Bradford	9,279	8.9	Birmingham	9,076	2.6
Leeds	8,466	4.9	Bradford	8,318	5.8
Newcastle	7,124	8.1	Edinburgh	8,031	3.3
Stockport	5,701	10.6	Newcastle	6,904	5.4
Preston	5,122	7.4	Sheffield	6,082	2.5
Bristol	4,761	3.5	Bolton	5,383	6.5
Sheffield	4,477	3.3	Paisley	4,703	9.8
Bolton	4,453	7.3	Preston	4,646	5.5
Paisley	4,036	12.7	Sunderland	4,469	4.6
Sunderland	3,601	5.5	Plymouth	4,093	6.2
Wolverhampton	3,491	7.0	Stockport	3,975	7.5
Merthyr Tydfil	3,051	11.3	Bristol	3,876	2.1
Hull	2,983	3.5	Middlesbrough	3,621	9.2

DESCRIPTIONS OF THE IRISH

Doc. 7.1: *The Glasgow Courier* on Irish Immigration, 1827

The Glasgow Courier, 11 November 1827.

Equally childish and absurd also are those complaints which we hear so loudly made, and so frequently repeated, about the great influx of Irish labourers amongst us, and the vicious characters which are thus thrown like so many brands amidst the community. That the best of the population of that country [Ireland] visit us, is not to be expected; and if we lend the prudent hand, which we ought to lend, and which we are bound in duty to lend, in order to improve and enlighten them in Ireland, and enable them to live in comfort in their native country, then, and not till then, will

Scotland and England cease to be inundated with Irishmen and Irish-women of idle habits and vicious dispositions. We do not stand forward to deny, to vindicate, or to gloss over the errors and the crimes which are but too frequently committed in Ireland; but we would, at the same time, bear in mind amongst ourselves perfection does not exist, and that wherever we find man uninstructed, uncivilised, idle and poor, we will find his passions always to run in extremes. But it is the cause of these things which we ought, and are called upon, to remove. To what place also ought the Irish to go to seek relief but amongst their fellow-subjects under the same sceptre; and why should we complain of the influx of numbers, while we do so little, we mean that is judicious and effectual, to give them profitable employment at home? The Irishman has just as good a right, in our opinion, to go to this country, trying to better his condition, as the Scotch-man or Englishman has to go to Ireland, or any other part of the British dominions, to try to better their fortunes and their conditions. Let us hear no more complaints, therefore, about the injurious effects of the influx of Irish into Great Britain, except to notice it only with a view to remove the cause; for we may depend upon it that the reproach which arises, and which will continue to arise from the Irish being obliged to do so, lies as much at our door as it does at the door of the people of Ireland.

Doc. 7.2: James Phillips Kay on Irish Immigration, 1832

James Kay (Shuttleworth), *The Moral and Physical Condition of the Working Classes employed in the Cotton Manufacture in Manchester* (1832), 20–21; 44–5.

Manchester, properly so called, is chiefly inhabited by shopkeepers and the labouring classes. Those districts where the poor dwell are of very recent origin. The rapid growth of the cotton manufacture has attracted hither operatives from every part of the kingdom, and Ireland has poured forth the most destitute of her hordes to supply the constantly increasing demand for labour. This immigration has been, in one important respect, a serious evil. The Irish have taught the labouring classes of this country a pernicious lesson. The system of cottier farming, the demoralization and barbarism of the people, and the general use of the potato as the chief article of food, have encouraged the population in Ireland more rapidly than the available means of subsistence have been increased. Debased alike by ignorance and pauperism, they have discovered, with the savage, what is the minimum of the means of life, upon which existence may be prolonged. The paucity of the amount of means and comforts necessary for the mere support of life, is not known by a more civilized population, and this secret has been taught the labourers of this country by the Irish. The hand-loom weavers still continue a very extensive class and though they labour four-teen hours and upwards daily, earn only from five to seven or eight shillings per week. They consist chiefly of Irish, and are affected by all the causes of moral and physical depression which we have enumerated. Ill-fed – ill-clothed – half-sheltered and ignorant; – weaving in those close damp cellars, or crowded workshops, it only remains that they should become, as is too frequently the case, demoralized and reckless, to render perfect the portraiture of savage life. Amongst men so situated, the moral check has no influence in preventing the rapid increase of the population. The existence of cheap and redundant labour in the market has, also, a constant tendency to lessen its general price, and hence the wages of the English operatives have been exceedingly reduced by this immigration of Irish – their comforts consequently diminished – their manners debased – and the natural influence of manufactures on the people thwarted. We are well convinced that without the numerical and moral influence of this class, on the means and on the character of the people who have had to enter into competition with them in the market of labour, we should have had less occasion to regret the physical and moral degradation of the operative population.

Doc. 7.3: Thomas Carlyle on Irish Immigration, 1839

Thomas Carlyle, *Chartism* (1839),181–3.

We English pay, even now, the bitter smart of long centuries of injustice to our neighbour Island . . . England is guilty towards Ireland; and reaps at last, in full measure, the fruit of fifteen generations of wrong-doing. But the thing we had to state here was our inference from that mournful fact of the third Sanspotato, coupled with this other well-known fact that the Irish speak a partially intelligible dialect of English, and their fare across by steam is four-pence sterling! Crowds of miserable Irish darken all our towns. The wild Milesian features, looking false ingenuity, restlessness, unreason, misery and mockery, salute you on all highways and byways. The English coachman, as he whirls past, lashes the Milesian with his whip, courses him with his tongue; the Milesian is holding out his hat to beg. He is the sorest evil this country has to strive with. In his rags and laughing savagery, he is there to undertake all work that can be done by mere strength of hand and back; for wages that will purchase him potatoes. He needs only salt for condiment; he lodges to his mind in any pighutch or doghutch, roosts in outhouses; and wears a suit of tatters, the getting off and on of which is said to be a difficult operation, transacted only in festivals and the hightides of the calendar. The Saxon man if he cannot work on these terms, finds no work. He too may be ignorant; but he has not sunk from decent manhood to squalid apehood; he cannot continue there. American forests lie untilled across the ocean; the uncivilized Irishman, not by his strength, but by the opposite of strength, drives out the Saxon native, takes possession in his room. There abides he, in his squalor and unreason, in his falsity and drunken violence, as the ready-made nucleus of degradation and disorder. Whosoever struggles, swimming with difficulty, may now find an example how the human being can exist not swimming but sunk. Let him sink; he is not the worst of men; not worse than this man. We have quarantines against pestilence; but there is no pestilence like that; and against it what quarantine is possible? It is lamentable to look upon.

Doc. 7.4: Frederick Engels on Irish Immigration, 1844

F. Engels, *The Condition of the Working Class in England* (1844), 122–5.

The rapid extension of English industry could not have taken place if England had not possessed in the numerous and impoverished population of Ireland a reserve at command. The Irish had nothing to lose at home, and much to gain in England . . . These people having grown up almost without civilization, accustomed from youth to every sort of privation, rough, intemperate, and improvident, bring all their brutal habits with them among a class of the English population which has, in truth, little inducement to cultivate education and morality . . . With such a competitor the English working-man has to struggle, with a competitor upon the lowest plane possible in a civilized country, who for this very reason requires less wages than any other. Nothing else is therefore possible than that, as Carlyle says, the wages of the English working-man should be forced down further and further in every branch in which the Irish compete with him. And these branches are many. All such as demand little or no skill are open to the Irish. For work which requires long training or regular, pertinacious application, the dissolute, unsteady, drunken Irishman is on too low a plane. To become a mechanic, a mill-hand, he would have to adopt the English civilization, the English customs, become, in the main, an Englishman. But for all simple, less exact work, wherever it is a question more of strength than skill, the Irishman is as good as the Englishman. Such occupations are therefore especially over-crowded with Irishmen: hand-weavers, bricklayers, porters, jobbers, and such workers, count hordes of Irishmen among their number, and the pressure of this race has done much to depress wages and lower the working-class. And even if the Irish, who have forced their way into other occupations, should become more civilized, enough of the old habits would cling to them to have a strong degrading influence upon their English companions in toil, especially in view of the general effect of being surrounded by the Irish. For when, in almost every great city, a fifth or a quarter of the workers are Irish, or children of Irish parents, who have grown up among Irish filth, no one can wonder if the life, habits, intelligence, moral status – in short, the whole character of the working-class assimilates a great part of the Irish characteristics. On the contrary, it is easy to understand how the degrading position of the English workers, engendered by our modern history, and its immediate consequences, has been still more degraded by the presence of Irish competition.

Doc. 7.5: J.R. McCulloch on Irish Immigration, 1854

J.R. McCulloch, *Account of the British Empire* (1854), 395.

Within the last few years, however, an immigration has taken place into England, and also into Scotland, that has already had a great, and promises to have a still greater, influence over the blood and character of the people. We allude to the immigration of Irish, or Celtic, labourers into Great Britain. Considering the want of employment, and the low rate of wages in Ireland, the temptation to emigrate to England is all but irresistable; and steam communication has reduced the expense of transit to almost nothing; having established, as it were, floating bridges between Dublin and Liverpool, Belfast and Glasgow, Waterford and Bristol. In consequence, very many thousands of Irish labourers have established themselves in Lancashire and other places, principally on the west coast of England and Scotland. So great indeed has been this immigration, that, at present, it is believed about a *fourth part* of the population of Manchester and Glasgow consists of native Irish and of the descendants of such; and in other places the proportion of Irish blood is even greater. Instead of being diminished, this influx, great as it has been, has latterly been augmented, and threatens to entail very pernicious consequences on the people of England and Scotland. The wages of the latter have been reduced by the competition of the Irish; and, which is still worse, their opinions in regard to what is necessary for their comfortable and decent subsistence have been lowered by the contaminating influence of example, and by familiar intercourse with those who are content to live in filth and misery. It is difficult to see how, with the existing facilities of intercourse between the two countries, the condition of the labouring classes in them should not be pretty much approximated; and there is too much reason to fear that the equalisation will be brought about rather by the degradation of the English than by the elevation of the Irish. Hitherto the latter have been very little, if at all, improved by their residence in England; but the English and Scots with whom they associate have been certainly deteriorated. Though painful and difficult, the importance of the subject gives it the strongest claims on the public attention. It were better that measures should be adopted to check, if that be possible, the spread of pauperism in Ireland, and to improve the condition of its inhabitants; but, if this cannot be done, it seems indispensable that we should endeavour to guard against being overrun by a pauper horde.

LIVING CONDITIONS

Doc. 8.1: The Irish Quarter of St Giles, London

Flora Tristan, *London Journal [Promenades Dans Londres]*(1840), 134–6.

[a]   Oxford Street, a fine long street thronged with carriages, a street of broad sidewalks and smart shops, runs almost perpendicularly into Totten-ham Court Road. Where the two streets meet, there is a small alley invariably blocked by an enormous coal wagon, so that there is scarcely enough room to squeeze by. The little alley is called Bainbridge Street and gives access to the Irish quarter.

The alley, entirely taken up by the great coal warehouse, is impassable. On the right we found another alley, this one not even paved and full of nauseating, stagnant pools of greasy, soapy water and other filth. In St.Giles one feels asphyxiated by the stench; there is no air to breathe nor daylight to find one's way. The wretched inhabitants must wash their own rags, and they hang them out to dry on poles that stretch from one side of the alley to the other, so that fresh air and sunlight are completely blocked out. Foul odours rise from the mire at your feet, and dirty water drips upon your head from the paupers' rags above.

Imagine men, women, children, all barefooted, ploughing through the nasty, filthy mire. Some were leaning against the wall for lack of place to sit, others were squatting on the ground, there were children lying about in the mud like pigs. No, unless one has seen it with his own eyes, it is impossible to imagine such squalid indigence, such utter debasement, nor a more total degradation of the human creature!

With my own eyes I saw children without a stitch of clothing, young girls, nursing mothers with no shoes on their feet, wearing only a tattered shift which barely covered their naked bodies. Old people huddling for warmth in rotten straw, young men dressed in tatters. Inside and out the decrepit hovels are like the rags of the people who live in them. Neither the windows nor the doors of most of these lodgings can be closed off; floors are mostly bare earth; each one has its own, crudely made oak table, a stool, a wooden bench, a few tin bowls; everyone sleeps in the one room, father, mother, sons, daughters and friends, like so many animals. Such is the comfort of the Irish quarter! It is a dreadful thing to see! and yet it is nothing compared to the expressions on the faces! They are all dismayingly thin, debilitated, sickly; their faces, necks, and hands are covered with sores; their skin is so dirty, their hair so filthy and dishevelled that they look like woolly-headed Negroes; their hollow eyes express intense stupor. How do these people earn their living? by prostitution and theft. At the tender age of nine or ten boys go out to steal. At eleven or twelve girls are sold to brothels. All of them, men and women alike, live off thievery; and old people beg. If I had seen this district before visiting Newgate, I would not have been surprised to learn that forty to sixty children and as many prostitutes are sent there every month. Theft is the logical consequence of poverty carried to its ultimate limits.

Montague Gore, *On the Dwellings of the Poor* (London, 1851), viii–xiv.

[b]   Rows of crumbling houses flanked by courts and alleys, cul de sac, etc., in the very densest part of which the wretchedness of London takes shelter . . . squalid children, haggard men, with long uncombed hair, in rags, with a short pipe in their mouths, many speaking Irish, women without shoes or stockings – a babe perhaps at the breast with a single garment, confined to the waist by a bit of string; wolfish-looking dogs; decayed vegetables strewing the pavement, low public-houses; linen hanging across the street to dry. In one house a hundred persons have been known to sleep on a given night. In these rooms are piled the wares by which some of the inhabitants gain their precarious living – oranges, herrings, water-cresses, onions seemed to be the most marketable articles; and there were sweepers, cadgers or beggars, stray luggage-porters, etc., lounging about. But nine-tenths of the inhabitants are Irish; do we then set down to Irish nurture this account of wretchedness and immorality? God forbid! We believe that female profligacy is more rare in Ireland than in England, though poverty is more excessive. But the Irish coming to London seem to regard it as a heathen city and to give themselves up at once to a course of recklessness and crime. The misery, filth and crowded condition of the Irish cabin is realized in St. Giles. The purity of the female character which is the boast of Irish historians here at least is a fable.

Doc. 8.2: 'Little Ireland' in Manchester, 1844

Frederick Engels, *The Condition of the Working Class in England* (1844), 934.

But the most horrible spot (if I should describe all the separate spots in detail I should never come to the end) lies on the Manchester side, immediately south-west of Oxford Road, and is known as Little Ireland. In a rather deep hole, in a curve of the Medlock and surrounded on all four sides by tall factories and high embankments, covered with buildings, stand two groups of about two hundred cottages, built chiefly back to back, in which live about four thousand human beings, most of them Irish. The cottages are old, dirty, and of the smallest sort, the streets uneven, fallen into ruts and in part without drains or pavement; masses of refuse, offal and sickening filth lie among standing pools in all directions; the atmosphere is poisoned by the effluvia from these, and laden and darkened by the smoke of a dozen tall factory chimneys. A horde of ragged women and children swarm about here, as filthy as the swine that thrive upon the garbage heaps and in the puddles. In short, the whole rookery furnishes such a hateful and repulsive spectacle as can hardly be equalled in the worst court on the Irk. The race that lives in these ruinous cottages, behind broken windows, mended with oilskin, sprung doors, and rotten door-posts, or in dark, wet cellars, in measureless filth and stench, in this atmosphere penned in as if with a purpose, this race must really have reached the lowest stage of humanity. This is the impression and the line of thought which the exterior of this district forces upon the beholder. But what must one think when he hears that in each of these pens, containing at most two rooms, a garret, and perhaps a cellar, on the average twenty human beings live; that in the whole region, for each one hundred and twenty persons, one usually inaccessible privy is provided; and that in spite of all the preachings of the physicians, in spite of the excitement into which the cholera epidemic plunged the sanitary police by reason of the condition of Little Ireland, in spite of everything, in this year of grace 1844, it is in almost the same state as in 1831! Dr. Kay asserts that not only the cellars but the first floors of all the houses in this district are damp; that a number of cellars once filled up with earth have now been emptied and are occupied once more by Irish people; that in one cellar the water constantly wells up through a hole stopped with clay, the cellar lying below the river level, so that its occupant, a hand-loom weaver, had to bale out the water from his dwelling every morning and pour it into the street!

Doc. 8.3: An Irish Household in Caribee Island, Wolverhampton, in 1851

Occupants of No. 8 Caribee Island, Wolverhampton, on 30 March 1851 from 1851 Census.

Name	Relation	Condition	Age	Occupation	Birthplace
Thomas McHale	Head	Married	42	Agricl. lab.	Ireland
Catherine McHale	Wife	Married	34	–	Ireland
Mary McHale	Daughter	Single	12	Scholar	Ireland
Bridget McHale	Daughter	Single	10	Scholar	Ireland
Michael McHale	Son	Single	2	–	Wolverhampton
Anne McHale	Daughter	Single	3m	–	Wolverhampton
William McHale	Brother	Married	44	Agricl. lab.	Ireland
David McHale	Brother	Married	39	Agricl. lab.	Ireland
Catherine McHale	Sister/law	Married	35	–	Ireland
Mary McHale	Sister/law	Married	30	–	Ireland
James Gerraghty	Cousin	Single	26	Agricl. lab.	Ireland
Martin Walsh	Visitor	Single	21	Agricl. lab.	Ireland
Michael McLynn	Visitor	Single	24	Agricl. lab.	Ireland
Anthony Cunningham	Visitor	Single	28	Agricl. lab.	Ireland
Bridget Cunningham	Visitor	Single	23	–	Ireland

Doc. 8.4: An Irish Lodging House in Bangor, 1851

Occupants of 91 Robert St., Bangor, from 1851 Census.

Name	Relation	Condition	Age	Occupation	Birthplace
Patrick Glasing	Head	M	64	Shoemaker	Ireland
Margaret Glasing	Wife	M	57		Ireland
Thomas Jeffrey	Lodger	M	25	Cotton Dealer	Salisbury
Catherine Jeffrey	Wife	M	21		Ireland
William Holland	Lodger	M	33	Labourer	Ireland
Edward Holland	Lodger	U	19	Labourer	Ireland
Mathew Digner	Lodger	U	33	Hawker	Ireland
David Jones	Lodger	M	45	Sweep	Caernarvonshire
Elizabeth Jones	Wife	M	46		Caervarvonshire
Edward (unknown)	Lodger	M	35	Sweep	Ireland
Mary	Wife	M	35		Anglesey
Mary	Daughter	U	4m		Ireland
Edward	Son	U	5	Beggar	Ireland
Caroline	Daughter	U	2	Beggar	Ireland

Doc. 8.5: The Distribution of the Irish-Born in Selected Liverpool Wards, 1841–51

From J.D. Papworth, 'The Irish in Liverpool 1835–71' (University of Liverpool unpublished PhD thesis, 1982).

Ward		1841			1851	
	Total pop.	Irish-born	Irish as %	Total pop.	Irish-born	Irish-as %
Scotland	35,290	6,095	17.3	60,065	18,275	30.4
Vauxhall	25,330	8,529	33.7	25,663	12,115	47.2
St. Pauls	18,086	3,853	21.3	14,051	3,563	25.2
Exchange	17,652	6,115	34.3	16,935	7,965	47.0
Castle Street	9,742	2,382	24.5	8,746	2,186	24.9
St. Peters	9,511	2,236	23.5	9,278	2,074	22.4
Pitt Street	15,393	3,793	24.6	12,144	3,328	27.4
Great George	19,331	4,354	22.5	20,181	6,009	29.8
Rodney	15,072	1,136	7.5	17,892	1,504	8.4
Abercromby	15,669	1,248	7.9	21,701	2,060	9.5
Lime Street	18,753	1,837	9.8	17,570	2,181	12.4
St. Annes	18,862	1,850	9.8	22,706	3,503	15.4
North Toxteth	21,714	2,275	10.5	28,270	3,681	13.0
South Toxteth	18,241	1,769	9.7	31,667	4,558	14.4
Total	258,646	47,472	18.4	306,869	72,978	23.8

Name	Relation	Condition	Age	Occupation	Birthplace
John	Son	U	11	Beggar	Ireland
Sarah	Daughter	U	8	Beggar	Ireland
Anne Butler	Lodger	U	9	Scholar	Monmouthshire
Patrick Hoon	Lodger	M	30	Hawker	Ireland
Bridget Hoon	Wife	M	30	Hawker	Ireland
Margaret Hoon	Daughter	U	7		Ireland
Mary Hoon	Daughter	U	9m		Ireland
John Canavan	Lodger	U	40	Hawker	Ireland
George Long	Lodger	M	41	Sawyer	Ireland
Ellen Long	Wife	M	40		Ireland
Ellen Long	Daughter	U	5		Ireland
John Long	Son	U	1		Liverpool
Elizabeth (unknown)	Lodger	U	37	Hawker	Pembroke
John	Lodger	U	2		Ireland

Doc. 8.6: The Irish in Birmingham, 1872

The Nation, 13 August 1872.

From Leicester to Birmingham, and we are in one of the most active centres of English political thought – a town as noted for the freedom and spirit of its people, as for the variety of its productions in art and manufactures. Here the Irish population is large, amounting to over 30,000 souls; and here the political influence which the Irish people exercise is most marked and beneficial. There is no interest, local or national, in which that influence is not felt – none in which it has not practically the power – under proper organisation and guidance – to direct the issues and control the designs of party. But here, as elsewhere among the Irish people, there is a lack of that coherent union and persistent energy so essential to the accomplishment of all that lies within their power. Trained in an excellent political school, and prompt on occasion to give evidence that its lessons have not been lost on them, our people in Birmingham have given such repeated proofs of their patriotism and fidelity, that to recite them would be only to repeat what is well and widely known: but they are too prone to relax effort when the occasion which called it forth is past, and so are unprepared to grapple with political contingencies as they arise, or exercise that amount of influence which their numbers, position, intelligence, and patriotism would ensure to them under a well-devised and permanent system of organisation. In few towns in England have the Irish people, as occasion required, come to the front and acted with more decision and effect than in Birmingham, and in scarcely any has there been less previously-organized preparation. This shows at once the strength and the weakness – the force and the fault of the people. If so much has been done without preparation, what could be effected if a people so numerous, influential, and intelligent were marshalled in their full force, and prompt, at the instance of their trained and deputed leaders, to act when called upon in the name of creed, country or principle?

Birmingham was one of the first towns in England in which a Home Rule Association was formed – the first, I believe, so publicly pledged to the principle and purpose of the movement. Since then it has scarcely kept pace with the other large towns. At present the Home Rule Association is being reorganised, and under its new management will, I have no doubt, realise the expectations of its early promise. Patriotism, ability, and public spirit are not lacking. The thing required is to combine these, and direct the whole force furnished by their combination in such a manner as to be practical and effective. To organise a complete system of registration and unite the elements of force thus obtained, to be ready for any emergency, appears to be the first essential preliminary to make the Irish power of the town felt and respected. It would be superfluous to suggest the many ways in which this would prove a source of power and an advantage. Under the guidance of a central body like the Executive of the Home Rule Association, besides furnishing the means of control in municipal and parliamentary affairs, it would bring into more close communion the thought and feeling of the Irish people, and supply one of the best means of counteracting the vitiating influences of English social life. Probably literary and political clubs in all the large towns – the programmes of which would include periodic reunions – would best effect this object. But I find I am directing instead of describing, forgetting, in my zeal to promote the good of our people, that my commission is but to see and to report on their state and condition.

In Birmingham there is to be found a larger percentage of the Irish people who are trained to skilled and artistic workmanship than in most of the other English towns; and here, as in all other cases where Irish taste and genius are cultivated, their peculiar adaptability for the higher kinds of manual art is evident. But the great body of the people earn their bread by the severest toil. Chiefly the young have been trained to skilled labour; and the numbers of those who have worked their way into middle class positions, though considerable, bear no proportion to the great toiling many. In all these classes the best elements of the Irish mind and character are to be found. The zeal – the charity – the sacrifice for others – the purity – the piety, which appear so conspicuously to distinguish the Irish race, is nowhere more marked than here. Indeed, this is true of all the Black Country, which – at least so far as relates to the Irish people – is not so black as it is painted by the Scribes and Pharisees of the Cockney press. But here in Birmingham there is a great loss – a loss that I am assured by an Irish priest who has laboured long and zealously for the welfare of his people, amounting to one in six of the Irish population. Two thousand of the young are on the road to ruin. Three thousand of the adult population in the gloom of indifference. This is the dread total. Their poverty at first drove them to live among the worst of the bad. The force of evil example dragged them to the earth. Some struggle on, good and virtuous to the last – often pinched by poverty and assailed by the most trying temptations. Others, weaker in spirit, yield to the influence of the corruption by which they are surrounded, and sink into its direful depths. The vice of drunkenness ruins hundreds. The force of example does the rest. The youth of careless or intemperate parents – (both male and female) – grow up themselves indifferent, or, it may be, imitate the example of their elders, only to surpass them in their degradation. The youth are taught indifference to parent control by their English associates, and this often in cases where the parents are examples of all that is good. Hundreds on hundreds of the Irish youth here and throughout England are thus ruined. Schooled in vice, they graduate to crime, became absorbed in the ranks of evil, and are lost. There is no shutting one's eyes to the fact. It is so here – it is so everywhere. There is just this, however, to be said about it which is highly creditable to the Irish of Birmingham. There are few – very few – Irish women who have sunk to the lowest depths of degradation. Though fallen away from what they were, they are not as those to whose example they owe their degradation – though habitually indifferent, they are rarely impure.

But when all deductions are made – and deductions there must be made everywhere in England – the condition of the Irish in Birmingham is one of power and promise. Politically – even in this most Liberal of towns – their power is sufficient to mar the Liberal programme and rule the destiny of an election; and it is a question if at the next election that power will not be used in opposition to the nominees of the Education League. Socially, the Irish here are more on an equality and in harmony with the English people than in most other places. Their patriotism is respected. Effort to obtain for Ireland her just rights not alone meets no active opposition, but, in nearly every instance, is cordially aided by Englishmen. Much of this is due to the just and liberal spirit of the people – much more to the earnest labours of a few Irishmen in combatting prejudice and promoting truthful and fair public opinion on Irish affairs – much more still to the work and example of the Rev. Arthur O'Neill – a Baptist Minister here of great local influence – whose power with the people has been one of the chief aids in destroying prejudice and creating good feeling among the English masses; and who never fails to take advantage of the occasion, whatever it may be, to proclaim the injustice of English rule in Ireland, and vindicate the right of the people to make their own laws and shape their own destiny. What has been done here can be done – nay, is being done – elsewhere; and here and throughout England the Irish people are as yet preparing for the struggle which they are determined to pursue till triumph crowns their labours, and the land of their hope and their affections is a crowned queen among the nations.

Part 3

Employment

William Darling McKay, RSA (1844–1923), *Field Working in Spring: At the Potato Pits*, reproduced by permission of the National Gallery of Scotland.

INTRODUCTION

Overall, among the country immigrants to British towns and cities, the Irish were generally the least prepared to succeed in their new environment. Indeed, the *Report on the State of the Irish Poor in Great Britain* concluded in 1836 that Irish immigration was 'an example of a less civilized population spreading themselves, as a kind of substratum, beneath a more civilized community, and, without excelling in any branch of industry, obtaining possession of all the lowest departments of manual labour'.[1] A variety of factors were seen to consign the Irish to the lowest occupations, including their lack of skill, capital and education; their low expectations and high leisure preferences, including a propensity for drink; the perceived impermanence of their residence in Britain, coupled with their contempt for authority, especially British authority; and the discrimination they faced from British employers and workers.[2] Nevertheless, the *Report on the State of the Irish Poor in Great Britain*, although presenting some evidence that the Irish lowered wages (**Doc. 9.1**), contained ample testimony from employers in regard to the importance of the contribution of Irish labour to Britain's economic development in industrial centres such as Greenock (**Doc. 9.2**) and Paisley (**Doc. 9.3**) and concluded that, on balance, Irish labour was invaluable. This said, much of the evidence given by employers to the *Report on the State of the Irish Poor* was partial, for many of these employers actually depended on cheap Irish labour and their evidence was designed to further their own interests.

The great majority of Irish-born, largely illiterate and unskilled, entered the lowliest and least healthy of urban occupations, unless they enlisted in the army, which was 30 per cent Irish in the mid-Victorian period. Most of those with limited or no skills were concentrated in unskilled occupations in mines, ironworks, textile mills and manufactories; in construction industries, notably as railway 'navvies' (**Doc. 9.4** and **10.1**), and in casual dock labour and street-selling. These were occupations for which a highly sophisticated city like London, with a highly specialised labour force, held very few rewards and the Irish could only enter the metropolitan economy with difficulty. Although a minority of skilled workers entered sweated industries like cobbling and tailoring (**Doc. 10.2**), street-selling was, as Henry Mayhew observed, the most common occupation among the Irish in London's East End (**Doc. 10.3**). By contrast, in Liverpool, which was a trading and commercial rather than an industrial centre, employment opportunities, housing and sanitation were overwhelmed by the sheer magnitude of Irish immigration during the 1840s, and the demand for labour lay largely in

---

[1] *Report on the State of the Irish Poor in Great Britain, Parliamentary Papers* XXXIV (1836), 456–7.

[2] E.H. Hunt, *British Labour History, 1815–1914* (London, 1981), 158–79.

unskilled occupations for which Catholics and Protestants were in active competition.[3] Similarly, although the Glasgow Irish were able to find employment in mills and mines, they were excluded from engineering by virtue of their lack of skill, from shipbuilding by the Orange Order and from skilled trades by the craft unions,[4] and in Edinburgh, a city of legal, literary and ecclesiastical institutions, the Irish were confined to such menial occupations as general labouring in building, domestic service, portering, street-cleaning and street-lighting.[5] In contrast, the expansion of the linen and jute industry in Dundee provided the greatest possibility of advancement to Irish migrants, and Irish immigration had a considerable impact on the subsequent development of this industry through the retention of hand-loom-weaving production by local manufacturers.[6] Nevertheless, although the nature and patterns of employment were invariably influenced by the local economic infrastructures of the towns inhabited by Irish migrants, one is struck by the sheer variety of jobs undertaken by the Irish-born, as the occupational profiles of Irish-born men and women in the Lancashire town of Leigh in 1851[7] illustrate (**Doc. 10.4**).

Yet it is both easy and dangerous to generalize. In the first place, not all Irish immigrants, whether Catholic or Protestant, were poor: even by mid-century there was a small middle-class world of professional men – doctors, lawyers, soldiers, shopkeepers, merchants and journalists.[8] Irish women also formed an important sector of the migrant labour force in textile mills, laundry work, street-selling and, most notably, domestic service, and in the longer term made notable contributions to a range of low-paid professional occupations, including social work and nursing.[9] Moreover, the economic position of the Irish was far less static than many contemporaries believed and there was a degree of differentiation in Irish

---

[3] T. Gallagher, 'A Tale of Two Cities: Communal Strife in Glasgow and Liverpool before 1914', in Swift and Gilley, *The Irish in the Victorian City*, 106–29.

[4] ibid.

[5] B. Aspinwall and J. McCaffrey, 'A Comparative View of the Irish in Edinburgh in the Nineteenth Century', in Swift and Gilley, *The Irish in the Victorian City*, 130–57.

[6] B. Collins, 'Irish Emigration to Dundee and Paisley during the First Half of the Nineteenth Century', in J.M. Goldstrom and L.A. Clarkson (eds), *Irish Population, Economy and Society* (Oxford, 1981), 195–212.

[7] For further details, see F. Neal, 'Irish Settlement in the North-east and North-west of England in the Mid-Nineteenth Century', in Swift and Gilley, *The Irish in Victorian Britain*, 76–100.

[8] See, for example, O. Dudley Edwards and P. Storey, 'The Irish Press in Victorian Britain', in Swift and Gilley, *The Irish in the Victorian City*, 158–78; J. Belchem, 'Class, Creed and Country: The Irish Middle Class in Victorian Liverpool', in Swift and Gilley, *The Irish in Victorian Britain*, 190–211.

[9] The potential for further work in this under-researched area is reflected in M. Lennon, M. McAdam and J. O'Brien, *Across the Water: Irish Women's Lives in Britain* (London, 1988).

occupational patterns. The survey of the Irish in Britain conducted by Hugh Heinrick in 1872 for *The Nation* argued that in relative terms the economic position of the Irish depended less on the structure of the Irish community in a given locality than on the economic infrastructure of the area where they worked. In developing this argument, the survey pointed to the emergence of a substantial Irish middle-class in London, to the presence of skilled workers in the Midlands (**Doc. 10.5**) and to the variable experience of the Irish in South Lancashire, where an Irish middle-class had emerged in Manchester (**Doc. 10.6**) whilst in neighbouring Wigan and St. Helens the Irish were almost wholly labourers of one description or another.[10] In 1892, John Denvir, an Irish nationalist, pointed to similar contrasts in Liverpool (**Doc. 10.7**).

Although most immigrants came from rural Ireland, subsistence agriculture in Ireland did not provide them with the skills for commercial agriculture in Britain. Moreover, they had little capital to invest in the British rural economy, and British landlords rarely needed or wanted them as tenants in the villages. In consequence, relatively few Irish immigrants worked on the land and Irish rural employment in Britain continued to be confined largely to seasonal harvest labour. Although statistical evidence of the numbers who were engaged in this form of employment is notoriously unreliable, it is thought that at least 60,000 seasonal workers crossed to Britain from Irish ports each year during the 1830s. Indeed, this process was described in some detail in the *Report on the State of the Irish Poor in Great Britain* of 1836 (**Doc. 11.1**). Thereafter, Irish men and women were a familiar ingredient of the British rural landscape until the early twentieth century, variously harvesting corn (**Doc. 11.2**), digging potatoes, collecting turnips, picking hops and draining land (**Doc. 11.3**). On the whole, relatively little is known of the nature and patterns of Irish rural employment in nineteenth-century Britain, and the whole subject is deserving of further research.[11] This said, it appears that, as mechanization increased, there was an overall decline in the annual number of Irish harvesters who travelled to England, Wales and Scotland between 1841 and 1900, although there were marginal regional fluctuations, as in Lincolnshire (**Doc. 11.4**). Yet the whole process acquired the force of tradition (**Doc. 11.5**) and even by the turn of the century, when Seebohm Rowntree witnessed Irish workers tramping from York to the chicory fields in the surrounding district (**Doc. 11.6**), there were about 30,000 Irish people engaged in seasonal rural labour in Britain. Moreover, the flow paths of Irish harvesters also changed during the period, influenced by certainty of work rather than harvest rates. Thus, whereas Irish harvesters had been generally dispersed throughout the agricultural districts during the 1840s and 1850s, by the 1880s they were

---

[10] A. O'Day, *A Survey of the Irish in England, 1872* (London, 1990), 153.

[11] The most important study to date is O'Dowd, *Spalpeens and Tattie Hokers: History and Folklore of the Irish Migratory Agricultural Worker in Ireland and Britain.*

increasingly active in the northern counties of Northumberland, Yorkshire and Cheshire, the midland counties of Gloucestershire, Worcestershire, Warwickshire and Shropshire (where they worked with Welsh reapers), and in Scotland (**Doc. 11.7**).[12] In contrast, despite the annual pilgrimage of many London Irish to the hop fields of Kent, relatively few harvesters operated in the southern counties of England, although Flora Thompson observed them in Oxfordshire in the 1880s (**Doc. 11.8**).

Discussion of the nature and patterns of Irish migrant employment has obvious implications for the broader, controversial and much-debated question of the impact of Irish immigration on the British economy during the industrial revolution. The 'classic view', epitomized in the findings of the *Report on the State of the Irish Poor in Great Britain*, presumed a labour shortage in industrial Britain, yet increasing Irish immigration occurred against the background of fears of the Malthusian 'trap', increased emigration from Britain, and native hostility to the importation of Irish labour which, it was feared, would reduce workers' living standards by taking work, reducing wages and weakening trade unions. Furthermore, much of the heavy work on turnpikes, canals, docks, harbours and, to a lesser extent, railways, was achieved by native labour before Irish immigration was of much consequence.[13] Hence it is possible that although the Irish-born comprised 8.8 per cent of the British labour force by 1861, their impact as a predominantly unskilled minority of workers on the British economy was perhaps not quite as significant as some contemporaries alleged.[14] It may well be of greater historical significance, particularly in the context of contemporary attitudes towards Irish migrants, that the Irish were believed to have reduced the living standards of the British working class than that they actually did so. Nevertheless, despite some evidence of upward economic mobility over time, it is clear that by the early twentieth century Irish migrants still remained overwhelmingly and disproportionately concentrated in unskilled and semi-skilled occupations, as the occupational profile of Irish-born workers in Scotland in 1911 illustrates (**Doc. 11.9**).

---

[12] For further details, see especially D. Morgan, *Harvesters and Harvesting, 1840–1900* (London, 1982), chap. 5, 'The Irish Harvesters', 76–87; J.H. Johnson, 'Harvest Migration from Nineteenth-Century Ireland, *Institute of British Geographers*, 41 (1967), 97–112; E.J.T. Collins, 'Harvest Technology and Labour Supply in Britain, 1790–1870', *Economic History Review*, XXII (1969), 453–73.

[13] Hunt, *British Labour History, 1815–1914*, 158–79.

[14] J.G. Williamson, 'The Impact of the Irish on British Labour Markets during the Industrial Revolution', *Journal of Economic History*, XLVI (1986), 693–721.

TYPES OF WORK

Doc. 9.1: The Impact of Irish Labourers in West Cheshire, 1834

Report on the State of the Irish Poor in Great Britain (Cornewall Lewis Report), Appendix, p. 41. *Parliamentary Papers* (1836), Evidence of Henry Potts, Clerk of the Peace in Chester, February 1834.

[Q] Would it be advantageous for this town and neighbourhood if the Irish immigration could of a sudden be completely stopped?

[A] The city of Chester and its immediate neighbourhood would no doubt be benefitted by stopping the immigration of Irish labourers; but many persons who have occasion for much manual labour would give an opposite opinion.

[Q] Could the work in the town be done, or could the harvest in the country be got in, without Irish labourers?

[A] The population of Chester and its immediate neighbourhood is considered abundantly sufficient for the work of the town and country, without the Irish; but I am informed, that in the less populous districts of the county their assistance is important to the harvest, and the expense of getting it in would perhaps be doubled; for the benefit, nevertheless, of the English labourer.

[Q] Has the Irish competition lowered the general rate of wages in this town and neighbourhood; and if so, in what departments of industry, and to what extent?

[A] Certainly; more particularly in harvesting hay, corn and potatoes, and in road-making to a considerable extent, and to some extent in other departments.

[Q] Has the Irish immigration increased the amount of the poor-rates in this town and neighbourhood?

[A] Yes, indirectly, in as much as the English labourer used to make his rent during harvest-time, for which he now frequently applies to the parish, and in case of refusal probably finds his way to the poor-house.

The answers above written contain the best information on the subject I have been able to collect; but of course there must be a variety of opinion upon such questions affecting the interests of the parties so differently. At Newton (a small town near the shore of the river Dee, ten miles from Chester), two or three years ago, there was a fight between the Irish labourers (who offer themselves to hire during harvest-time there in considerable numbers) and the Lancashire, Cheshire and Welsh labourers. I am told the quarrel was provoked chiefly by the English party, who look upon the Irish with much jealousy. There was a similar affair, on a smaller scale, in Chester last week, when a party of Irish road-makers were attacked by Chester labourers, and two of them were much beaten and abused; the offenders have been punished. The following information was furnished by a gentleman on the spot:– 'The native labourers in this part of the country exceed the demand for labour at all times of the year excepting harvest; in harvest-time some Welsh and a few Irish (but very few) are employed to reap. The Cheshire men are very jealous of the Irish, who undersell them, and use all means to prevent their coming; they beat them, steal their sickles etc. I could not find that any Irish families had settled in the neighbourhood.'

Doc. 9.2: Irish Sugar-Workers in Greenock, 1836

Report on the State of the Irish Poor in Great Britain, Parliamentary Papers, (1836) xxiv–xxvii.

Many statements will be found in the appendix as to the importance of the supply of Irish labourers to the growing trade and manufactures of the north-western parts of England and the western lowlands of Scotland. Mr Thomas Fairrie, sugar manufacturer, of Greenock [stated] 'If it was not for the Irish, we should be obliged to import Germans, as is done in London. The Scotch will not work in sugar-houses; the heat drives them away in the first fortnight. If it was not for the Irish, we should be forced to give up trade; and the same applies to every sugar-house in town. This is a well-known fact. Germans would be our only resource, and we could not readily get them. Highlanders would not do the work'. Other opinions will be found from persons who, not being engaged in business, are more awake to the moral evils than to the economic benefits which have flowed from the migration of the Irish into Britain. We ought not, however, to overlook the advantage of the demand for labour in England and Scotland being amply and adequately supplied, and at a cheap rate and at very short notice, by Irish, simply because they are a potato-fed and a disorderly population. Their irregular habits and low standard of comfort may be regretted; but it is to be remembered that these Irish have been, and are, most efficient workmen; that they came in the hour of need, and that they afforded the chief part of the animal strength by which the great works of our manufacturing districts have been executed.

Doc. 9.3: Irish Textile-Workers in Paisley, 1836

Report on the State of the Irish Poor in Great Britain, Parliamentary Papers (1836), 133–4. Evidence of Alexander Carlile.

The Irish in Paisley almost uniformly belong to the poorer classes; I only remember one Irish shopkeeper; there may be a few more. They are employed in the more disagreeable and lower descriptions of labour; the employment in the cotton mills is considered of this class. A cotton spinner does not hold the same rank in society as a fancy weaver. The moral condition of the Paisley fancy weavers has been raised in the last forty years, since they have worked in their own houses, instead of being collected together in weaving factories; few of the Irish become fancy weavers; the girls in the cotton mills are chiefly Irish; there are few Irish among the sewing girls or in thread works. It is my decided opinion that our manufactures never would have extended so rapidly if we had not had large importations of Irish families; for the work of this town requires women and children as well as men. Sufficient hands for the manufacture of this neighbourhood would not have been procured from Scotland.

Nothing is more mischievous than to give to any person wages beyond his degree of civilisation. There is a complete proof of this in the comparative states of the Irish employed in common labour and those employed in cotton factories. Those employed in common labour, who can seldom earn above 9s. a week, are in general steady and industrious; while those employed in cotton factories who can earn from 20s. to 30s. a week, are a comparatively degraded class, spending the quarter part of their high earnings in gross animal indulgences. Scarcely one of these cotton spinners lives in the slightest degree of comfort; his house is ill-furnished, and himself and family ill-clothed.

Doc. 9.4: Irish Railway Labourers in the 1840s

John Denvir, *The Irish in Britain* (1892), 157–9.

The decade from 1840 to 1850 was a period of great railway development and large numbers of Irishmen were employed in the construction of the various lines which seemed to be springing up like mushrooms all over the country. The bad feeling against them often developed into open violence, and in the early years of railway construction there were frequent desperate conflicts. These untutored Irish labourers often at these times displayed courage as great as was ever seen on a regular field of battle. Such conflicts had now been going on for about ten years, and mostly arose out of the rivalry between the Irish and English 'navvies', as the labourers were called who worked on the railways . . . Encounters like these were of such constant occurrence that, in their efforts to gain a living, the Irish were literally fighting for their existence in more ways than one, in the midst of what was too often a hostile population. The famine drove them here in such numbers as to glut the labour market, which would tend to bring down wages, and thereby rouse the animosity of the native labourers. It would not be right to describe our people as having been on every occason innocent of giving provocation, though they generally were. Their native pugnacity, particularly when roused by drink, sometimes provoked these quarrels. This, however, even by the accounts in the English newspapers, was not the case in connection with some desperate rioting in and about Penrith, on the Lancaster and Carlisle railway, then in course of construction. These riots commenced on Monday, February 16th, 1846, and lasted for several days. According to the local newspaper, the rioting was commenced by the English navvies, who were unwilling to allow the Irish to work on the same part of the line. The Irish, on the whole, appear to have been fairly well able to hold their own. Some of them were attacked by their opponents in a lodging-house – probably one kept by an Irishman for the accommodation of his fellow-countrymen. Some four years after this affray a Catholic chapel was opened in Penrith, so that it would appear that the ubiquitous Irish Celt managed to hold his ground here after all, and is on good terms with his neighbours throughout Cumberland.

EXPERIENCES OF WORK

Doc. 10.1: A Navvy's Life

Patrick MacGill, 'Padding It', *Songs of the Dead End* (1920).

Hashing it out like niggers on a two and a tanner sub,
Everything sunk with our uncle, little to burn at the pub,
Fifty and six were our hours, and never an extra shift,
And whiles we were plunging at banker, and whiles we were studying thrift
Sewing and patching the trousers, till their parts were more than the whole,
Tailoring, cobbling, and darning, grubbed on a sausage and roll –
Thrift on a fourpenny hour, a matter of nineteen bob,
But we glanced askew at the gaffer, and stuck like glue to the job,
We of the soapless legion, we of the hammer and hod,
Human swine of the muck-pile, forever forgotten of God.

Was it the highland slogan? was it the bird of the north,
Out of its frost-rimmed eyrie that carried the message forth?
'Jackson has need of navvies, the navvies who understand
The graft of the offside reaches, to labour where God has bann'd,
Men of the sign of the moleskin who swear by the soundless pit,
Men who are eager for money and hurry in spending it.
Bluchers and velvet waistcoats, and kneestraps below their knees,
The great unwashed of the model – Jackson has need of these.'

Then the labourer on the railway laughed at the engine peals,
And threw his outworn shovel beneath the flange of the wheels.
The hammerman at the jumper slung his hammer aside,
Lifted his lying money and silently did a slide,
The hod was thrown on the mortar, the spade was flung in the drain,
The grub was left on the hot-plate, and the navvies were out again.

All the roads of the Kingdom converged, as it were, to one.
Which led away to the northward under the dusk and the dawn,
And out on the road we hurried, rugous and worn and thin,
Our cracking joints a-staring out through our parchment skin,
Some of us trained from our childhood, to swab in the slush and the muck,
Some who were new to the shovel, some who were down on their luck,
The prodigal son half home-sick, the jail-bird, dodger and thief,
The chucker-out from the gin shop, the lawyer minus a brief,
The green hand over from Oir'lan', the sailor tired of his ships,
Some with hair of silver, some with a woman's lips,
Old, anaemic, and bilious, lusty, lanky and slim,
Padding it, slowly and surely, padding it, resolute, grim.

Through many a sleepy hamlet, and many a noisy town,
While eyes of loathing stared us, we who were out and down,
Looking aslant at the wineshop, talking as lovers talk,
Of the lure of the gentle schooner, the joy of Carroll's Dundalk;
Sometimes bumming a pipeful, sometimes 'shooting the crow',*
But ever onward and onward, fitfully, surely, slow,
On to the drill and the jumper, and on to the concrete bed,
On to the hovel and card school, the dirt-face and slush ahead.

* Ordering drink, having no intention of paying for it.

Doc. 10.2: Irish Tailors in London, 1849

Henry Mayhew, *The Morning Chronicle*, 18 December 1849.

The system adopted by wily sweaters to entrap inexperienced country and Irish hands into their service I heard described in various terms. The wife of a sweater (an Irishman, long notorious for such practices), herself a native of Kerry, visited her friends in that town, and found out two poor journey-men tailors. She told them of her husband's success in trade and of the high wages to be got in London by those who had friends in the trade, and engaged the two for her husband. Their wages were to be 36s. a week 'to begin with'. When the Irishmen reached the sweater's place, near Hounds-ditch, they found him in a den of a place, anything but clean, and anything but sweet, and were at once set to work at trowser making, at 1s. a pair, finding their own trimmings. Instead of 36s. a week, they could not clear more than 5s. by constant labour, and the sweater then offered to teach them, if they would bind themselves apprentices to him. During the year they were to have board and lodging, and £5 each, and a sort of document was signed. They then went to work on this new agreement, their board being this. For breakfast, half a pint of poor cocoa each, with half a pound of dry bread cut into slices, between the two, no butter. Dinner was swallowed, a few minutes only being allowed for it, between four and five. It was generally a few potatoes and a bit of salt fish, as low priced as could be met with. At seven, each man had half a pint of tea and the same allowance of bread as for breakfast. No supper. They slept three in a bed, in a garret where there was no ventilation whatever. The two men therefore seized an opportunity to escape. The sweater traced them to where they had got work again, took with him a policeman, and gave them in charge as runaway apprentices. He could not, however, substantiate the charge at the station-house, and the men were set at liberty.

Doc. 10.3: Irish Costermongers in Mid-Victorian London

Henry Mayhew, *London Labour and the London Poor*, vol. 1 (1861), 7–10.

The number of costermongers – that is to say, of those street-sellers attending the London 'green' and 'fish' markets – appears to be now 30,000 men, women and children. At the time of the famine in Ireland, it is calculated that the number of Irish obtaining a living in the London streets must have been at least doubled. Among the street folk there are many distinct characters of people – people differing as widely from each in tastes, habits, thoughts and creed, as one nation from another. Of these, the costermongers form by far the largest and certainly the most broadly marked class. They appear to be a distinct race – perhaps, originally, of Irish extraction – seldom associating with any other of the street-folks, and being all known to each other. The costermongering class or order also has its many varieties. These appear to be in the following proportions: One-half of the entire class are costermongers proper, that is to say, the calling with them is hereditary, and perhaps has been so for many generations; while the other half is composed of three-eighths Irish, and one-eighth mechanics, tradesmen and Jews. Under the term 'costermonger' is here included only such 'street-sellers' as deal in fish, fruit and vegetables, purchasing their goods at the wholesale 'green' and fish markets. Of these, some carry on their business at the same stationary stall or 'standing' in the street, while others go on 'rounds'. The itinerant costermongers, as contradistinguished from the stationary street-fishmongers and greengrocers, have in many instances regular rounds, which they go daily, and which extend from two to ten miles. The longest are those which embrace a suburban part; the shortest are through streets thickly peopled by the poor, where duly to 'work' a single street consumes, in some instances, an hour. There are also 'chance' rounds. Men 'working' these carry their wares to any part in which they hope to find customers. The costermongers, moreover, diversify their labours by occasionally going on a country road, travelling on these excursions, in all directions, from thirty to ninety and even a hundred miles from the metropolis.

Doc. 10.4: The Occupational Profile of the Irish-Born in Leigh, 1851

Census Enumerators' Sheets, Leigh, Lancashire, 31 March 1851.

[a]   Irish-Born Males

Description	Number	Description	Number	Description	Number
Cotton Industry		**Labourers**		Grinder (factory)	1
Carder	2	Agricultural	90	Joiner	1
Grinder	1	Chemical works	5	Lodging house kpr	7
Handloom weaver	4	General	35	Miner	4
Piecer	3	Vitriol works	5	Miller	1
Labourer	1			Painter	2
Spinner	2	**Other Jobs**		Rag collector	1
Stripper	1	Baker	1	Shoemaker	12
Tenter/Carder	1	Brickmaker	1	Tailor	10
Weaver	2	Cordwainer	1	Umbrella maker	1
Worker	4	Dealer (fruit)	2	Chelsea Pens.	1
		Drawer (colliery)	1	***Total Jobs***	**224**
Silk Industry		Factory worker	8	No data on jobs	48
Weaver	6	Farmer	1	At home	3
Worker	6	Doctor	1	Scholars	4
				Overall Total	**280**

[b]   Irish-Born Females

Description	Number	Description	Number	Description	Number
Domestic & Household Services		Nurse	6	**Other Jobs**	
Cook	1	Shoemaker	1	Labourer (agric.)	32
Charwoman	2	Seamstress	1	Chemical works	
Domestic duties	11			labourer	2
Housemaid	1	**Cotton Mills**		Factory worker	15
Laundress	2	Bobbin winder	1	General labourer	4
Servant	24	Carder	2	Nailmaker	1
Washerwoman	17	Doubler	1		
		Hand twister	1	***Jobs Total***	**181**
Other Services		Piecer	2		
Assistant in		Worker	10	**No Data on Jobs**	
Beerhouse	1			Wife	25
Bookbinder	1	**Silk Industry**		Daughters	12
Boot & Shoe binder	1	Handloom weaver	1	Lodgers	41
Dealer	3	Weaver	10	Rest	20
Dressmaker	3	Powerloom weaver	2	Scholars	7
Hawker	2	Winder	3	At home	4
Lodging house kpr	5	Worker	2	***Overall Total***	**290**

Doc. 10.5: Irish Employment in the Black Country, 1872

The Nation, 13 August 1872.

The 'Black Country' is the distinguishing name given to a district of the English Midlands, noted for its coal and iron mines, and for various and extensive manufactures in the latter commodity – chiefly in articles requiring great strength and not demanding high artistic taste or superior and delicate manual skill. Roughly estimated, the Black Country includes a district of about 200 square miles, extending from Birmingham to Wolverhampton in the one direction, and from Stourbridge to Walsall in the other. All this space is covered with mining buildings – furnaces for smelting the iron ore – and manufactories in which the metal is afterwards prepared and wrought into the curious and multifarious shapes in which it is sent out to the markets of the world. Here can be seen iron work in nearly all its manufactured forms. With the exception of cutlery, there is scarcely any form in which iron and steel may not be seen in this district. From the most delicate needle to the anchor, from the curiously wrought and highly polished 'steel toy' to the light-house, the marine boiler, and the iron and steel plates of which vessels are constructed, or by which – in the case of naval vessels their sides are defended – from the newest and most perfect weapons of death to the most precise and elaborately finished engines of progress and prosperity – iron work can be seen here in its fullest manufactured perfection, as well as in the various processes by which it is converted from the ore and the oxide into its last stage of finished perfection. Mars and Minerva alike engage the brain of the designer and direct the hand of the workman. On the borders of the district, and in Birmingham and Wolverhampton, the more finished and delicate kinds of workmanship are executed, the coarser and stronger in the centre, which is the 'Black Country' proper. In the one case the most cunning machinery has to be employed as well as the highest manual skill. In the other, the roaring and flaming furnace and the ponderous, though precise, steam hammer executes the work. Were the rites of Paganism not abolished, and a temple to be erected to Vulcan, the most fitting site on earth for the gloomy edifice would be in the centre of the Black Country.

   This district consists of a series of towns and villages, all linked together by chains of works and furnaces, which make the whole space look like one continuous town. In these towns and villages there is a very large Irish population. Their modes of life and position in any one of them apply generally to all – but for our purpose it will be necessary to note their numbers, position, and power in the chief centres, with the view of forming a just estimate of their present influence and their future prospects.

   The position and condition of the Irish population in Birmingham I have pointed out – but this description would not in any sense apply to the Irish in the other towns of the 'Black Country'. In the former there are various trades and callings in which the Irish people – and particularly the young – are trained to skilled and artistic labour. In the latter, the coal pit, the iron mine, the pit-head labour, and the furnace, furnish the chief sources of employ for the people, both English and Irish. The Irish people, in proportion to their numbers, supply a fair quota to the ranks of the more skilled employees in the manufactories; but the great bulk of Irish labour is either confined to the occupations mentioned or employed by railway companies, builders, etc. in the lowest and most laborious positions, and at a wage rate considerably below what can be obtained by those employed at the mines or in the works connected with the iron manufactures.

Doc. 10.6: William Reynolds: A Prosperous Irish Migrant, 1901

Extract from a letter from William Reynolds to his nephew, James William Reynolds, of Chicago, 18 January 1901, from Lawrence McBride (ed.), *The Reynolds Letters: An Irish Emigrant Family in Late Victorian Manchester* (Cork, 1999), 85–6. William Reynolds was one of six children who had left Mohill, County Leitrim, with their widowed mother during the Great Famine. The Reynolds family subsequently acquired wealth and respectability in Manchester as the dyeing and cleaning works of William Reynolds prospered.

Dear James, I will now tell you a few perticulers about myself and the business. I have got on very well considering. The Year 1898 was a record year for me but 99 went down through the war [Boer War]. Coal and Spirit advanced double. I think this year will be better commincing the New Century. The Laundry is going on pretty well. I lost Some of the old workers, Ferguson and Woolford. I still have Martin and he is now the Foreman. He has turned out a good man. I have Dan also. He is a good man. Mathue Park is also with me and nearly all the other workers.

The building I have had built is between the shed and the railway line. I purchased the land from the Canons. Between the works and the railway line thare is over 2000 yards. The building is on the bottom po[r]tion near the brook. It is a good building, 3 storeys & 91 feet long. I am going to Let off to Tennants. Mr Williams the grocer Dickenson Road is taking half 12 Stalls for his horses. A Bill posting Co has taking the Side facing the Railway, 600 square yds of Brick work without windows. What do you think about this spec. I was paying chief rent £24 per year for 3 years and never received one penny, So I was obliged to do Something. You can See I have not been idle. I never worked so hard in my life as I did last year all through the war. If I have good luck with the building it will be one of the best investments I have made. My health has been very good Since we went to live in Fallowfield. Mary Ann has had much better health. Our house is fine, by far the best house we have lived in yet and it is quite a treat to get home at night. All the shops are doing well. Stockport Shop has not been opened So long, So it is doing as well as we could expect . . .

The new building will cost me between 7 & 8 hundred pounds. I bought

5 houses of Slade Lane for Maryann about 2 years ago and paid £1000 pounds for tham. She has them in her own right and receives an income of £2 per week from tham. Her living is now I think secure.

Doc. 10.7: The Economic Condition of the Irish in Late-Victorian Liverpool

John Denvir, *The Irish in Britain* (1892). 435–7.

There has been, however, a vast change for the better in the surroundings of our people, and, indeed, in every other way, so that there is no town in the country in which we have made greater progress than in Liverpool. Irishmen are gradually emerging from the ranks of unskilled labour and becoming more numerous among the artisans, shopkeepers, merchants and professional classes. Among these latter they have most distinctly made their mark. Among other Irish lawyers of the highest reputation, Sir Charles Russell may be said to have graduated on this circuit. The Irish doctors of Liverpool are also numerous, and the first in their profession.

Notwithstanding this success, however, there is probably also more wretchedness among our people here than anywhere else in the country. But take them at their worst – take the jail statistics that cannot possibly give the whole truth, and take the lying statements of the no-popery orators – and there cannot be a doubt but that the overwhelming mass of the Irish of Liverpool will compare favourably with the people of any town. Intemperance, and the violence begotten of it, which caused Irish names to figure so often in the police courts, are confined to one wretched class; but even amongst them, these are generally their worst offences. You seldom hear of Irishmen in connection with more serious crimes.

It is often a source of wonder why Liverpool, with such a large Irish population, remains, on the whole, so persistently Tory. Reference has already been made to the Irish-Orange element in Liverpool. This, in point of numbers, would have been insignificant in itself, but that at its head were a number of bigoted, virulent, and eloquent Irish parsons, chief amongst whom was Dr. M'Neill, a native of County Antrim. These raised the no-popery cry on every occasion, and encouraged their ignorant followers – men of the Belfast Sandy Row type – to infuse their own venom into their fellow-workmen. As a consequence you find more of the bigoted, ignorant, anti-Irish, no-popery type of Toryism in Liverpool than probably in any other place in Great Britain. In fact, owing to the contagion brought in by the Irish-orangemen, many have had such a spirit developed in them that whatever party the Irish supported, they would range themselves on the opposite side.

Irish intellect and Irish courage have, in thousands of cases, brought our people to their proper place in the social scale, but it only too often happens that adverse circumstances drive the great bulk of them to the hardest, the most precarious, and the worst paid employments in the English labour market. The Irish of Liverpool frequently show a remarkable aptitude for dealing, which goes to show that, under the fostering care of a native government, ours would develop into a great commercial people. It is often noted that where an Irishman is steady and has got a good wife – for that is more than half the battle – he is frequently able to save enough from his earnings to open a marine store – a business our people seem partial to throughout the country – a coal yard, or a small shop. By degrees he gets on, as a rule, our people are more quick-witted in bargaining than even the jews – the difference being that Moses sticks to all he gets, whilst Pat's often too generous nature frequently lets go easily what he has won so hardly. There are, however, hard-headed Irishmen too – men who know how to keep what they have earned. So by degrees they get into the higher circles of the commercial world, and of these there are to be seen, among the merchant princes on 'Change, men who either themselves or whose fathers before them commenced life in Liverpool as corn or cotton porters, or even in some humbler or precarious occupation.

AGRICULTURAL WORK

Doc. 11.1: Irish Harvesters, 1836

Report on the State of the Irish Poor in Great Britain, Parliamentary Papers (1836) xliii–xlvii.

It remains to speak of those persons who periodically migrate from Ireland to Great Britain, and after a short absence return to their own homes; or of those who leave their country for an uncertain period, but revisit it occasionally, and never altogether lose their connection with it. Irish labourers come in large numbers to England and Scotland for the corn, and sometimes for the hay harvests, landing for the most part in the ports of Glasgow, Liverpool and Bristol. It is well known that they are for the most part labourers from the western and mountainous counties of Ireland; that they often shut up their houses and leave their wives and children to beg about the country during their absence; and that they frequently pay their rent with the money which they earn in England. Their conduct is in general orderly, their habits remarkably frugal and sober, and they appear to give satisfaction to their employers.

Mr George Forwood, Assistant Overseer of the parish of Liverpool [stated] 'The Irish come over from 500 to 700 in a steam-packet, principally in the harvest-time; a considerable number of these have families with them, and others have their families follow. They have been brought over in numbers for 1s. a head, and they never pay more than 5s. for the passage to England; the latter is the common price for their passage back to Ireland, exclusive of provisions. Those who have been over before become a description of leaders of gangs. All these are agricultural labourers when they are in England.'

John Thomas, [who] has a farm four miles from Birmingham on the Warwick Road [stated] 'In harvest-time Irish labourers get 12s. a week, a quart of beer a day, and they are lodged at night in a barn; frequently a dinner is given them on a Sunday, and sometimes also on Thursday. Frequently too many come, and will work for low wages, as low as 8s. a week. When they leave us they go on to Staffordshire, and get back in time for their own harvest. Most of them have a little land. Those that worked for me were exceedingly frugal; out of seven persons, six were very orderly; the seventh was disorderly, and the others refused to work with him. The English dislike their being employed; the master is forced to protect them from abuse.'

Doc. 11.2: Irish Reapers in Scotland, 1844

The Glasgow Examiner, 28 September 1844.

Harvest work being now nearly completed in this district, the Irish reapers that lend their valuable assistance are daily leaving the Broomielaw in crowds on their way back to the sister isle. Many of these hardy sons of Erin, we are glad to notice, are not a little improved in external appearance, the tattered garments in which they landed having given place to clothes of quite a different description; while others, restrained, it may be, by hard necessity, are returning home in the same miserable garb in which they left. All of them, however, must be considerably richer than they were upon landing here, and well do they merit their hard-won earnings. Their privations and fatigues during the season of harvest work are unexampled, and could only be borne by Irishmen.

Doc. 11.3: Irish Agricultural Workers in Scotland, 1862

R. Skirving, *Landlords and Labourers* (1862), 4–5.

The boasted peasantry of Scotland, instead of advancing in numbers, has sensibly decreased, and the soil is now to no inconsiderable extent culti-vated by the poorest, the most destitute and too often, I fear, by the most degraded class of Irish immigrants. This Hibernian invasion has in many respects stamped its impress upon the country. The regular ploughmen are still, with few exceptions, natives, but every extra hand is almost invariably an Irishman. Go, for example, into any field of drainers where twenty or thirty men are at work, and you will find that the whole, with perhaps the exception of the contractor, are Irishmen. In any town or village, on a Sunday morning, you may see groups of persons hanging about in their working clothes, in most un-Scotch-like fashion; these are sure to be parties of our friends from the Green Isle; and local police reports are not unfrequently swelled on Monday mornings by such names as those of Pat Flynn, Mike Fury or Denis McLusky . . . These Irish immigrants appear to range themselves into two totally different classes; one, chiefly scattered over the country, quiet, orderly, inoffensive, ignorant and religious; the other, huddled for the most part in the narrow little lanes of towns, noisy, reckless, turbulent, and caring quite as little for priest as for parson. Good and bad, quiet and disorderly, their labour is absolutely necessary. They have come to fill up a great gap. Without them it is simply impossible that, under present circumstances, the agriculture of some parts of Scotland could be carried on. While this is the state of things as regards the men, the female workers on the farm are still more exclusively immigrants, probably one-half of the whole number being either natives of Ireland or of our own Western Highlands.

Doc. 11.4: Irish Agricultural Labourers in Lincolnshire, 1892

John Denvir, *The Irish in Britain* (1892), 153–4, 412–14.

The numbers of the Irish peasantry who each year crossed the channel to reap the harvest in England and Scotland had enormously increased. In Lincolnshire, in that year (1841) there were but 1244 settled natives of Ireland. In 1851 there were 2344. They had about doubled their number – simply keeping pace with the total increase of Irish throughout the country; yet each year vast numbers of Irish came over for the harvest, for we find that in three or four days in August 1850, according to the *Stamford Mercury*, 12,000 of them passed through Liverpool from Ireland, on their way to the Fens of Lincolnshire. The census figures show how few must have remained each year.

The Fen country is in Lincolnshire, where there are places almost as well known, and spoken of as familiarly by the firesides of Mayo, as if they were in Ireland itself. Up to 1885 the number coming into Lincolnshire had been gradually decreasing, but after that there set in a slight increase, according to the observation of a patriotic Irish priest of the district. He noticed in 1885 a newspaper paragraph stating that eight hundred Irish harvestmen had left the North Wall, Dublin, for England. He met the same company on their arrival in Boston, one of the Lincolnshire towns called after St. Botolph. The same men, as a rule, came over year after year to the same farmers, and many of the fathers of the present race of harvestmen came over year after year to the fathers of their present employers. They encounter much hardship and real persecution, although not so much as formerly. Frequently the priests of these Lincolnshire Missions have to go many miles into remote districts to say Mass on Sundays for the harvest-men, it being no uncommon thing to have a congregation of five hundred or more hearing Mass in a barn lent for the occasion. The reverend gentle-man before referred to is one who believes that if these labourers can be made good Irishmen there is a better hope of keeping them good Catholics. He, therefore, used to get a dozen copies of one or more of the national newspapers for each Sunday and leave them for as many farm-houses, and he was always delighted to hear how intelligently the men discussed the contents on the following Sunday. The self-denial some of these poor fellows exhibit in hoarding up their earnings to send home to their families is heroic.

The settled Irish population is by no means so great in the Lincolnshire towns as formerly. During the harvesting and potato-digging many slept in the barns, which enabled them to save their lodging money. In the towns there were lodging houses which were often kept by Irishmen, and mostly used by their fellow-countrymen passing through, as well as by those working in the immediate district within a convenient radius. One street in Boston, North Street, was formerly nearly all lodging houses of the kind named. The Irish are now nearly all gone. Our people are tolerably numer-ous in the city of Lincoln, and there are small colonies at Louth and Grantham. It is in remote places that you come across relics of the great Famine in the persons of Irishmen, chiefly agricultural labourers, who have been here forty years or more. Of course, as might be expected, in some cases this long absence has sadly deteriorated the character of the people, but in the main the Lincolnshire Irish, in the second and third generation, many of them, are as sound at heart as if they had just left Ireland.

Doc. 11.5: Irish Harvesters in Leicestershire, 1883

M. Ellis, *Letters and Memorials of Eliza Ellis* (1883), 11–12.

I cannot here omit one other feature of the agricultural life of those days. Every summer the children at Beaumont Leys were accustomed to notice the arrival – regular as that of the swallows – of certain small, spare, active men, clad in grey frieze coats, with lapels and brass buttons, and they knew that the Irishmen had come again to help in the great work of the corn reaping. They settled steadily to their work by day, and at night the hay barn was their sleeping room. I wish I could give you a true idea of the devotion of these labourers to your grandfather, or of his trust in their honesty, and his appreciation of their characters. One family of Quins, from Roscommon, came to Beaumont Leys for a period of many years, growing at last too old and infirm to undertake the long journey. Your older aunts can remember an incident which always delighted our father, and which illustrated the sympathy existing between himself and genuine Irishmen. A party of reapers arrived one night at our home, asking for permission to sleep in the barn. Their request was granted, and I have little doubt that a supper was also supplied to them. Your grandfather was ever an early riser, but on this occasion he was not prepared for a diligence surpassing his own. When he went out in the early morning to superintend the work of the day, the barn was empty, but the gratitude of the poor Irishmen had expressed itself with palpable, irresistible eloquence. They had reaped part of a field of oats before continuing their journey!

Doc. 11.6: Irish Chicory Workers in York, 1901

B.S. Rowntree, *Poverty: A Study of Town Life* (1901), 10.

These poor Irish people, whose early experiences of the city were so unpropitious, were probably attracted to York by the prospect of obtaining work in connection with the cultivation of chicory, for which the district was then noted. This industry is now practically disappeared, and the number of Irish in the city has begun to decline, but is still considerable. Of those who remain, many find work as general labourers, while some of the women pick up a more or less precarious livelihood by working in the fields outside the city, often tramping out for miles in the early morning to their work. On summer evenings it is a common sight to see the women in the Irish quarter sitting on the kerbstone outside their cottages, smoking clay pipes.

Doc. 11.7: Irish Potato-Pickers in Scotland, 1914

Patrick MacGill, *Children of the Dead End* (1914), 68–75.

The Foyle was a sheet of wavy molten gold which the boat cut through as she sped out from the pier. The upper deck was crowded with people who were going to Scotland to work for the summer and autumn. They were all very ragged, both women and men; most of the men were drunk, and they discussed, quarrelled, argued, and swore until the din was deafening. Little heed was taken by them of the beauty of the evening. Many of the passengers were singing songs of harvest-men, lovers, cattle-drovers, and sailors. There were many on board who were full of drink and fight, men who were ready for quarrels and all sorts of mischief. All over the deck and down in the steerage the harvestmen and labourers fought one with another for hours on end.

The potato merchant met us at Greenock quay next morning, and here Mickey's Jim marshalled his squad, which consisted in all of twenty-one persons. Seventeen of these came from Ireland, and the remainder were picked up from the back streets of Greenock and Glasgow. With the exception of two, all the Irish women were very young, none of them being over nineteen years of age. The potato merchant hurried us off to Buteshire the moment we arrived, and we started work on a farm at mid-day. The way we had to work was this. Nine of the older men dug the potatoes from the ground with short three-pronged graips. The women followed behind, crawling on their knees and dragging two baskets a piece along with them. Into these baskets they lifted the potatoes thrown out by the men. When the baskets were filled I emptied the contents into barrels set in the field for that purpose. These barrels were in turn sent off to the markets and big towns which we had never seen. The first day was very wet, and the rain fell in torrents, but as the demand for potatoes was urgent we had to work through it all. The job, bad enough for men, was killing for women. All day long, on their hands and knees, they dragged through the slush and rubble of the field. The baskets which they hauled after them were cased in clay to the depth of several inches, and sometimes when emptied of potatoes a basket weighed over two stone. The strain on the women's arms must have been terrible. But they never complained. Pools of water gathered in the hollows of the dress that covered the calves of their legs. Sometimes they rose and shook the water from their clothes, then went down on their knees again. The Glasgow women sang an obscene song, 'just by way o' passing the time', one of them explained.

We left work at six o'clock in the evening, and turned in to look up our quarters for the night. We had not seen them yet, for we started work in the fields immediately on arriving. A byre was being prepared for our use, and a farm servant was busily engaged in cleaning it out when we came in from the fields. He was shoving the cow-dung through a trap-door into a vault below. The smell of the place was awful. There were ten cattle-stalls in the building, five on each side of the raised concrete walk that ran down the middle between two sinks. These stalls were our sleeping quarters.

Doc. 11.8: Reminiscences of Irish Harvesters in Oxfordshire

Flora Thompson, *Lark Rise to Candleford* (1939), 257–8.

One of the smaller fields was always reserved for any of the women who cared to go reaping but, by the 'eighties, there were only three or four, besides the regular field women, who could handle the sickle. Often the Irish harvesters had to be called in to finish the field. Patrick, Dominic, James (never called Jim), Big Mike and Little Mike, and Mr O'Hara seemed to the children as much a part of the harvest scene as the corn itself. They came over from Ireland every year to help with the harvest and slept in the farmer's barn, doing their own cooking and washing at a little fire in the open. They were a wild-looking lot, dressed in odd clothes and speaking a brogue so thick that the natives could only catch a word here and there. When not at work, they went about in a band, talking loudly and usually all together, with the purchases they had made at the inn bundled in blue-and-white check handkerchiefs which they carried over their shoulders at the end of a stick. 'Here comes they jabberin' old Irish', the country people would say, and some of the women pretended to be afraid of them. They could not have been serious, for the Irishmen showed no disposition to harm anyone. All they desired was to earn as much money as possible to send home to their wives, to have enough left for themselves to get drunk on a Saturday night, and to be in time for Mass on a Sunday morning. All these aims were fulfilled; for, as the other men confessed, they were 'gluttons for work' and more work meant more money at that season; there was an excellent inn handy, and a Catholic church within three miles.

Doc. 11.9: Occupational Profile of Irish-Born Workers in Scotland, 1911

Based on the *Report on the Twelfth Decennial Census of Scotland*, H.C. (1913–14), cited by D. Fitzpatrick, 'The Irish in Britain, 1871–1921', in W.E. Vaughan (ed.), *A New History of Ireland, vol. 6, Ireland Under the Union, II, 1870–1921*, 695, Table 5. Index = index of over-representation, dividing Irish natives as a percentage of all workers of the same sex thus occupied in Scotland by the Irish-born percentage of the entire Scottish male or female workforce.

	Occupation	Percentage	Index
Males	Building	32.0	531
	Drainage	18.4	305
	Docks	21.8	329
	Chemicals	27.9	325
	General labour	17.6	292
	Gasworks	21.9	363
	Navvying	15.5	257
	Iron and steel	24.4	404
	Railway labour	10.3	171
	Farm labour	2.8	46
	Shoemaking	8.5	141
	Engine driving	9.8	163
	Hawking	9.3	154
	Iron founding	10.4	173
	Shipbuilding	14.6	242
	Mining	7.4	123
	Insurance	6.1	102
	Publicans	6.5	108
	Carters	4.6	76
	Waiters	4.5	74
	Tailors	3.2	53
	Grocers	2.7	45
	Clerks	1.4	23
	Total	**6.0**	**100**

	Occupation	Percentage	Index
Females	Hawking	8.9	340
	Farm labour	2.8	108
	Charwomen	5.5	213
	Waitresses	5.5	210
	Hemp and jute	3.4	129
	Teaching	3.2	121
	Domestic service	2.4	92
	Nursing	3.5	135
	Dressmaking	2.2	84
	Cotton	3.6	138
	Clerks	1.0	38
	Total	**2.6**	**100**

Part 4

Social Conditions:
Poverty, Health and Crime

INTRODUCTION

Poverty was a driving force of Irish migration to Britain during the nineteenth century. Once disembarked, a majority of the new arrivals crowded into slum tenements, lodging-houses and cellar dwellings in the long-established and already-overcrowded districts of Irish settlement in Lancashire and London, and even in the smaller centres their poverty and destitution tended to consign them to the filthiest and foulest of neighbourhoods. These displayed the full spectrum of social evils: appalling overcrowding, little or no sanitation, unhealthy diet, inadequate clothing, vagrancy, disease, alcoholism and general squalor, a high quota of unemployed paupers or of underemployed casual labourers, and a high incidence of casual violence.

Against this background, the Irish became an easy target and the poor Irish, who were the only visible Irish, became convenient scapegoats for environmental deterioration.[1] Yet the plethora of urban social problems which comprised the 'Condition of England Question' was clearly not the product of Irish immigration: these conditions had existed long before large-scale Irish migration during the Famine, which served only to magnify and exacerbate them. Nevertheless, for many middle-class observers during the 1840s and 1850s, Irish migration was widely regarded as a root cause of some contemporary social ills, most notably poverty, low standards of public health, and crime.[2]

Irish pauperism and vagrancy had informed the debates on Poor Law reform during the 1820s and 1830s and the poverty of Irish migrants in Britain loomed large in the Cornewall Lewis Report of 1836, as the Reverend T.M. MacDonald's description of the Irish in Birmingham illustrates (**Doc. 12.1**). However, as several recent studies have shown, the sheer scale of Irish migration during the Famine and the horrific manifestations of destitution, disease and death that were so visible in many British cities exposed the inadequacies of public and private provisions for relieving poverty.[3] In five months during 1847 some 300,000 pauper Irish landed in Liverpool alone, swamping a town with a native population of 250,000; in Glasgow it was observed that 'the misery which many of these poor creatures endure can scarcely be less than what they have fled or been driven from at home' (**Doc. 12.2**); whilst it was reported from South Wales that 'the principal cause of the excessive overcrowding found to prevail in Cardiff is the vast influx of destitute Irish from Cork and Waterford, who have been partly attracted in the hope of obtaining employment on the

---

[1] M.A.G. Ó Tuathaigh, 'The Irish in Nineteenth-Century Britain: Problems of Integration', *Transactions of the Royal Historical Society*, 31 (1981), 149–74.

[2] See, for example, MacRaild, 'Irish Immigration and the "Condition of England" Question', 67–85.

[3] Neal, *Black '47*, 239–76.

public works'.[4] In this broader context, the tragic case of the McAndrew
family from Sligo, described graphically by *The York Herald* in June 1848,
provides an all-too-familiar reminder of the horrendous experiences of
some Famine migrants in British towns (**Doc. 12.3**). Others were more
fortunate, including Marie Matthews and her child, admitted to the House
of Charity in Soho, London, in August 1850 (**Doc. 12.4**).

Even before the Famine, Irish migrants had been widely regarded as a
burden on the poor rates, and the dependence of the Irish poor on parish
relief in the northern manufacturing districts in the late 1840s and early
1850s, when the costs of relieving the Irish poor were, albeit temporarily,
disproportionate to their numbers, undoubtedly reinforced this perception
in the public mind. In Leeds, for example, expenditure on the Irish-born in
1850–51 comprised 67.7 per cent of total expenditure on outdoor relief.[5] Yet
studies of Irish employment patterns in other towns, including Bristol[6] and
York,[7] have shed doubt on this popular view by suggesting that, at least
before 1860 and the relaxation of the settlement provisions of the 1834 Poor
Law, the Irish made a much smaller demand on public and private charity
than their poverty and English prejudice might lead one to suppose. Nevertheless, faced with questions of morality and cost arising from the Famine
exodus, some local authorities sought to repatriate Irish paupers to Ireland
under the removal clauses of the Poor Law. The case of Timothy Keife and
his wife, removed to Cork by the West London Board of Guardians in June
1854, offers a useful illustration of how removal was effected (**Doc. 12.5**).
Between 1846 and 1853 there were 62,779 Irish removals from Liverpool
alone,[8] and in 1854 the Liverpool Select Vestry petitioned the House of
Commons against rescinding legislation for the compulsory removal of
Irish poor (**Doc. 12.6**). Similar concerns were also expressed in Glasgow,
although *The Commonwealth* provided a rare voice for caution and modera-
tion (**Doc. 12.7**). Yet repatriation was itself an expensive solution for Poor
Law Guardians to apply, particularly on a large scale, and it was often
counter-productive, especially when persons removed to Ireland subsequently found the means to return to England. Thus some local Boards of
Guardians, including those of Cardiff (**Doc. 12.8**) and Chester (**Doc. 12.9**),
were more discriminating and less zealous in exercising their powers in
regard to compulsory repatriation.

After 1860, when many of the popular anxieties attending Irish migration during the Famine period had somewhat abated, relatively few of

[4] *Report of the Select Committee on Poor Removal, Parliamentary Papers* XVII (1854), 396,
Minutes of Evidence, 474–6.

[5] MacRaild, *Irish Migrants in Modern Britain*, 64.

[6] D. Large, 'The Irish in Bristol in 1851: A Census Enumeration', in Swift and Gilley, *The
Irish in the Victorian City*, 37–58.

[7] Finnegan, *Poverty and Prejudice*, 110–18.

[8] Neal, *Black '47*, 222.

those Irish applicants for English relief who could not prove their permanent residence in the chargeable union for a period of one year were removed to Ireland, although they were technically subject to removal. In Scotland both Poor Law legislation and practice were more rigorous, and 7,000 paupers were removed to Ireland between 1875 and 1910. But here too the number of removals was progressively declining, whilst the persistent excess of Irish paupers was largely attributable to an ageing population of Irish inmates in Scottish workhouses.[9] Nevertheless, the notion that the Irish received a disproportionate share of poor relief persisted in some quarters (**Doc. 12.10**). Moreover, despite some evidence of marginal upward social and economic mobility, life for the majority of the Irish-born and their descendants in late-Victorian and Edwardian Britain continued to comprise an endless struggle against poverty, if not simply pauperism. Their plight was by no means unique at a time when the surveys conducted by Charles Booth in London and B.S. Rowntree in York suggested that one-third of Britain's urban population was living in poverty.[10] Nevertheless, Booth's description of Shelton Street provides an evocative illustration of the character of a poor Irish district in London's East End at the turn of the century (**Doc. 12.11**), whilst the reminiscences of Tom Barclay, born of Irish parents in Victorian Leicester (**Doc. 12.12**), and Pat O'Mara, born of Irish parents in Edwardian Liverpool (**Doc. 12.13**), illustrate in rather different ways not only what it meant to be poor but also that the experience of poverty, particularly during childhood, was indelible.

If the Famine served to reinforce contemporary perceptions of the association between Irish migration and poverty, it was also influential in shaping public attitudes in regard to the relationship between Irish migration and low standards of public health in British cities.

The experience of Liverpool usefully illustrates this issue.[11] During the 1830s the city was widely held to possess the most insanitary of urban conditions, with a higher mortality rate than that of London. However, the Liverpool Corporation, reformed in consequence of the Municipal Corporations Act of 1835, showed a real sense of commitment in attempting to remedy this situation. In 1842 Dr W.H. Duncan produced his *Report on the*

---

[9] Fitzpatrick, 'A Curious Middle Place?', 19–70.

[10] For the work of Booth and Rowntree, see especially the relevant sections in D. Englander and R. O'Day (eds), *Retrieved Riches: Social Investigation in Britain, 1840–1914* (Cambridge, 1995).

[11] The relationship between Irish migration and public health in Liverpool awaits detailed scholarly analysis, but see W.M. Frazer, *Duncan of Liverpool* (1947; rev. ed., Preston 1997); E.C. Midwinter, *Old Liverpool* (Newton Abbot, 1971), 85–114; G. Kearns, P. Laxton and C.J. Campbell, 'Duncan and the Cholera Test: Public Health in Mid-Nineteenth Century Liverpool', *Transactions of the Historic Society of Lancashire and Cheshire*, 143 (1993), 85–115; R.J. Scally, *The End of Hidden Ireland: Rebellion, Famine and Emigration*, Chap. 9, 'Liverpool and the Celtic Sea' (Oxford, 1995), 184–216; Neal, *Black '47*, 123–56.

Sanitary State of the Labouring Classes of Liverpool, which was included in Edwin Chadwick's famous Report of the same year. In this report, Duncan suggested that insanitary conditions and low standards of public health were in part the product of poverty and required a comprehensive programme of sanitary reform. However, he also linked insanitary conditions to the habits of the Liverpool Irish (**Doc. 13.1a**). In 1843 Duncan delivered a series of lectures on the physical causes of the high mortality rate in Liverpool to the Liverpool Literary and Philosophical Society, thereby pressing the case for public health reform among the city's elite and mobilising influential opinion; in 1844 he gave evidence to the Royal Commission on the State of Large Towns and Populous Districts; and in 1845 he helped to establish the Liverpool Health of Towns Association, which further publicized the need for sanitary reform. In 1846 the city secured a local Act of Parliament, the Liverpool Sanitary Act, which provided the Corporation with wide powers of environmental control, prohibiting the habitation of some cellar-dwellings, compelling house-owners to install privies, and authorising the appointment of a Medical Officer of Health (Duncan duly accepted the appointment). In 1847 the Liverpool Waterworks Act enabled the Corporation to embark upon an ambitious scheme to provide the city with adequate supplies of fresh water.

The immediate impact of these reforms was undermined by the sheer scale of Irish migration to Liverpool during the Famine, which, as the *Liverpool Mercury* observed (**Doc. 13.1b**), posed enormous problems for the authorities. The problem of numbers was compounded by the debilitated condition of those who disembarked at the Clarence Dock; not only were many migrants starving when they began their voyage to Liverpool, but they had also endured horrendous conditions during their passage, either exposed on deck or cramped below with animals. Most Irish poor arrived in an exhausted physical condition, with a low level of resistance to disease, even if they were not already carrying those illnesses most associated with malnutrition – dysentery, typhoid and typhus. The scale of Irish migration also precipitated a housing crisis of immense proportions. Even the lower-valued houses in the city were beyond the means of Irish paupers: they were offered space in the already overcrowded cellars and courts of the Irish districts in the North End by existing tenants; they illegally occupied empty cellars, already considered unfit for human habitation; as a last resort, they crowded into the cheapest lodging houses. Many who were absolutely destitute sought shelter where they could find it – in outhouses and, in one much-publicized case, in an old boiler on waste ground in the North End (**Doc. 13.1c**).

A typhus epidemic struck the city in 1847, with an estimated 100,000 cases. *The Times* attributed the epidemic solely to the recent arrival of thousands of Irish paupers (**Doc. 13.1d**). The authorities found it difficult to contain the disease because as soon as patients were transferred to the city's hospitals, further cases were reported among more recent waves of immigrants. Temporary fever sheds were erected, and some victims were isolated in two vessels moored in the Mersey. Duncan, who linked the habits of the Irish poor to the spread of the disease (**Doc. 13.1e**), warned the authorities that typhus was spreading outside the Irish districts and threatened not only the English working classes but also the middle classes. Indeed, the epidemic took a heavy toll of 'respectable and useful citizens' whose duties brought them into contact with typhus victims, notably priests, doctors, nurses and relieving officers (**Doc. 13.1f**).

By January 1848 the epidemic had run its course. Yet Duncan's Report for 1847 makes interesting reading. It showed that the total number of deaths in Liverpool in 1847 was 17,280, an increase of 100 per cent on the 1846 figures. Deaths from typhus and dysentery combined totalled 7,475 (or 43 per cent of all deaths), of which 51 per cent occurred in those wards with the greatest concentration of Irish (Vauxhall, Scotland and Exchange). Moreover, typhus was widely described in the local press as 'Irish fever', thereby projecting the Irish as the harbingers of disease, whilst frequent references to the 'disgusting state' of many of the Famine migrants, irrespective of the conditions which had brought this about, reflected the widely held view that dirt and disease were the inevitable outcomes of Irish migration.

Yet although the Famine migration retarded the Corporation's ambitious public health programme, it also gave a further impetus to public health reform in Liverpool by showing the urgency of the situation and the need for further action. By 1858, Duncan was able to direct the Corporation to suitable environmental solutions: 80 miles of sewers and 60 miles of street drains had been constructed, 300 street-cleaners had been employed, and 8,000 cellars forcibly emptied. Nevertheless, by the end of the century the most overcrowded and insanitary districts in Liverpool continued to be those with the largest concentrations of Irish – Scotland, Vauxhall, St Pauls and Exchange.

The belief that Irish migrants threatened standards of public health was evident in other towns during the late 1840s and early 1850s,[12] including Edinburgh (**Doc. 13.2**), The Potteries (**Doc. 13.3**) and Gateshead (**Doc. 13.4**), where the incidence of fever was variously ascribed to the prevalence of overcrowded and insanitary living conditions and to the habits of the Irish themselves. Particular concern focused on conditions in Irish lodging-houses, as the examples from Church Lane, in London's notorious St Giles district, illustrate (**Docs. 14.1, 14.2**). However, many of these concerns, which virtually comprised a moral panic during the exceptional circumstances of the Famine years, appear to have abated during the late

---

[12] For a useful local study, see A.P. Coney, 'Mid-Nineteenth Century Ormskirk: Disease, Overcrowding and the Irish in a Lancashire Market Town', *Transactions of the Historic Society of Lancashire and Cheshire*, 139 (1990), 33–111.

nineteenth century when the Irish were conspicuous by their absence from government inquiries into the health of towns.

It was also widely held that Irish migrants were the harbingers of crime and disorder, the ancillaries of urban poverty and environmental deterioration. Indeed, whilst crime and disorder had long been regarded as Irish traits, it was also held that the Irish were more criminal than other sections of British society and, as such, represented a challenge on the part of 'the dangerous classes', in which the Irish bulked large, to authority and order in nineteenth-century Britain.[13] This was certainly the view advanced by the *Report on the State of the Irish Poor* of 1836, which devoted four pages to the subject, by reference to the evidence of police officers in Birmingham, Liverpool, Manchester, Stockport, Glasgow, Paisley, Kilmarnock and Edinburgh (**Doc. 15.1**). Statistical evidence suggests that throughout the Victorian period the Irish-born were almost three times as likely to face prosecution than their English neighbours, and more than five times as likely to be convicted and imprisoned (**Doc. 15.2**).

Some important qualifications should be made. First, Irish criminality was overwhelmingly concentrated in less serious or petty categories. Although there were undoubtedly some professional Irish criminals in Victorian cities, including the receivers of stolen property or 'fences' described by the *Glasgow Argus* (**Doc. 15.3**), the Irish were not noted either for serious crimes or for crimes of great violence. Second, the Irish were not over-represented in all categories of petty crime; local case-studies indicate that Irish criminality was highly concentrated in the often inter-related categories of drunkenness, disorderly behaviour and assault (including assaults on the police) and, to a lesser extent, petty theft and vagrancy.[14]

Moreover, many of the so-called 'Irish disorders' which so concerned contemporary opinion were essentially multi-causal and came in various shapes and sizes. Sometimes they comprised disturbances among the Irish themselves; on other occasions they involved collective violence either by the Irish or against the Irish, or a combination of both. Hence they operated on both intra-communal and inter-communal levels within specific communities, revealing different types of behaviour according to time and place.[15] The most common disorders consisted largely of drunken brawls,

---

[13] The relationship between Irish migration and crime is relatively under-researched, but for further details see especially R. Swift, 'Crime and the Irish in Nineteenth-Century Britain', in Swift and Gilley, *The Irish in Britain, 1815–1939*, 163–82, and R. Swift, 'Heroes or Villains?: The Irish, Crime and Disorder in Victorian England', *Albion*, 29, 3 (1998), 399–421.

[14] See, for example, H. Peavitt, 'The Irish, Crime and Disorder in Chester, 1841–1871', (University of Liverpool PhD thesis, 2000), especially chap. 3, 100–135.

[15] Recent studies of Irish disorders include F. Neal, 'English-Irish Conflict in the North-East of England', in Buckland and Belchem, *The Irish in British Labour History*, 59–85; F. Neal, 'English-Irish Conflict in the North West of England: Economics, Racism, Anti-Catholicism or Simple Xenophobia?', *North West Labour History Journal*, 16 (1991–2),

quarrels between neighbours and domestic disputes which were confined to Irish districts. Much of this violence was between rather than against Irish people. There was, for example, a good deal of faction fighting in rural Ireland, and a tradition of hostility between men from rival villages, counties and provinces. These rivalries were sustained in English cities, where the drunkenness, noise and casual violence associated with Saturday night saturnalia in the public houses, beershops and lodging-houses of 'Little Irelands' – not to mention the celebration of weddings, wakes, and St. Patrick's Day – made the Irish more visible, reinforcing the popular perception of the Irish predilection for drunkenness and disorderly behaviour, as the extract from *The Glasgow Herald* illustrates (**Doc. 15.4**). Such disorders, commonly described by the provincial press as 'Irish rows', which so horrified 'respectable' opinion, were of little interest to the police or magistrates unless they spilled over into the public domain, which was sometimes the case with violence bred of sectarian rivalries, most notably in Liverpool and Glasgow.

Clashes between the Irish and the police had a character of their own, as the observations of Gilbert Hogg, the Chief Constable of Wolverhampton, illustrate (**Doc. 15.5**). The attempts of provincial police forces after 1835 to monitor more closely the working-class areas of English towns and cities made Irish districts particularly vulnerable to police surveillance. The essential targets of the 'New Police' were varieties of street crime – drunkenness, disorderly behaviour, petty theft, vagrancy and unruly forms of popular leisure and recreation – in short, the very offences for which the Irish had acquired a legendary reputation. The Irish were, therefore, particularly vulnerable to police surveillance, and this was subsequently reflected in the level of Irish-born prosecutions in these petty criminal categories. Similarly, police attempts to quell intra-communal disorders, to enforce the licensing laws, to trace illegal stills, to regulate lodging-houses (regarded by the police as nurseries of crime and havens for criminals) and to apprehend suspicious characters in Irish districts were perceived by the Irish as examples of police violence and often led to more generalised disorders, at which point the distinction between 'intra-communal' and 'inter-communal' violence became blurred.

It was, of course, the 'lowest Irish' – the poorest Irish men and women – who were associated in the public mind with crime and disorder, as the Rev. Joseph Dare's comments on juvenile crime in Leicester indicate (**Doc. 15.6**), although such comments also mirror the more negative attitudes of the period towards the poorest sections of working-class society in general. Some contemporaries, including Henry Mayhew, found difficulty in

---

14–25; P. Mulkern, 'Irish Immigrants and Public Disorder in Coventry, 1845–1875', *Midland History*, 21 (1996), 119–35; L. Miskell, 'Irish Immigrants in Cornwall: The Camborne Experience, 1861–1882', in Swift and Gilley, *The Irish in Victorian Britain*, 31–51.

pinpointing the exact causes of Irish criminality (**Doc. 15.7**), but it is clear that much Irish crime was the by-product of a poverty-ridden and brutalizing urban slum environment. Nevertheless, the stereotype of the brutalized 'Paddy' was well entrenched in the public mind even before the large-scale migration of the Irish during the 1840s and 1850s; thereafter, Irish districts were expected to be hotbeds of crime and disorder, and anti-social behaviour by the Irish merely confirmed preconceived notions regarding the irresponsibility and criminality of the Celt.

It is important to acknowledge that Irish migrants were sometimes the *victims* of crime and, more particularly, of communal violence,[16] and although there was a gradual and relative decline in the recorded incidence of anti-Irish violence in late-Victorian Britain, it is possible that anti-Irish sentiment continued to be expressed in more subtle and less public ways within working-class communities via psychological terror, smale-scale brawls, attacks on individuals and a routine diet of discrimination rather than by regularized mob violence.

POVERTY AND POOR RELIEF

Doc. 12.1: State of the Irish Poor in Birmingham, 1834

Report on the State of the Irish Poor in Great Britain, Parliamentary Papers (1836), Appendix I, State of the Irish Poor in Birmingham, xlix; Evidence of Rev. T.M. MacDonald, Roman Catholic Priest, of St. Peter's Place, Birmingham.

I think there are about 6,000 Irish in Birmingham, not more. I have from 1,000 to 2,000 in my charge. The number fluctuates very much. There are about 1,000 non-Irish Catholics in Birmingham. As compared with the English, the Irish belong to a very low class. None of the non-Irish are in a state of destitution, very many of the Irish are. I attribute their poverty to their want of means of rising, to the national and religious prejudice against them (this operates very partially, and is wearing away), and to their recklessness. They are not as good managers as the English; they don't live equally well on equal wages; they don't aspire to the same comforts. They live more for the present moment. They have more reputation for drunkenness than they deserve, because they are so noisy and brawling. They give money to one another when in distress and sickness, and they send money to their parents and wives and poor relations in Ireland, especially to their sisters; they are very fond of their sisters and try to send them marriage

---

[16] For further details, see A. O'Day, 'Varieties of Anti-Irish Behaviour in Britain, 1846–1922', in P. Panayi (ed.), *Racial Violence in Britain* (1993), 26–43; see also R. Swift, 'Anti–Irish Violence in Victorian England: Some Perspectives', *Criminal Justice History*, 15 (1994), 127–40.

portions. If they marry at all they marry very young, but very many men live unmarried. There is hardly any prostitution among the Irish girls, I don't know a single case. That is also the case among the non-Irish part of my flock . . . I am disposed to recommend early marriages on the principle of virtue, and sometimes do so. Their marriages are very fruitful, and they rear many children; of an average they have four or five children. They are very fond of their children, but from poverty neglect them. They let them run about the streets a good deal and have their fling. A few send their children out to beg. They are honest and chaste, and rarely commit crime . . . They are not very importunate in applying for charitable relief; they are enduring of privation. I have often spoken to them about vaccination, reproving them for neglecting it. They do not seem to be aware of its advantage.

Constantly their excuse for not sending their children to school, or not attending chapel is want of clothes and shoes, which they would not have or think of in Ireland. I think that their mixture with the English raises their habits of economy and increases their love of comfort, but deteriorates their morality. In all things the Irish are less moderate than the English, both in virtue and vice.

The Irish are principally employed for their manual labour; they are rarely employed in departments which require considerable mechanical skill. I think there may be a few cases where a poor Irishman has raised himself to business. The Irish from the North are, generally speaking, more managing and thinking than the others; generally they are in rather comfortable circumstances. The Irish of Birmingham chiefly come from Mayo and Roscommon; those settled emigrate on account of their poverty. The harvestmen come to pay their rent. In my opinion the reform and political union have allayed the national dislike between the English and Irish. I think the introduction of poor laws into Ireland, continued to the relief of the impotent, would have hardly any effect on the Irish emigration to England.

Doc. 12.2. Irish Migrants in Glasgow, 1847

The Glasgow Herald, 11 June 1847.

The streets of Glasgow are at present literally swarming with vagrants from the sister kingdom, and the misery which many of these poor creatures endure can scarcely be less than what they have fled or been driven from at . home. Many of them are absolutely without the means of procuring lodging of even the meanest description, and are obliged consequently to make their bed frequently with a stone for a pillow. Others, however, have managed to find shelter in various ways, and with an ingenuity sometimes illustrative, to a considerable degree, of that invention which is given birth to by necessity. A rather remarkable case of this kind was discovered in Gorbals about a fortnight ago. In Buchanan Street there is an old granary and maltbarn, purchased some time ago by the Caledonian Railway Company to form the site of a terminus, which was standing unoccupied, and this having come under the notice of some of the destitute Irish immigrants, they took possession of it, and the colony has continued increasing till the beginning of this week, when the number of persons congregated together amounted to upwards of fifty. Fever having broken out in the place, the parochial authorities of Gorbals were applied to, and for sometime past they have done all in their power under the circumstances to alleviate the sufferings of their wretched horde of human beings by giving money and medicine, and procuring admission lines to the Fever Hospital.

Doc. 12.3. Irish Migrants in York: The Case of the McAndrew Family, 1847

The York Herald, 10 July 1848.

The wife of the deceased, who was herself apparently much indisposed, stated that some weeks ago, she, her husband and four children came to this country from the county Sligo in Ireland, having in that time in their possession the sum of £2, the proceeds of their little property previous to their leaving their native country. Having reached Bradford they remained there until after she was confined and the whole of their money expended. The infant and three of the children died in the town of hunger and measles combined. Deceased, his wife and the remaining child afterwards proceeded to Leeds and from thence to York, where they slept in the Vagrant Office one night, and the next night in a barn. They applied for admittance into several of the lodging houses but the inmates, thinking they had fever, refused to take them in, saying that the priests and the doctors had told them they were not to admit them.

On the evening of Thursday 2nd July they found their way to the vicinity of the Union Hospital and here they were seen (among others) by Mr Thomas, the surgeon to the institution. They were laid on the bank with their feet in a dry ditch. Having inquired into the circumstances, he told the deceased there was no room for him at that time in the hospital, but recommended him to go to the Relieving Officer whose duty it was to provide for them if they were destitute.

The deceased did apply to the city Relieving Officer who informed him that the case was not in his district and directed him to the rural officer. The deceased went to him but found that he was from home.

On Friday evening Mr Thomas found the deceased and family still on the roadside and he, along with Mr Tuke junior, endeavoured to provide some place of shelter for them. Being unable to do so, Mr Tuke furnished them with some straw and an additional blanket, they having had one previously, and he was determined to get the deceased into hospital the next day if possible. One Saturday morning the poor fellow expired suddenly at about 10 o'clock. The deceased was, in Mr Thomas's opinion, 'with the blankets and other coverings better off than he would have been in many of the lodging houses, therefore his sleeping under a hedge had nothing to do with accelerating his death'.

Doc. 12.4: Charitable Relief, 1850

Extracts from the Register of the House of Charity, Soho, London, 1851–2.

Maria Matthews and child: Admitted, 7 August 1850; Religion: RC; Birthplace: Ireland; Recommended by: Rev. T.S. Evans.

Details: Met by her recommender in the street and induced by him to abandon the sinful life she was leading. She came for a few days until she could be removed to a more definitely penitential establishment. Finding that she was RC, application was made to the Convent of the Good Shepherd where she was at once received with the understanding that every effort be made to provide for her child. The system was too rigorous for her and after having been there a short time she gave notice to quit and again threw herself on the House. Feeling certain that if she was not received her only alternative would be to return to her sinful way of life, she was again sheltered and by God's blessing in the course of a month induced to return to the convent. Her conduct there has been quite satisfactory and on 22 April 1851 she is still an inmate of it. Through the kindness of some friends sufficient interest has been roused in the case to induce some RCs to provide for the child's maintenance and education and he is now about to leave the House to be placed with a respectable woman in St John's Wood very near the school. Child discharged: 17 August 1851.

November 2 1852 she was readmitted at the urgent request of Mr Evans. She had been 11 months in the service of Mme de Macedo, wife of the Brazilian Ambassador, where she appears to have met with much annoyance because the fact that she has a child to support has been found out by her fellow servants. She conducted herself very well and obtained another situation at Brook House, Clapton. Discharged: 9 November 1852.

Doc. 12.5: Irish Pauper Removals in London: The Case of Timothy Keife, 1854

Letter from William Chamberlain, Relieving Officer, to J. Pontifex, Clerk to the West London Board of Guardians, 3 June 1854, *Report of the Select Committee on Poor Removal, Parliamentary Papers* (1854). Minutes of Evidence, 583.

Sir, – In reply to your letter of the 31st ultimo, respecting the removal of Timothy Keife, his wife, and six children, from the parish of St. Sepulchre, in the city of London, to Ireland, that being his legal place of settlement by birth and apprenticeship.

I beg to inform you, that on the 9th of January last my attention was called to the distressed state of Timothy Keife, his wife, and six children, a tailor living at No. 21 Union-court, in the parish of St. Andrew, City. I visited the case, and, upon inquiry, I found they had removed from St. Luke's, Middlesex, the day previous, to No. 21, Union-court; they were in a very dirty, destitute condition, and I recommended them to come into the workhouse that evening, which they declined to do. I then gave an order, the same evening, upon Mr. Phillips, the assistant relieving-officer, who keeps the books and pays the poor, for 1s. 6d. in necessaries and three loaves of bread; on the 11th January, an order for 1s. 6d. in necessaries and three loaves of bread more, and on the 14th January, an order for 6d. in necessaries and three loaves of bread; total, in bread and necessaries, 8s. 9d. for the week; the family then removed from this place of residence, and I could not ascertain where they were gone to, until Friday, the 20th January. The Rev. James Jackson, rector of St. Sepulchre's Church, city of London, called my attention to a distressed family of the name of Timothy Keife, his wife and six children, living at No. 8, Brazier's-buildings, in the parish of St. Sepulchre, in the city, which I found to be the same family that removed from No. 21, Union-court. I gave them an order for relief, 2s. 6d. in necessaries, six loaves of bread, and 1s. 2d. in meat, total 7s. 2d.; and an order for the applicant, Timothy Keife, to attend our Board on Tuesday, the 24th January, which he did, and the guardians ordered him relief to the amount of 20s.

On Monday evening, the 27th March, an application was again made by Timothy Keife, living at No. 8, Brazier's-building, for assistance. I gave him an order for two loaves of bread, and an order to appear before our Board the next morning; Keife and his wife both came to the Board, stating it was impossible for them to maintain their family, and asked to come into the workhouse, to be passed to Ireland; the Guardians granted their application, and the family was admitted the same day.

Mr. Wright, the messenger of the union, conveyed Timothy Keife in a cab to Guildhall, to be sworn to his parish in Ireland, on Saturday, the 1st of April; he was sworn, and Sir George Carrol signed the order for their removal to Ireland on the following Thursday, the 6th April.

Tuesday, the 4th April, being our Board-day, Timothy Keife and his wife applied to the Guardians as inmates of the workhouse, through Mr. Rentell, the master, for assistance, they having a long distance to travel when landed at Cork; they were allowed 25s. 6d., and they were conveyed in a cab, by Mr. Wright, the messenger, from the workhouse to the vessel, on Thursday morning, the 6th of April, at half-past six o'clock in the morning.

Keife has one daughter married, named Walker, who frequently applies for relief, in consequence of her husband having no employment, also in cases of temporary sickness; she is, in my opinion, quite unable to assist her parents; they have another daughter in place of service, earning 2s. per week and her maintenance. The above is a true statement of the case, to the best of my recollection.

Doc. 12.6: Demands for the Removal of Irish Paupers from Liverpool, 1854

Report of the Select Committee on Poor Removal, Parliamentary Papers (1854). Petition from Liverpool Select Vestry to the House of Commons for the compulsory removal of Irish paupers. Minutes of Evidence, 364–5. Evidence of the Rev. A. Campbell.

To the Honourable the Commons of the United Kingdom of Great Britain and Ireland in Parliament assembled. The humble petition of the select vestry of the parish of Liverpool in the county of Lancaster, showeth, that your petitioners, who are the elected representatives of a parish containing, by the last census, a population of 258,000 souls, submitted to your Honourable House, on Friday last, a petiton praying for the reasons therein assigned, that the Bill introduced by Mr. Baines, to abolish in England and Wales the compulsory removal of the poor on the ground of settlement, and to make provision for the more equitable distribution of the charge of relief in unions, might not pass into law. That your petitioners have since observed, with the greatest apprehension, that it is the purpose of Her Majesty's Government to introduce another Bill effecting a most vital change in the nature and objects of that introduced by the President of the Poor Law Board; no less, indeed, than to abrogate the compulsory removal of paupers to Ireland and Scotland. That your petitioners feel that they should be wanting in their duty, not only towards the ratepayers, but the poor of the said parish, did they not humbly, but earnestly, protest against the proposed legislation, certain as it is to inflict upon both the ratepayers and the poor hardship and injustice at all times, and occasionally the most disastrous consequences. That in 1847, as often represented to your Honourable House, the pauperism of Ireland was relieved at the expense of Liverpool to a very enormous extent, by the immigration of destitute men, women, and children, in overwhelming numbers, who straightway applied to the parish for relief, and by their crowding into the low lodging-houses of the town, generated fever of a malignant character, which caused a most calamitous increase of mortality in the town and the deaths of several of the medical and relieving officers; 47,194 persons (not to mention many thousands whose relief it was impossible to record in the outset of the crisis) cost the parish upwards of £70,000. That this enormous expenditure, which was of a temporary character, has been succeeded by a permanent burthen of a still more oppressive kind, in the operation of the Five Years Residence Act, which has increased the ordinary expenditure of the parish by £16,000 a year in relief, given mainly to poor persons belonging to Ireland. That the immigration of 1847 may, by the favour of cheap transit and now by the additional privilege of irremovability, be at any time repeated with the like calamitous results; in short, the burthen of relief to Irish paupers may, under such circumstances, be indefinitely transferred to the cost of Liverpool ratepayers, and by numbers nullify the application of the indoor labour test, considered to be one of the most valuable provisions of the Poor law. Your petitioners, therefore, humbly pray that the parish of Liverpool, from its peculiar position, may be exempted from the operation of any act abrogating the compulsory removal of Irish poor; and your petitioners, as in duty bound, will ever pray. Signed in and on behalf of the said select vestry, this 28th day of March, 1854, Augustus Campbell, Rector of Liverpool, chairman of the said select vestry.

Doc. 12.7: Irish Paupers in Glasgow, 1854

The Commonwealth, 9 September 1854.

It appears from the report presented the other day to the City Parochial Board that we have in the City Parish 400 pure Irish paupers, and 1,600 who claim to be Scottish in their native growth . . . But this is not all. Of the 1,600 who claim the soil of Scotland as their birthplace, a large proportion have sprung immediately from Hibernian parents; so that the fact is noted as explaining the existence of 2,000 paupers in the heart of the city of Glasgow. To Ireland, it appears, we are indebted for this somewhat large mass of civic poverty, drinking, and swearing, and sometimes fighting in our midst. It was moved and seconded that this Scot-Irish fact be noted in the reported condition of the parish affairs of our thriving community.

Now, we are not sure . . . whether our parochial senators are about to petition Parliament against further incursions from the Sister Isle, or demand that the progeny of the Irish, to the third and fourth generation, shall have no claim on the parish charity . . . Whatever the issue, to what good, we ask, is this record made if these paupers have established their claim in law to parochial aid? They come hither in quest of employment. They have laboured, in various ways, in the public and private works of the city. They may be improvident, they may be worse than improvident; but still they are, as labourers, doing much of the toilsome work of the city. Throw the Irish labour overboard, and we question much whether our city's expansion in parks, and crescents, and streets without end could be so cheaply carried forward. If these hard-working fellows should leave behind, when cropped by cholera, or typhus, or other social evil, some widows, or orphans, or other wretched dependents, shall we snuff at once because the blood is of the Emerald Isle? At the very moment that Ireland is feeling the incursion of Saxon farmers, and Saxon possessors of the soil, would it not be well to discontinue these invidious references to race, and name, and national distinctions, and – as our Government is one, our armies one, our national interest one – feel that, in parochial matters, while all is conducted according to law, it is not patriotic to stigmatize the poor on the parish roll wholly Irish, or three-fourths Irish, or simply in habiliments bearing the odour and aspect of the ragged Irish? As toiling amid the onward progress of our city, as ministering sinew and blood to its greatness, let them in their fair, inevitable poverty, share as others in the provision made by law for the relief of the poor. To act otherwise only irritates and perpetuates national animosities, which ought in haste to die and be for ever forgotten.

Doc. 12.8: Irish Pauper Immigration into Cardiff, 1854

Report of the Select Committee on Poor Removal, Parliamentary Papers (1854). Minutes of Evidence, 474–6. Evidence of Evan David, Chairman of the Cardiff Board of Guardians.

[Q] Have the Irish paupers been varying much lately?

[A] In the last two or three years we find that they are increasing; of course, they are not equal to what they were in 1847 and 1848, during the potato failure in Ireland, but latterly they are rather increasing . . .

[Q] Where do they come from chiefly, as far as you can make out?

[A] Chiefly from Cork; they are brought over in the coal vessels. We have a large export of coal from Cork, and the vessels generally return in ballast, and they are enabled to bring deck passengers, of course at a very low rate; and we have them in very large numbers; we have had as many as 100, 150 and 200 landed at once, all in the most wretched condition . . .

[Q] Are they landed at Cardiff?

[A] They were formerly landed at Cardiff, but our union ascertained that the captains of those vessels had no licenses for carrying passengers, and they offered a reward for information against them. After considerable difficulty, they fined only one; we then found that they left the paupers on our coast near Cardiff, and went on themselves to Newport, consequently we were unable to get at the captains. We find the paupers very reluctant to state by what vessel they come, or the name of the captain; they are very loathe to give us any information; they also stated that their passage was paid, but they did not know by whom.

[Q] Have you another document to which you are about to refer?

[A] I have Mr Rammell's report, the superintending inspector from the Board of Health, who visited Cardiff some few years ago . . . Mr Rammell states 'The principal cause of the excessive overcrowding found to prevail in Cardiff, is the vast influx of destitute Irish from Cork and Waterford, who have been partly attracted in the hope of obtaining employment on the public works, and partly by the extraordinary facilities of conveyance offered by the captains of vessels trading to this port . . . and the same observation has been made by others that these poor wretches are brought over as ballast, without any payment for their passage. The captains, it appears, find it cheaper to ship and unship the

living ballast than one of lime or shingles. They are generally landed,
however, on the coast before the vessels arrive at the port; and from
thence they make their way into the town, and throng the lodging-
houses, bringing pestilence on their backs, famine in their stomachs . . .
and that it has been from this source that fever has subsequently spread
through the town . . . At the time the epidemic broke out in 1847, in
addition to the cases given before as attended by myself, 186 were
admitted into a temporary hospital in the suburbs of the town; 61 of
them were fatal. This large proportion of mortality is to be accounted
for by the circumstance of nearly all the cases being those of Irish
suffering from fever at the time of their landing, and in a half-famished
state, immediately going to the hospital. The cases, in fact, may be said
to have been imported direct from Skibbereen and Clonakilty'. . .

[Q] Will you be so good as to describe what is your mode of dealing with
those cases when they come before the Board of Guardians?

[A] We generally give them relief at the time. But when there is any proba-
bility of their continuing paupers we are obliged to tell them that we
shall send them back to Ireland. We do not, perhaps in the first instance
do so, but if the application is repeated or if the parties are completely
destitute, they are then sent back, or at all events threatened to be sent
back.

Doc. 12.9: The Chester Board of Guardians and Removal, 1855

Report of the Select Committee on Poor Removal, Parliamentary Papers (1855), Minutes of
Evidence, 270, S.3433–4, 3446–7, 21 May 1855. Evidence of J. Trevor, Chairman of the
Chester Board of Guardians.

We had a case which I wish to mention to the Committee as illustrating the
system, when you resort to compulsory removals, how the people return
upon you. It was a case in which at the time I felt great sympathy; it was the
case of Bridget Mulloy, the mother of six legitimate children, and a widow.
I considered at the time, as all her children had been born in England, that
it was an exceedingly great hardship to remove the woman to Ireland, and
the Board of Guardians expressed themselves to the relieving officer not to
put the law in force. She unfortunately had an illegitimate child; that disen-
titled her to out-door relief, except with the sanction of the Poor Law
Board; it had been our rule never to transmit a case of that kind to the Poor
Law Board, except we could allege an extenuation of the misconduct.
However, the parish officers removed her, and, as I said before, I felt great
sympathy with the woman; she was removed on the 3rd of April; she came
back in a very few days, and had an order given her to go into our workhouse. On her being brought before the Board, I asked her how she had
come back; she said that she had been taken before the Lord Mayor of
Dublin; that she had represented the case; that the case had been explained

by some of the officials in the administration of the Poor Law in Dublin, and that the Lord Mayor had given her 10s. to come back. She came back and she was again removed on the 26th; and I am sorry to say I can give the Committee no further account of her. Perhaps the Committee will wonder, as her removal and that of her family, in the first instance, cost £2. 18s. 2d., how she came back with 10s. In the first place, we are obliged to pay the expense to put the law in motion; there is then the cost of the conveyance by railway, and the packet fare from Liverpool to Dublin; sometimes it is 2s. 6d., sometimes it is 5s. There are two prices in those packets; one in going from England to Ireland, but a less charge in coming back; and the woman would get herself brought from Dublin to Liverpool for 1s., two of her children brought for another shilling, and she could get back to Liverpool with her family, perhaps, for 4s. Then she could come upon the railway for about four railway fares, at 1s. 3d. each; so that the 10s. which the Lord Mayor of Dublin gave her amply covered the expense back. I merely mention this as an illustration of what I know is an exceedingly common occurrence. I recollect a case perfectly well; I have not the name here; I think it occurred before 1851, soon after the Irish famine, where a family of, I think, the name of Branigan were removed compulsorily from Chester; the neighbours made a collection to bring them back again; it was given to the woman in the presence of the removing officer, and she was back as soon as the removing officer. I merely mention this, to show that where there is a will there is a way; and if England is better than Ireland, they will find their way back . . . There is scarcely a Board-day when an Irish case does not come before us, or even an English case which is unsettled, when the question is not debated in principle. I have illustrated it by bringing to notice, if the power of removal were put into operation, whether in cases of English or Irish removal, the hardships to which it would subject the poor, and I have never heard from our guardians a dissenting remark.

[Q] Are you of opinion that the Irish poor in the large manufacturing districts, Liverpool for instance, Manchester, Wolverhampton, and those districts in your neighbourhood, occasion an undue burden on the rates, taking into account the advantages which their labour must necessarily confer?

[A] Certainly not; if you look at the increase of population in the manufacturing districts of Lancashire, and some parts of Cheshire and Derbyshire, if you look to the great increase of population which has occurred, which cannot have occurred by breeding, but by the importation of labourers, either from the agricultural districts of England, but principally from Wales and Ireland, and the great advantages resulting to the capital and the wealth of the country, I am strongly of opinion that, notwithstanding the temporary pressure which was imposed upon these districts by the Irish famine, which perhaps threw an undue proportion upon them, and rather overstocked them, yet, from what I read of the statistics of those towns, the paupers in them are not receiving more than a due proportion of relief . . . I do not find that either in Chester, or Birkenhead, or Liverpool, previous to the Irish famine, there was any undue pressure upon the rates from Irish poor; that unfortunate event did operate certainly, not only as a great blight in Ireland, but it operated in certain places in this country very disadvantageously upon the funds of the ratepayers, and also upon the labour market. It brought a great deal of disease with it, for this reason; the densely crowded courts of Liverpool were not adequate to the great influx of population; they were not sufficiently drained or ventilated; there were no sanitary arrangements, and fever was the natural consequence in the town. It operated in a less degree, but certainly also very prejudicially, in the city of Chester, and we felt it necessary to remove these unfortunate people into temporarily constructed fever hospitals. That cost us £700 or £800; we got rid of it very well and cheaply, but I did not find that the Irish convalescents when fit to go to labour at all pressed upon the rates.

Doc. 12.10: Relief of the Irish Poor in Birmingham, 1895

Report of the Royal Commission on the Aged Poor, Parliamentary Papers, XV (1895), Evidence of Mr. H. Allen, Birmingham City Councillor, 6 March 1894, S.16571–72.

[Q] Have you taken any pains to ascertain the general character of those who are receiving relief in the workhouse other than the infirmary?

[A] Well, you cannot very well get statistics. Of course, the guardians of Birmingham, so far as I know, are very particular, and have a call-over of the house, very frequently, I think, to ascertain whether there are those in who should be outside. But from what I see of people who get into the house I think a great number of them have got there through their own fault; and in Birmingham we find that one class of individuals especially take a much larger share of the rates.

[Q] What class is that?

[A] Well, that would be the class that I designate as the third section in the definition of the working classes. They are those who have never had any settled occupation in life, but have picked up odd jobs occasionally which are soon ended; and when old age comes upon them of course they are not able to do that kind of thing as they have done before, and they naturally drift there and take it as a matter of course; and we find in Birmingham that, compared with the natural population, the Irish take a very large percentage of relief in the house.

Doc. 12.11: Irish Poverty in Late-Victorian London

Charles Booth, *Life and Labour of the People of London* (1889–1903), vol. II, 46–7.

Shelton Street was just wide enough for a vehicle to pass either way, with room between curb-stone and houses for one foot-passenger to walk; but vehicles would pass seldom, and foot-passengers would prefer the roadway to the risk of tearing their clothes against projecting nails. The houses, about forty in number, contained cellars, parlours, and first, second, and third floors, mostly two rooms on a floor, and a few of the 200 families who lived here occupied more than one room. In little rooms no more than eight feet square would be found living father, mother and several children. Some of the rooms, from the peculiar build of the houses (shallow houses with double frontage) would be fairly large and have a recess six feet wide for the bed, which in rare instances would be curtained off. If there was no curtain, anyone lying on the bed would perhaps be covered up and hidden, head and all, when a visitor was admitted, or perhaps no shyness would be felt. Most of the people described are Irish Roman Catholics getting a living as market porters, or by selling flowers, fruit, fowls or vegetables in the streets, but as to not a few it is a mystery how they live. Drunkenness and dirt and bad language prevailed, and violence was common, reaching at times even to murder. Fifteen rooms out of twenty were filthy to the last degree, and the furniture in none of these would be worth twenty shillings, in some cases not five shillings. Not a room would be free from vermin, and in many life at night was unbearable. Several occupants have said that in hot weather they don't go to bed, but sit in their clothes in the least infested part of the room. What good is it, they said, to go to bed when you can't get a wink of sleep for bugs and fleas? A visitor in these rooms was fortunate indeed if he carried nothing of the kind away with him. The passage from the street to the back door would be scarcely ever swept, to say nothing of being scrubbed. Most of the doors stood open all night as well as all day, and the passage and stairs gave shelter to many who were altogether homeless. Here the mother could stand with her baby, or sit with it on the stairs, or companions would huddle together in cold weather. The little yard at the back was only sufficient for dustbin and closet and water-tap, serving for six or seven families. The water would be drawn from cisterns which were receptacles for refuse, and perhaps occasionally a dead cat. At one time the street was fever-stricken; the mortality was high, and the authorities interfered with good effect so that the sanitary condition of the street just before it was destroyed was better than it had been formerly. The houses looked ready to fall, many of them being out of the perpendicular. Gambling was the amusement of the street. Sentries would be posted, and if the police made a rush the offenders would slip into the open houses and hide until danger was past. Sunday afternoon and evening was the hey-day time for this street. Every doorstep would be crowded by those who sat or stood with pipe and jug of beer, while lads lounged about, and the gutters would find amusement for not a few children with bare feet, their faces and hands besmeared while the mud oozed through between their toes. Add to this a group of fifteen to twenty young men gambling in the middle of the street and you complete the general picture.

Doc. 12.12: Reminiscences of a Leicester Childhood in the 1850s

Tom Barclay, *Memoirs and Medleys: The Autobiography of a Bottle Washer* (Leicester, 1934; revised edition, Coalville, 1995), 2–4.

My next remembrance is one of disappointment, unsatisfied desire. How low must that state of poverty be in a family where the child, and he the only child, has to scratch a brick of the floor with a splinter of slate for want of a pencil. I had toddled into the street and saw a fragment of slate-pencil – a strayed two-inch fragment – below the threshold of a doorway; I knew instinctively that it would write and drew smoothly. I desired it with a great desire, but – alas! I dared not reach for it. I hesitated, and while hesitating another little one put forth his hand, and it was his. What a monotonous childhood! No toys, no picture-books, no pets, no going 'ta-ta'. No carpet on the uneven brick floor, no mat, no wall-paper; what poverty! There was neither doctor nor midwife present at my birth; of that I am convinced. Indeed I have heard mother boast that she never needed a midwife. She was very hardy, brought up in the wilds of the 'county Mayo, God help us!' After all, why shouldn't a woman be able to bring forth like cats and cows and other mammals?

Here in this eighteen foot square court off Burley's Lane, Leicester, St. Margaret's bells rang dismally every Sunday morning as I tried to play with duckstones for toys. I'm afraid the one door and one chamber window of the two-roomed crib we lived in were seldom opened, though not six feet from the muck hole and the unflushed privies, and air could only get in from one side of the house. How did we remain healthy?

After the monotony and dreariness of that Burley's Lane hut, I somehow find myself in a similar two-roomed hut in a similar court in a similar slum – Abbey Street: our walls are now plastered with wood-cuts from newspapers, and there are mounds of thick ice all around the gutters. Now there are five of us sleeping in one little upper room . . . We were commanded to remain shut in, father and mother being out most of the day earning a living. Father knew no trade and to dig was not able: he collected rags and bones, rag-bag on back, without as much as a truck (or handcart): mother worked at a rag-shop or marine store dealer's, or she got blocks of wood from the woodyards, chopped them small and sold the chips in pen'norths for fire-lighting round the neighbouring streets.

Doc. 12.13: Reminiscences of a Liverpool Childhood in the Early 1900s

Pat O'Mara, *The Autobiography of a Liverpool Irish Slummy* (London, 1934; revised edition, Liverpool, 1998), 32–3.

Shortly after I was born, the old fiddler-barber, convinced like all the other people who knew him, that my father was mad, had us put out. Next we went to live in Court No. 6, and from here, a few years afterward, mother, Alice and I went into Brownlow Hill Workhouse. Desperate for ale money, my father had been caught stealing some lead piping from the New Branch then being added to the Queen's Dock. Unable to work because of my recent birth, my mother appealed to the Parish and was given four shillings a week to support the three of us.

At the end of the month my father returned with ten shillings earned in jail, all of which was spent in Cain's public house at the top of the street. Then, he repaired to our shack and gave my mother another fearful beating. Though I was very young, the picture of her, covered with blood, lying on a stretcher and being carried to the ambulance, is still very vivid in my mind. For this my father was given two months in Walton.

As soon as my mother recovered sufficiently we were again dispossessed. We had by this time acquired quite a neighbourhood reputation and no one wanted to take us in. But somehow we got a little room in Kent Square and, though very hungry, we lived happily in the new peace and quiet we found, on the four shillings a week contributed by the Parish. After his two months were up, my father asserted his legal rights and again rejoined us, stayed normal for about a week, then broke loose once more. He attempted to throw my mother bodily down the stairway – and failed in this only because of the combined efforts of all three of us. It was a strange thing that he would listen to us children, particularly to me, whom he liked very much. But although he was thwarted at the stairway episode, he beat my mother so badly that she was again carried to the Southern Hospital for a week's stay, while he was taken to Walton jail, this time for four months.

When my mother returned with bandaged head the landlady, gripped with fear, asked us to leave. It was the last straw. Broken in spirit, my mother trudged, with us wonderingly at her side, up to the Workhouse and surrendered. This was indeed gall for her to take, since, despite her seeming lack of spirit, she was an inherently proud woman and would work off her fingertips, as proved in later years, if only she could get something to do and if she could reconcile the desertion from my father with her very Catholic conscience. If there had been any decent government institution into which to put us children without fear of losing that vital faith she cherished, my mother would have done so immediately and put my father out of her life. But there seemed no such haven. The governmental tendency as I have said, was to frown upon any slummy woman with two children, seeking matrimonial separation – particularly when opposed to her plea, denying everything alleged against him, was a man as tricky as my father.

Alice was five and I was three when we entered the big iron gate so dreaded by the slummies; and though our stay was only to be brief – three weeks, enough time for my mother's head and crushed spirit to heal – for a while it looked as though we were to go the way of all permanent inmates.

But upon recovery, frightened at this rigid necropolis, my mother applied for release. What visible means had she of support with her husband in jail? asked the Board. Then my mother told of her sister's (Auntie Janie) working as a charwoman in Heilbron's Emigrant House, a Cunard Line passenger agency in Great George's Square, inferring that Janie would obtain work for her. It was a plausible story and the Board was sympathetic. Off came our little red frocks and my mother's grey striped dress and on went our old rags reeking with fumigation gas. Outside in the street my mother proudly brought forth two shillings which she had concealed in her hair (for fear that it might be taken from her in the workhouse). She treated us all to meat pies and tea in such a nice peaceful shop that I still remember it and her contented look.

SICKNESS AND HEALTH

Doc. 13.1: The Irish and Public Health in Early Victorian Liverpool

Dr Duncan, *Report on the Sanitary State of Liverpool* (1842).

[a]   The custom prevalent among the Irish of keeping pigs in the cellars and even garrets which they inhabit ought to be noticed in connection with the present subject. On one occasion I had to grope my way (at noon-day) into a house in a court in Thomas Street; and on a candle being lighted I discovered my patient lying on a heap of straw in one corner, while in the opposite corner of the room a donkey was comfortably established, and immediately under the window was the dunghill which the donkey was employed to assist in gathering from the street. The general fact of the unhealthiness of dirty streets has already been noticed, and I may add that the three streets which appear to have yielded the largest proportion of fever cases (Lace Street, North Street and Oriel Street) are three of the most notoriously dirty streets in Liverpool, being very ill-supplied with ash-pits and chiefly inhabited by the lowest class of Irish. Of 58 front houses in Lace Street, 51 have no yard, privy or ash-pit; of 50 in Oriel Street, 41 are similarly situated; and of 29 in North Street, only 6 are supplied with any convenience. The disinclination, especially among the Irish, to be removed to the hospital on the very first appearance of fever in their dwellings is a circumstance which favours very much the extension of disease. In illustration of this, many instances could be given, if necessary. But it is to be remembered that many of the evils which I have pointed out are, perhaps, the inevitable results of poverty; and I believe that fever, to a certain extent, is an inseparable accompaniment of extreme poverty affecting large masses of the community. Among the causes of fever in Liverpool I might have enumerated the large proportion of poor Irish

among the working population. It is they who inhabit the filthiest and worst-ventilated courts and cellars, who congregate the most numerously in dirty lodging-houses, who are the least cleanly in their habits, and the most apathetic about everything that befalls them. It is among the Irish that fever especially commits its ravages; and it is they who object the most strongly to be removed to the hospital from their miserable abodes.

Liverpool Mercury, 15 January 1847.

[b]   The fact is that in the cold and gloom of a severe winter, thousands of hungry and half naked wretches are wandering about, not knowing how to obtain a sufficiency of the commonest food nor shelter from the piercing cold. The numbers of starving Irish men, women and children on our quays is appalling; and the Parish of Liverpool has at present the most painful and most costly task to encounter, of keeping them alive, if possible.

E. Rushton (Liverpool JP), Evidence to the *Select Committee on Poor Removal, Parliamentary Papers* (1847).

[c]   They lodge in cellars and rooms of the lowest character, fifteen or sixteen in a room. There is no adequate provision for the offices of nature, no one convenience of civilised life; they are sleeping in the clothes they wear in the day, without beds and without utensils. Their relief consists of baked meat and soup, and this is that state in which many thousands of Irish people are now abiding in that town.

The Times, 4 May 1847.

[d]   The return shows a great increase in the mortality of this district (the North End), which is without doubt solely attributable to the many thousands of Irish paupers who have landed here within the last three months, bringing with them a malignant fever, which is very appropriately called 'the Irish fever', and many hundreds of them were suffering from diarrhoea and dysentery when they arrived, which will account for so many deaths from those causes. Everything which humanity could devise and money carry out for their cases has been adopted by the Select Vestry but so many thousands of Irish are continually pouring in, and their habits are so disgustingly filthy, that little can be done as yet to stay the great mortality among them. Perhaps there is not a parallel case to Liverpool for the last two months in the history of the country.

Dr Duncan, Minutes of the Liverpool Health Committee, 15 March 1847.

[e]   I would like to draw the attention of the Health Committee to the objectionable custom of retaining the bodies of the dead, especially those who have died of infectious fevers, in the sleeping rooms of the living. On Sunday last a man died of typhus in a small room in Thomas Street in which seven or eight other inmates slept, two of whom were also ill with fever. Their friends objected to the burial taking place before Sunday (tomorrow)

and in the meantime the other occupants continued to sleep in the same room with the dead body. I myself have seen, last week, the body of a child who had died of smallpox lying in a cellar where fifteen individuals slept.

Dr Duncan, Liverpool Medical Officer of Health's Report (1850).

[f]   During that calamitous season we had to deplore the loss of many respectable and useful citizens. Among them may be enumerated the Roman Catholic clergymen, a Missionary Minister to the poor, ten medical practitioners, a number of relieving officers and others whose duties brought them into contact with Irish paupers, and many hundreds of English residents in comfortable circumstances, most of whom might have been alive had Liverpool not been converted for a while into 'a City of Plague' by the immigrant Irish who inundated the lower districts.

Doc. 13.2: Famine Migrants in Edinburgh, 1848

Edinburgh Medical Journal, 69 (1848).

These poor people, wretchedly clothed, exposed to cold and wet as deck passengers, many of them starving, and not a few of them actually labouring under disease, were ushered into our densely populated towns, there to seek the cheapest and most wretched lodging-houses or places of shelter. Fever thus became induced into these abodes, and after its induction it was kept up by a system as loathesome as culpable until the authorities, in many instances, interfered for its removal. It was impossible to put it down, however, as whenever they had their houses whitewashed and cleansed and their bedclothes washed at the public expense, they resumed the same system. I had several opportunities of visiting these lodging-houses occupied by the poor Irish. They in general consist of large-sized rooms, in dirty and badly-aired localities (generally the poorest in the town) in which beds are arranged on the floor as thickly as they can be placed. Here all sexes and ages occupied; and when one took fever and was removed to the hospital, no cleansing took place, but the next applicant was admitted into the bed just vacated by the fever patient. In this way the disease was spread. In Edinburgh almost every case admitted into the Infirmary at the beginning of the epidemic was from Ireland; and for nearly three months they continued so.

Doc. 13.3: The Sanitary Condition of Irish Migrants in the Potteries, 1850

Report on the Sanitary Condition of Newcastle-under-Lyme, Parliamentary Papers (1850).

The lodging houses in Newcastle are so numerous, and exert so great influence upon the sanitary condition of the borough, that I have thought it right to give them a special consideration . . . Newcastle appears to be a convenient centre for the whole of the district, and therefore the Irish make it their place of abode. Men, women and children are ostensibly traders in something, and all the towns in the Potteries are accessible from Newcastle. The consequence is that many Irish reside in the town, not exactly as a fluctuating population like tramps, but going out in the daytime with their various articles of petty merchandize and returning in the evening when they crowd together in large numbers for the night, the houses which accommodate them being chiefly in the most unhealthy parts of the town. From information for which I am indebted to Mr Cotter-ill, it appears that there are 52 common lodging-houses in the borough: 1 is for respectable Jew pedlars; 24 for Irish labourers, few of whom, he says, have any visible means of living, except harvest-men; 6 for decent working men, with clean beds, and not crowded; and 21 harbouring low prosti-tutes, travelling dog-cart thieves, mendicants, etc. In most of these places the rooms are crowded to excess; the sexes indiscriminately mix: the houses are very filthy, and without ventilation. Such places afford every facility for crime.

As seats of excessive mortality I should name the Upper and Lower Greens, Fletcher Street, Holborn, Lower Street, Pool Dan, Goose Street, and the alleys opening into those streets, and, indeed, the whole of the lower parts of the town, and the Higher Land. If the mortality of those were separated from the better parts of the town, it would be very high indeed, probably amounting to 4 per cent. The habits of the people residing in those parts are not so good as they might be. Many of the inhabitants reside there. I should think the Irish population amounts to not less than 800. They suffered severely from typhus fever in 1847, but not to the same extent from cholera this year. In many of the streets there is no drainage, and the public arrangements are not such as to secure the health of the inhabitants. In many places which I have visited during the prevalence of cholera I have found accumulations of filth, overflowing privies, and general want of drainage, sufficient to engender disease, irrespective of the habits of the occupants. In those parts of the town where fever prevails the defects are – want of sewerage and drainage, great and neglected accumu-lations of refuse, dirty habits, and an overcrowded state of lodging-houses, where men, women, and children are huddled together indiscriminately on straw, five or six in beds packed together in one room. Where fever raged in 1847, so has cholera in 1849. I draw from this and other facts that the devel-opment of fever and cholera has been promoted by the same exciting causes, and certainly they are to a great extent within the meaning of the term preventible.

Doc. 13.4: Typhus Fever in Gateshead

Report on the Sanitary Condition of the Inhabitants of the Borough of Gateshead, Parliamentary Papers (1850).

Typhus fever appeared in the borough of Gateshead and its neighbouring villages as an epidemic of a very serious nature in the summer of 1847 and carried off a great number of people. This epidemic, from its symptoms being peculiar to itself, and from its supposed importation by the immense droves of poor Irish, who came over in the summer of 1847, many of them harbouring fever; Gateshead, from it being at that time the residence of a great number of Irish who were labouring at the Public Works, was very heavily visited . . . The localities principally affected were Leonard's Court, Pipewellgate, and Hillgate, which are notoriously dirty places, where people are living huddled together amongst filth without the necessaries of life. In Pipewellgate and Hilgate the lodging-houses were the chief foci of the disease; these are principally resorted to by the Irish and other trampers; they are ill-ventilated houses in both districts, continually overcrowded. We have counted so many as 26 individuals in one room . . . During September, October and November the fever was what is termed Irish or starvation fever, a mild form of low typhus; during December and January it was mixed with influenza, latterly the cases were pure typhus.

   The borough contains 26 [lodging] houses of this class. They are situated for the most part in low and crowded neighbourhoods. Of the keepers, 17 are Irish, 7 English and 1 German; and they comprise in the whole 74 rooms (if I do not misapply the term). Many of the dormitories are little better than hovels, whether as regards size, cleanliness, ventilation or drainage, and they are such as are calculated to engender disease in its most malignant form. This opinion I have seen fully borne out during the prevalence of the late epidemic. I have had opportunities of witnessing, in rooms not measuring more than 14 feet square, from 15 to 20 men, women and children lodged; the women with nothing more than a shift, which, from length of time and filthy habits of the wearer, had the appearance more of oil cloth than the under garment of a female; they were all breathing an atmosphere pestilential in the extreme. Added to this, unrestrained sexual intercourse takes place in the presence of the youth of both sexes, not a screen of any kind intervening; indeed, in my experience, I have witnessed, along with other officers, sights of this kind such as would disgrace a savage life, but which, to the inmates of these dens from familiarity and their low standard of morality, went unnoticed, except in the shape of vulgar jest or ribald remark.

HOUSING

Doc. 14.1: A Lodging-House in Church Lane, St Giles, London in 1847

Report on the State of the Inhabitants and their Dwellings in Church Lane, St Giles, *Journal of the Statistical Society of London*, XI (1848), 2–3.

[House No. 2] Parlour of Ground Floor: Size of room, 14 ft. long, 13 ft. broad, 6 ft. high; size of window, 5 ft. 3 in. by 5 ft.; rent paid, 8s. weekly for two rooms; under-rent paid, 3d. per night for each adult; time occupied, 28 years by landlady. Number of families, 3; consisting of 8 males above 20, 5 females above 20, 4 males under 20, 5 females under 20, total 22 souls. Number of persons ill, 2, fever and measles; deaths in 1847, 1, measles. Country, 7 English, 15 Irish; trade, dealers and mendicants. State of rooms, filthy; state of furniture, bad and dirty; state of windows, 21 whole and 9 broken panes. Number of beds, 6; number of bedsteads, 6 in two rooms. A man and his wife and children, occupying a bed for a week pay 3s., but 12 adults, at 3d. per night, Sunday not counting, give the landlady 18s. a week for the 8s. she pays, or a profit of 10s. The rent paid for the ground-floor of this house is 3s. above the ground-floor of other houses in the street. 1,092 cubic feet of air, 1st room, 815 cubic feet of air, 2nd room; total, 1,907 cubic feet of air for 22 persons.

Back Room, Ground Floor: Size of room, 11 ft. 4 in. long, 11 ft. 3 in. broad, 6 ft. 5 in. high; size of window, 3 ft. 4 in. by 3 ft. 3 in. The yard of this house, 6 ft. square, in a very bad state. The privy has no seat or door; night-soil scattered about the yard. Liquid filth under the broken pavement. This room is rented with the preceding, and may be said to form part of it; the twenty-two tenants being common to the two rooms.

The Cellar of this House: Was found occupied. 3 beds, 3 bedsteads, dirty. 1 male above 20, 3 females above 20, 4 males under 20, 3 females under 20; total 11 persons: adults pay 3d. per night. This is the only cellar found with beds in the houses examined.

First Floor: Only one room. Size of room, 17 ft. 6 in. long, 13 ft. 9 in. broad, 8 ft. 3 in. high; size of window, 5 ft. 9 in. by 4 ft. 4 in.; rent paid 3s. weekly; under-rent paid, 1s. 6d. and 2d. each family; time occupied, 3 months. Number of families, 3, and 1 widow with 4 children; comprising 3 males above 20, 3 females above 20, 4 males under 20, 6 females under 20, total 16. Number of persons ill, – ; deaths in 1847, – ; Country, Irish; trade, dealers. State of rooms, dirty; state of furniture, bad, dirty; state of windows, 24 whole, 6 broken. Number of beds; 3; number of bedsteads, 3.

Second Floor: Size of room, 17 ft. long, 13 ft., broad, 8 ft. 3 in. high; size of window, 5 ft. 4 in. by 3 ft. 3 in.; rent paid, 3s. weekly; under-rent paid, 2s.;

time occupied, 2 years. Number or families, 2; consisting of 3 males above 20, 2 females above 20, 3 males under 20, 4 females under 20; total 12. Number of persons ill, 1, asthma; deaths in 1847, none. Country, Irish; trade dealers. State of rooms, dirty; state of furniture, bad, dirty; state of windows, 21 whole, 8 broken. Number of beds, 3; number of bedsteads, 2. Three females sleep in one bed. A son, aged 22, sleeps with his mother.

Doc. 14.2: The Inhabitants of Church Lane, St Giles, London, in the 1850s

Henry Mayhew, *London Labour and the London Poor* (1861).

In company with a police officer we proceeded to the Seven Dials, one of the most remarkable localities in London, inhabited by bird-fanciers, keepers of stores of old clothes and shoes, costermongers, patterers, and a motley assemblage of others, chiefly of the lower classes . . .

From the windows of the three-storied houses in Church Lane were suspended wooden rods with clothes to dry across the narrow streets – cotton gowns, sheets, trousers, drawers and vests, some ragged and patched, others old and faded giving a more picturesque aspect to the scene, which was enhanced by the dim lights in the windows, and the groups of the lower orders of all ages assembled below, clustered around the doorways, and in front of the houses, or indulging in merriment in the street. Altogether the appearance of the inhabitants was much more clean and orderly than might be expected in such a low locality. Many women of the lower orders, chiefly of the Irish cockneys, were seated, crouching with their knees almost touching their chins, beside the open windows. Some men were smoking their pipes as they stood leaning against the walls of their houses, whom from their appearance we took to be evidently out-door labourers . . . At the corners of the streets, and at many of the doorways, were groups of young costermongers, who had finished their hard day's work, and who were contentedly chatting and smoking. They generally stood with their hands in their breeches pockets.

Most of these people are Irish, or the children of Irish parents. The dark-ness of the street was lighted up by the streetlamps as well as by the lights in the windows of two chandlers' shops and one public house . . . Here a house was pointed out to us, No. 21, which was formerly let at a rent of £25 per annum to a publican that resided in the neighbourhood. He let the same in rooms for £90 a year, and these again receive from parties residing in them upwards of £120. The house is still let in rooms, but they are occu-pied, like all others in the neighbourhood, by one family only . . . In Church Lane we found lodging-houses, the kitchens of which are entered from the street by a descent of a few steps leading underground to the basement. Here we found numbers of people clustered together around several tables, some reading the newspapers, others supping on fish, bread, tea, and potatoes, and some lying half asleep on the tables in all imaginable positions. These, we were told, had just returned from hopping in Kent, had walked long distances, and were fatigued . . .

Other houses of a less reputable character were very numerous. One stood at the corner of Church Street and Lawrence Street, occupied by the most infamous characters of the district. On entering the house from Lawrence Lane, and proceeding upstairs, you would find on each floor several rooms connected by a kind of gallery, each room rented by prostitutes. These apartments were open to those girls who had fleeced any poor drunken man who had been induced to accompany them to this den of infamy. When they had plundered the poor dupe, he was ejected without ceremony by the others who resided in the room; often without a coat or hat, sometimes without his trousers, and occasionally left on the staircase naked as he was born . . . The old Crown public house in Church Lane, formerly the resort of the most notorious cadgers, was inhabited by Irish people, where often from twelve to thirty persons lodged in a room . . . Now, however, the district is considerably changed, the inhabitants are rapidly rising in decency, cleanliness, and order, and the rookery of St Giles will soon be ranked among the memories of the past.

CRIMINAL ACTIVITY

Doc. 15.1: Crime and the Irish, 1836

The Report on the State of the Irish Poor in Great Britain, Parliamentary Papers, XXXIV (1836), xx–xxiii.

The number and the character of the crimes committed by the Irish settlers in Great Britain further require consideration, as throwing much light on their moral habits, and on the change produced on them by their withdrawal from the various elements of disturbance which are at work in their own country. It appears then, from the best evidence on this subject which I was able to collect, that the Irish in the larger towns of Lancashire and Scotland commit more crimes than an equal number of natives of the same places; but that their crimes are not in general of a very dangerous character, being for the most part brutal assaults committed in a state of drunkenness; crimes against the person, committed after long premeditation and with unrelenting cruelty, by several persons, such as murders, nightly attacks on houses, beatings, vindictive rapes, &c., which are unhappily so frequent among the Irish in their own country, scarcely ever occur among them in Great Britain. The violence to which the Irish are prone, when excited by spirits, and the habit of disrespect for the law and resistance to its officers, which they had formed in their own country, are naturally increased when they find themselves under a feebler police and less rigorous administration of the law than they had hitherto been accustomed to. The evil effects of this weakness of the executive power are particularly seen at Manchester, as well as in some other towns of Lancashire. In Scotland, the large towns have a much more efficient police.

The crimes of violence most frequently committed by the Irish are the result of drunken broils, in which several persons are generally engaged on each side. As they fight not with fists, but with any weapons which they can reach at the moment, such as pokers, sticks, clubs &c., they frequently inflict grievous wounds on each other. The following statements of various witnesses will explain this subject.

Mr. Redfern, Prison-keeper and Deputy Constable, Birmingham:– 'The Irish are not so dishonest as the English of the same class, but more riotous when drunk. They get drunk on Saturday evening and Sunday; having eaten little in the week, a small quantity of spirits has much effect on them. Their general habits appear frugal and sparing; they are rarely drunk on week-days after Monday. They fight with one another in public houses and in the streets; the quarrel is frequently about the merits of their respective counties. Irish rows are more frequent in the summer than in the winter, because the weather tempts them into the open air. Sometimes at that time there are eight or ten Irish drunken rows on a Sunday. The English never make drunken rows of this kind; an English row is between two persons, who generally fight with their fists. The Irish fight with anything, sticks, pokers, or any weapons, but never with fists.'

Mr. Whitty, Superintendent of the Watch of Liverpool:– 'As to crimes against the person, deliberate murder is very rare among the Irish in Liverpool. Manslaughter is not frequent; wounding, maiming, and doing grievous harm, which if death ensued would be manslaughter, are frequent. Aggravated assaults are frequent among them, arising from some sudden provocation or drink. These are the result of the drunken rows, in which women and men are indiscriminately engaged. I never knew an Irish row in which women were not concerned. On these occasions they use everything that comes to their hand; if there is nothing, they fight with their fists; they never fight with fists if they can get a weapon. The Irish give infinitely more trouble, and are infinitely more riotous and disorderly in the streets than any other class of persons, or than all others put together. They make a great deal of noise; they are in fact more accustomed to a country than to a town life. I do not think that, because they make so much noise in the streets, they get more credit for drunkenness than they deserve. Hundreds, I might say thousands of them spend all their wages on a Saturday night.'

Mr. Barrett, Gaoler and Superintendent of the Police of Stockport:– 'Very aggravated assaults committed in a state of drunkenness are particularly frequent [among the Irish of Stockport]. They fight with weapons, as fire-pokers, pieces of iron, or shillelaghs, and rarely with fists. Frequently on these occasions they stab one another: these fights are principally among the Irish of different parties, and not so often between English and Irish; the parties depend on the part of the country whence they came; the women very often join in these encounters. Of the whole number of persons brought before the magistrates of Stockport, about a third are Irish. I think that they are not a tenth part of the population of the borough. Of the persons brought up for drunken and disorderly conduct, the Irish are the majority. The Irish are the most violent and troublesome set of people we have to do with. In consequence of so many living in a house, and the manner in which they support one another, whole crowds will turn out at a minute's notice, and will set upon the first person they meet, and maltreat him cruelly in order to revenge themselves.'

Mr. William Blane, Surveyor of the Police of Kilmarnock:– 'Generally throughout the year, there are more drunken rows among the Irish than the Scotch, in proportion to their numbers; it is only a few of the young Scotch who are not settled in life that make disturbances, whereas the Irish of all ages are engaged in rows of this sort. Of the persons brought to the police office for drunken broils and assaults, the absolute majority are Irish.'

Among the crimes against property, those of a serious nature do not seem often committed by Irish; thus Mr. Thomas states that at Manchester, although highway robberies are common, the Irish have rarely any part in them; though at Stockport it is said that, 'of the highway robberies which occur in the outskirts of the town, and even in its streets, the majority are committed by Irish'. The professional thieves of Liverpool are stated by Mr. Whitty to be generally from London and Yorkshire; as this craft probably requires as much dexterity and skill as many of the mechanical trades. The Irish, not having been regularly trained to house-breaking, are contented with stealing small articles, and this they practise to a very considerable extent. Their pilfering habits are usually acquired at an early age, and are generated by the vagrant and mendicant life which the parents, and especially the mothers, too often follow. It is, moreover, not uncommon for the Irish to send out their children into the streets, in order to get what they can, either by begging or any other mal-practice. Occasionally a certain sum is prescribed, which the child is required to bring home at night, and is beaten, or otherwise punished, if it is not forthcoming. Hence the male children become thieves, and the female children both thieves and prostitutes. It is much to be lamented that these abuses prevail to a considerable extent among the Irish settled in Great Britain, even those whose circumstances afford no excuse for such conduct, as appears from the following statements.

Mr. Redfern, Deputy Constable of Birmingham:– 'They (the Irish) bring up their children very ill; they send them out begging, and, according to their ages, so much money are they to get. Sometimes the children, when sent out to beg, learn from others to steal.'

Mr. Parlour, Superintendent of the Police of Liverpool:– 'There is a great deal of pilfering among the Irish; many Irish women send children out to steal, and maintain them for the purpose of thieving.'

Mr. Thomas, Deputy Constable of the Township of Manchester:– 'There is a great deal of crime in Manchester, among Irish, both boys and girls, of very tender years. This arises from desertion; the children are forced into the streets to beg or steal, and are punished when they come home if they do not bring money; the sum required is generally 1s. or 1s. 6d., according to the adroitness of the children. This practice prevailed to a great extent among the Irish of St. Giles's and the purlieus of Drury Lane; it rarely occurred among the English. I consider the Irish very negligent of the morals, cleanliness, and care of their children.'

Mr. Davies, Superintendent of the Manchester Watch:– 'A great many Irish live in entire idleness on the money collected by their children. They send them out to beg or steal, as it may be, and require them to produce a certain sum at the close of the day; if they do not produce it they are severely beaten, and it often happens that we find them in the street at midnight, not daring to go home for fear of being punished. Some children will collect 2s. or 3s. in a day in this manner. The parents who treat their children in this way lead most drunken, disorderly, and dishonest lives. I have no doubt that there are in Manchester a hundred Irish families that live in this manner. I cannot recollect a single English family that does the same. A greater proportion of the youthful thieves, especially of the females, in Manchester, are Irish than of the grown-up ones. The low Irish treat their children with great cruelty, even of the labourers some send their children out to beg.'

Mr. Barrett, Gaoler of Stockport, after stating that 'a third part of the depredations committed in the borough [of Stockport] are committed by Irish,' remarks, 'Many Irish who earn from 12s. to 15s. a-week as labourers send their wives and children out begging. Irish children have often stated before the magistrates that their parents sent them out begging and made them bring things home, without asking how they obtained them, and beat them and refused food or lodging if they failed to do so. Many felonies have been committed in Stockport on this account by Irish children between 10 and 12 years of age. I never knew an instance of this among the English.'

Mr. Watson, Superintendent of the Police of Glasgow:– 'There is little serious crime within the jurisdiction of the police. Petty thefts are very common, and the majority of the juvenile delinquents are descended from Irish parents. This is owing to the improvident and intemperate life that the parents lead, and their want of attention to their families and children. They very often send out their children to beg and get what they can, by all means in their power; but it is not a common practice for the parents to punish their children if they do not bring a stated sum at the close of the day. It is very rare for Irish children to be brought to the police, saying that they dare not go home without a certain sum. There are hundreds of boys, girls, elderly people, and worn-out prostitutes, who find employment in gathering bones for manure, old iron, rags, and similar articles from dunghills; almost all these are Irish. There is also a great deal of prostitution among the low Irish. Among the young prostitutes there are more Irish than Scotch.'

Mr. Stuart, Superintendent of the Police of Edinburgh:– 'The majority of petty pilferers are children of Irish. The Irish are in the habit of sending out their children to beg. We know some instances where they encouraged their children to steal. It frequently happens that children are brought into the office, saying that they dare not go home for fear of being beat as they have not made any money; these are generally Irish, but not always.There are not many Irish among the grown-up prostitutes, but among the very young, from twelve to sixteen years of age, a considerable portion are Irish, or of Irish extraction. It seldom happens that a grown-up Irishman is convicted of theft; but there is much stealing among the young Irish born in this country.'

Mr. Murtrie, Superintendent of the Police of Paisley:– 'Of the petty thefts, more are committed by Irish than Scotch, in proportion to the population. Some Irish families are nearly all addicted to thieving, children as well as parents. There is more begging among the Irish than the Scotch, especially among the children; the parents send them out begging.'

Mr. Blane, Surveyor of the Police of Kilmarnock:– 'As far as I can recollect, most of the petty thefts in the town have been committed by Irish, particularly by boys of seven to fourteen years of age; nearly all these are of Irish parents.'

Illicit distillation prevails to a considerable extent among the Irish in England; and it is to them that the practice is confined, as the English are generally ignorant of the process of distilling, whereas the Irish were much accustomed to it in their own country, especially before the reduction of the duty on spirits. Mr. Pritchard, an excise officer at Manchester, who had taken much pains to suppress illicit stills in that town, calculated the annual loss to the revenue from illicit distillation in the Manchester collection at £20,000. In the large towns of Scotland, it appears that there is now little illicit distilling, either among the Irish or the natives.'

Doc. 15.2: The Statistics of Irish Criminality

Sources: R. Swift, 'Heroes or Villains?: The Irish, Crime and Disorder in Victorian Britain', *Albion*, 29, 3 (1999), 401; D.M. MacRaild, *Irish Migrants in Modern Britain, 1750–1922*, 163; H. Peavitt, 'The Irish, Crime and Disorder in Chester, 1841–1871' (University of Liverpool, PhD Thesis, 2000), 103. IOR = index of over-representation, being the extent to which the percentage of Irish prosecutions was greater than their proportion of the population.

[a]   Prosecutions of Irish-born in selected towns 1851–1891

| | IB% | IOR | IB% | IOR | IB% | IOR | IB% | IOR | IB% | IOR |
		1851		1861		1871		1881		1891
Barrow	–	–	–	–	–	–	31	2.9	36	4.4
Bradford	–	–	19	3.3	24	4.2	15	3.5	5	2.0
Chester	26	3.5	29	4.1	28	4.0	–	–	–	–
Liverpool	–	–	37	2.0	34	2.2	24	1.9	16	2.1
Manchester	–	–	30	1.9	22	2.3	17	2.3	13	2.8
Preston	–	–	26	3.1	28	5.2	27	6.1	26	8.4
Wolverhampton	22	2.8	–	–	–	–	–	–	–	–
York	26	3.6	21	2.6	16	2.1	–	–	–	–

House of Commons Papers, Judicial Statistics, England & Wales 1861–1901, cited by D. Fitzpatrick, 'A Curious Middle Place?: The Irish in Britain, 1871–1921', in R. Swift & S. Gilley (eds.), *The Irish in Britain 1815–1939*, 26.

[b]   Irish-born committals to prison 1861–1901

| | IB% | IOR | IB% | IOR | IB% | IOR | IB% | IOR | IB% | IOR |
		1861		1871		1881		1891		1901
England & Wales	15	4.9	14	5.7	12	5.7	8	5.3	7	5.6
Lancashire	31	3.5	28	4.0	24	3.9	15	3.7	12	3.7
Middlesex	16	4.2	12	4.2	8	3.6	5	3.1	5	3.9

Dec. 15.3: Irish 'Fences' in Glasgow, 1834

Glasgow Argus, 21 April 1834.

Few of our readers, we believe, have any idea of the immense traffic carried on betwixt Scotland and Ireland in the articles of stolen wearing apparel, watches, jewellery etc., or of the facility which is at all times given in the Sister Island to the disposal of goods of the above description . . . The encouragement in this traffic is so great that it has brought into existence a numerous body of nefarious traders, who keep up an almost perpetual intercourse with Ireland, realising on their merchandise profits, compared with which those of the most lucrative mercantile concerns at home sink into insignificance. In this city these traders are generally to be found in the

classic lanes adjoining the Bridegate, and may be recognised by the rakish-
ness and half gentility of their Irish looks, well fed and portly, wearing
fashionable clothes, soiled and muddied, and ornamented with the dashing
gold appendages, it may be, of gold watches. They are the swells of Irish
life in Glasgow, who drink and gamble all the week, mount a horse of a
Sunday, and bet boldly and largely on all contests of the ring etc. They are
known to all thieves in the city, who convey to their shops articles of
plunder, immediately after the perpetration of their robberies, for which the
poor wretches receive scarcely a tithe of their real value. These are momen-
tarily conveyed to places of safety and secrecy unknown to the police, from
which they are removed on the earliest possible opportunity, after amounting in all to a sizeable package, and placed on board the most eligible
conveyance for Belfast or Londonderry . . . After the whole of the ill-gotten
spoil has been disposed of, the trader returns with heavy pockets. Some
idea of the small return to thieves by these fellows for stolen property, and
the profit which they afterwards contrive to realise, may be formed when it
is mentioned that a supply of wearing apparel, valued at about £30, has
been sold for 30s., a watch worth £5 sold for 10s. or 20s., and so on with
other articles in proportion . . . A noted dealer in this way, who was transported at a recent Circuit, was not merely able to retain the most eminent
Counsel for his defence, but left behind him a large sum for the benefit of
his wife.

Doc. 15.4: Saturday-Night Saturnalia in Glasgow

The Glasgow Herald, 16 December 1861.

Crowds are also flowing and surging like troubled waters up and down the
centre of the street, and every now and then they are divided or pushed
aside by cabs, fish-barrows, hurleys and donkey-carts laden with coals.
Along the outside of the pavement huxters with stalls, and without them,
are busy roaring, gesticulating and selling their fish, oranges, cheese, handkerchiefs, note-paper, braces and Brummagen razors. One long wiry
Milesian bawls out the contents of the 'Sensation song-book', containing a
fabulous number of the 'most popular and sinitimintal songs' ever
published . . . A little further down the street a melancholy man is blowing
away at a pair of Irish pipes . . . On the opposite side of the street an old
blind fiddler is earnestly thrashing out the refractory notes of a piece of
music, intended for 'Rory O'More' . . . Sometimes family parties are seen
wending their devious way among the stalls, fish-barrows, and knots of
loungers, laden with the Sunday's provender . . . Well-doing navvies who
'mind the main thing' may be seen trudging along encased in their white
moleskins and tremendous laced boots, bearing loaves, salted fish, lumps
of beef, onions, potatoes and cabbages, greens, slices of strong-scented
pork ham, and packages of coffee, sugar and tea. From the entrance to the

various pawnshops dissipated-looking women are pouring in and out, carrying little bundles away with them, which are likely to be returned on the Monday forenoon . . . The eating-houses or tripe shops are, however, deserving of something more than a passing notice, as they appear to the longing eye of the hungry pedestrian, with their tempting sights of riotous living, their familiar sounds of jingling spoons, knives, forks and crockery, and their indescribable and overpowering smells. We take our station outside the window of one of these hunger-dispelling repositories . . . Inside the counter of this gastronomic temple is a little, bustling, hard-featured Irishwoman, ladling out tripe 'brue' and dividing the leather-like substance into thrippeny bowls. Loud, impatient and angry voices are repeating their demands from the boxes and back rooms and every now and then we catch the phrases: 'a pig's fut', 'troipe', 'coo heel', 'pottit head', or 'saut fish and tatties' . . . Brokers' shops next claim our attention, distinguished as they are by the variety of the wares, which appear to compromise every conceivable necessary and personal convenience to men and women . . . It is now, however, eleven o'clock and the public houses and singing saloons are pouring forth their tenants at will, and noisy, troublesome tenants assuredly they are. The old Saltmarket and Bridgegate are now more crowded, more noisy, and more tumultuous than ever. Rings are formed in all directions and quarrelling and fighting become the business of the hour. Blows are exchanged with a word, and sometimes without one, and the fun becomes fast and furious. Windows are thrown up, and towsy heads protruded, smoking away at dirty tobacco pipes, and watching the fun and fighting going on below . . . Patrols of police constables enter upon the scene, and make their exit without disturbing the hilarity of the proceedings, or appearing to be greatly disturbed themselves. Men and women are roaring, and screaming, and swearing, and laughing, and every now and then a top-heavy weight tumbles into the gutter.

Doc. 15.5: Policing the Irish District of Wolverhampton, 1848

Report on the Sanitary Condition of Wolverhampton, Parliamentary Papers 28–9. Evidence of Gilbert Hogg, Chief Constable of Wolverhampton, to Robert Rawlinson.

The following remarks and statements are founded upon the experience which I have had of the general condition of Wolverhampton during the period that I have filled the post of chief officer of police in this town. I have ever found that in those districts where there is the greatest amount of filth, deficiency of comfort, want of proper accommodation in dwellings, and an absence of cleanliness amongst the inhabitants, that there prevails much the largest amount of drunkenness and disorderly conduct. This remark applies more especially to the neighbourhood of Stafford-street, Canal-street, Berry-street and Salop-street, in which localities the dwellings of the poor are crowded together in confined courts and alleys. These districts are regarded as the most dirty parts of the town: Stafford-street has obtained an unenviable notoriety by the number of disturbances which have taken place from time to time. I have frequently been obliged to remove police-men from other parts of the town and place them in Stafford-street, in order to maintain tranquillity in that neighbourhood. The great majority of the lower classes living in this locality are Irish, and whenever any distur-bance takes place, these overcrowded lodging houses pour forth their inmates in almost incredible numbers, attacking a single policeman or two with great ferocity and savageness, but being equally expert in beating a retreat when faced by a sufficient force to repel their lawless proceedings. I have at times been compelled to have as many as 20 men parading the streets with cutlasses, to assert the supremacy of the law. The majority of commitments from this part of the town are mainly for offences against the public peace, and not for the crime of felony; the number of commitments of that kind being comparatively few.

The neighbourhood of Stafford-street is crowded with public houses and beershops, kept open up to a late hour at night, and I am of the opinion, after an experience of six years in this town, that many of the poorer classes are tempted to spend their money in these places from the total want of comfort at their own houses; indeed, many of them have told me, after having been turned out of the public house, and ordered to go home, that the place in which they lived was in such a miserable state that they would rather remain out in the open air if the weather was not severe. I must, however, remark that a great improvement has lately taken place in the state of the streets on Sundays. Formerly on the Sabbath morning, the streets were crowded with drunken men and women, but since the recent Act has come into operation requiring publicans to close their house at 12 o'clock on Saturday night, the streets on Sunday morning have been comparatively quiet. This observation applies to the town and district generally; and by reference to the police books it is found that the number of drunken cases brought before the magistrates has greatly decreased since the introduction of the salutary enactment of the legislature.

With reference to the crowded state of the lodging-houses in those localities to which I have adverted, I may remark that there can be no doubt that the habitual mixture of all sexes and ages in such houses tends greatly to disseminate vice and demoralization of every kind, and to impart to the young, especially, a total disregard for those decencies of life which prevail among the more favoured classes of society. Most of the houses to which I refer are not provided with any place for the recreation and amusement of the children of the poor, and consequently they are to be found in different parts of the town, some begging and others thieving, whilst many of them become the associates of older persons, too well versed in crime, and are thus gradually led on to the commission of graver offences.

The number of persons transported from this town within the last six years has been very great. Many of the inmates of these lodging houses are to be seen in the streets on Sundays in their tattered and dirty clothes, standing at the corner of the streets as the respectable inhabitants are on their way to church, and gazing with apparent indifference at what is passing around them. Such was the total disregard for the observance of the sabbath in the neighbourhood of Stafford-street, that until recently, Sunday trading was almost universal, many of the shopkeepers being obliged to keep open their shops to accommodate their customers on that day, or lose them during the other parts of the week. The Mayor has now put a stop to the system by a public proclamation, expressing his determination to fine all persons offending against the law with respect to Sunday trading. The intervention has had the desired effect, and the shops in question are now closed on the sabbath day.

Doc 15.6: Irish Juvenile Crime in Leicester, 1854

Rev. Joseph Dare, *Ninth Report of the Leicester Domestic Mission Society* (1854), 10–11.

Two or three Irish children were observed by a benevolent lady on the race course the Sunday before last: these children were in such a 'ragged filthy condition as to be a disgrace to a Christian country. Could anything be done for them?' I made inquiries of a respectable neighbour whom I have known for twenty years, and who has known these same Irish families four or five years. The mother of two of the said children lives in that respectable locality 'Pork-shop Yard.' She has offspring by several men – is enceinte and perpetually drunk. She sends out her children in this condition on purpose to excite commiseration; if the children were dressed up tidy today, the clothes would all be stripped off, sold for drink and the children driven forth half-naked to play the same game tomorrow. The other Irish case is that of a man, a widower, who shortened his wife's existence by ill-treatment. He lives, himself, by gathering rags and bones and begging. He takes no care whatever of his children. They are sent at large in rags and dirt to obtain subsistence in any manner they are able. A better garment or a pair of shoes would be immediately taken from them for drink: the boy seen on the race-course was recently in prison for theft. Should not the Irish generally be referred to their own priest? They are a great calamity to our large towns. Wherever they locate they introduce crime, disease, and wretchedness. There is scarcely an Irish case deserving of relief. The police should have orders to clear the public walks and race-courses, especially on a Sunday, of all such objects as referred to above. They are sent there for the express purpose of preying on the unwary.

Doc. 15.7: 'Irish Cockneys' and Crime in London, 1862

H. Mayhew and J. Binny, *The Criminal Prisons of London* (1862), 402–3.

As a body, moreover, the habitual criminals of London are said to be, in nine cases out of ten, 'Irish Cockneys', ie. persons born of Irish parents in the Metropolis . . . what is called the Irish-cockney tribe; and at the boys' prison at Tothill Fields we can see the little Hibernian juvenile offender being duly educated for the experienced thief. Some bigots seek to make out that the excess of crime in connection with the Irish race is due directly or indirectly to the influence of the prevailing religion of that country; and small handbills are industriously circulated among the fanatic frequenters of Exeter Hall, informing one how, in Papal countries, the ratio of criminals to the population is enormously beyond that of Protestant Kingdoms. From such documents, however, the returns of Belgium are usually omitted, for these would prove that there is really no truth in the theory sought to be established . . .

As to what may be the cause of crime in Ireland we are not in a position to speak, not having given any special attention to the matter; but the reason why there appears to be a greater proportion of Irish among the thieves and vagrants of our own country, admits of a very ready explanation. The Irish constitute the poorest portion of our people, and the children, therefore, are virtually orphans in this country, left to gambol in the streets and courts, without parental control, from their earliest years; the mothers, as well as the fathers, being generally engaged throughout the day in some of the ruder forms of labour or street trade. The consequence is, that the child grows up not only unacquainted with any industrial occupation, but untrained to habits of daily work; and long before he has learned to control the desire to appropriate the articles which he either wants or likes, by a sense of the rights of property in others, he has acquired furtive propensities from association with the young thieves located in his neighbourhood.

He has learnt, too, what is much worse, thieves' morals – which once in the heart, it is almost hopeless to attempt to root out. He has learnt to look upon 'pluck', or daring, as the greatest virtue of life; he has learnt to regard all those who labour for an honest living as 'flats', or, in plain English, fools; he has learnt to consider trickery, or 'artful dodges' as he calls them, as the highest possible exercise of the intellect, and to believe that the main object in life is amusement rather than labour. His attention has never been trained to occupy itself with any one subject for five minutes together, nor have his impulses been placed under the least restraint. What wonder, then, that he grows up a mere savage amongst civilised men! But whatever be the cause, the fact is incontestible, that a very large proportion of the juvenile prisoners are the children of Irish parents.

Part 5

Catholicism, Protestantism and Sectarianism

AGRICULTURAL HALL

SNOW HILL, WOLVERHAMPTON

ROMANISM AND PUSEYISM
UNMASKED.

Roman Catholic Priests and Laymen of Wolverhampton,
YOU ARE AFFECTIONATELY INVITED TO THE

ADDRESSES

TO BE DELIVERED (D.V.) AT THE ABOVE HALL, BY

MR. W. MURPHY,

Of the Protestant Evangelical Union, 3, Craven Street, Strand; Lieutenant-Colonel Brockman, President; on the following Evenings at Eight o'clock.

MONDAY, FEBRUARY 18th,
SUBJECT :   Purgatory, the Scapular, and the Blessed Virgin Mary coming down from Heaven to release Souls out of Purgatory.

TUESDAY, FEBRUARY 19th,
SUBJECT :   Transubstantiation and the Sacrifice of the Mass.

WEDNESDAY, FEBRUARY 20th,
SUBJECT :   The Glories of Mary and the Glories of Jesus.

THURSDAY, FEBRUARY 21st,
SUBJECT :   The Seven pretended Sacraments of the Church of Rome Unscriptural.

Admission to the above Meetings---Reserved Seats, 2d.; Back Seats, 1d., to defray expenses.

ON FRIDAY, FEBRUARY 22nd, SUBJECT :

MAYNOOTH AND ITS TEACHING,
AND THE
"CONFESSIONAL UNMASKED."

Shewing the depravity of the PRIESTHOOD and the IMMORTALITY of the CONFESSIONAL.

CHAIR TO BE TAKEN AT EIGHT O'CLOCK, BY THE

REV. J.E. ARMSTRONG,
DD., LL.D., RECTOR OF BURSLEM.

LADIES not admitted to the Lecture on the Confessional except those who frequent it, nor Gentlemen under 21 years of age.
PROTESTANTS : Come and hear the questions put to the married and unmarried in the Confessional, and save your wives and families from the Contamination of the Confessional.
Admission to the Confessional Sixpence. The "Confessional Unmasked," will be sold after the Meeting, price One Shilling

HILDRETH & CHAMBERS, PRINTERS, OPPOSITE QUEEN STREET CHAPEL, WOLVERHAMPTON.

Murphy Advertisement, Wolverhampton, 1867.

INTRODUCTION

The majority of Irish people who settled in Victorian Britain were Roman Catholics, and the survival of an Irish identity was crucially bound up with the survival of Catholicism, as the Roman Catholic Church in England, Scotland and Wales was the only native institution with a fundamental claim on Irish loyalties.[1] This relationship was reflected in the unique role and status of the Roman Catholic priest within Irish communities in British towns and cities, as Henry Mayhew observed in mid-Victorian London (**Doc. 16.1**).[2]

The rise of an expatriate Irish Catholicism was part of the transformation of nineteenth-century Irish religion from a faith based chiefly on the home and on family prayers, and Gaelic devotion and pilgrimage or 'patterns' in a sacred rural landscape, to a much more chapel-orientated religion of weekly attendance at Mass.[3] This transformation, which can be dated from Archbishop Paul Cullen's remaking of the Irish church in the Roman mould in the 1850s, has been described as a 'Devotional Revolution',[4] and by the end of the century the Irish had become the most practising Catholics in the world. But more was involved in the change than simply higher mass attendance, for the Irish clergy sought also to suppress the folklore, superstition, drunkenness and even obscenity which accompanied wakes, weddings and other religious patterns. Thus Irish religion in the nineteenth century became more modern, more decorous, more Victorian, more disciplined and more Puritan; and what happened in rural Ireland also happened in England, where the 'Devotional Revolution' witnessed the polarisation of a whole new range of chapel and priest-centred devotions to the Blessed Sacrament, the Virgin and Saints. These

---

[1] This is the subject of an extensive historiography, but see especially D. Gwynn, 'The Irish Immigration' in G.A. Beck (ed.), *The English Catholics, 1850–1950* (London, 1950), 265–90; E.R. Norman, *The English Catholic Church in the Nineteenth Century* (Oxford, 1984); D. McRoberts (ed.), *Modern Scottish Catholicism* (1979); S. Gilley, 'Irish Catholicism in Britain, 1880–1939', in S.J. Fielding (ed.), *The Church and the People* (Warwick, 1988), 1–28; S.J. Fielding, *Class and Ethnicity: Irish Catholics in England, 1880–1939*; S. Gilley, 'Roman Catholicism and the Irish in England', in MacRaild, *The Great Famine and Beyond*, 147–67.

[2] See, for example, S. Gilley, 'The Catholic Faith of the Irish Slums: London, 1840–70', in H.J. Dyos and M. Wolff (eds), *The Victorian City: Images and Reality*, 2 vols. (London, 1973), vol. 2, 837–53; R. Samuel, 'The Roman Catholic Church and the Irish Poor', in Swift and Gilley, *The Irish in the Victorian City*, 267–300; J. Turton, 'Mayhew's Irish: The Irish Poor in Mid-Nineteenth-Century London', in Swift and Gilley, *The Irish in Victorian Britain*, 122–155.

[3] D. Miller, 'Irish Catholicism and the Great Famine', *Journal of Social History*, IX (1975–6), 81–98.

[4] E. Larkin, 'The Devotional Revolution in Ireland, 1850–75', *American Historical Review*, 77 (1972), 625–52.

were taken from the popular public religion of Italy and France, called 'ultramontane' from their association with papal Rome, because Rome lay 'ultra montes', beyond the mountains.

Yet the Catholic revival in Britain was not simply of Irish origin, for the English Catholic church was strongest in Lancashire, one of the principal areas of Irish immigration.[5] However, as a traditionally lay and gentry-dominated institution, it was a very different body from the Catholic church in Ireland and had developed a very English restraint and reserve during the long period before Catholic Emancipation in 1829. Thereafter, English Catholics moved away from this tradition as they increasingly came under Roman continental influences. By the time the Pope reorganized English Catholics under Cardinal Archbishop Wiseman in 1850, the church had become more aggressive in seeking English converts, partly under the influence of the Oxford Movement. For this new Roman Catholic crusade for converting England, the huge number of pauper Irish who needed priests and chapels was to some extent a distraction, not least in reinforcing English notions and prejudices that Catholicism was 'un-English'.

Nevertheless, the churches of the Irish diaspora began by re-evangelizing the nominally Irish Catholic faithful in secularized towns and cities where English, Scottish and Welsh priests devoted themselves to the creation of missions for the Irish poor, despite shortages of money and sittings. During the 1840s and 1850s the Catholic clergy were overwhelmed by the number of Irish they were trying to reach, who even included itinerant railway navvies (**Doc. 16.2**), and often worked themselves to exhaustion. This heroic age of missionary Catholicism included Father Mathew's famous temperance tour of England in 1843 (**Doc. 16.3**): in the Irish centres, Mathew was greeted by huge crowds who, much to his embarrassment, expected him to work miracles as well as administer the pledge.[6] Subsequently, Mathew's work was continued by other priests, most notably Father Lockhart in London in the early 1870s (**Doc. 16.4**). By contrast, the second half of the nineteenth century witnessed the development of the parochial system, an increase in the number of priests, and a boom in church building which transformed the austere and simple Catholic chapels of the past into people's palaces, awash with the new iconography of altars, statues and pictures which in Britain were the

---

[5] See, for example, G. Connolly, 'Irish and Catholic: Myth or Reality? Another Sort of Irish and the Renewal of the Clerical Profession among Catholics in England, 1791–1918', in Swift and Gilley, *The Irish in the Victorian City*, 225–54; W.J. Lowe, *The Irish in Mid-Victorian Lancashire: The Shaping of a Working Class Community* (New York, 1989), 109–144; Fielding, *Class and Ethnicity*, 38–77.

[6] For Mathew's work, see E. Malcolm, *'Ireland Sober, Ireland Free': Drink and Temperance in Nineteenth Century Ireland* (Dublin, 1986), 101–50; B. Harrison, *Drink and the Victorians: The Temperance Question in England, 1815–1872* (Keele, 1994), 167–81.

expression of communal pride and self-assertiveness, a challenge to their Protestant counterparts, and a genuine working-class attraction away from the gin palaces which were their neighbourhood rivals.

The Catholic Church not only reshaped Irish Catholicism but also served as an avenue of cultural adaptation for the Irish in Britain. Few communal rituals survived transplantation from Ireland. The wake, a major folk cere-mony in Ireland, gradually disappeared in Irish communities in Britain, outlawed as it was by the Church, although wakes were held in South Wales as late as the 1870s (**Doc. 16.5**). The traditional belief in the magical powers of priests, epitomized in the anecdote about Father Carroll in Merthyr (**Doc. 16.6**), was also shed, although the belief that priests could lay ghosts or cure illnesses persisted into the 1890s. Irish superstitions, including fairy lore, were undermined by the Church, whilst even staple religious festivities, including pilgrimages and the celebration of Saints' days, failed to survive transplantation, apart from the celebration of St Patrick's Day. The Gaelic language also declined, due largely to the rela-tively small number of Irish-speaking priests and the fact that the Roman Catholic Church in England had no interest in saving it.

The Catholic Church helped Irish migrants to adapt to urban life by providing a social and cultural world based on the parish church whose provisions included schools – promoted by the Jesuits, the Franciscans, and the Sisters of Mercy, founded by Catherine McAuley in 1828 (**Doc. 16.7**) – social clubs, lectures, dinners, bazaars, temperance groups, festi-vals, church suppers, choral societies, bands and excursions. These exercised a particular influence over women and children.[7] However, the Catholic Church was also a force for social discipline among Irish adult males through clubs such as the Total Abstinence Society, the Catholic Association for the Suppression of Drunkenness, and the Brotherhood of St Patrick. The larger impact of Roman Catholic culture was ideological in that the religious symbols of the Catholic Church in England sanctified the ideals of work, poverty, virginity and moderate Irish nationalism. Priests used Irish themes and symbols to draw Irish migrants into church activities, as the proceedings at St Briget's Confraternity, Soho, illustrate (**Doc. 16.8**), whilst elaborate St Patrick's Day celebrations of the kind

---

[7] For Catholic social and welfare provisions, see Devine, 'The Welfare State within the Welfare State: The Saint Vincent de Paul Society in Glasgow, 1848–1920', in W.J. Shiels. and D.Wood (eds), *Voluntary Religion*, Studies in Church History, 23 (Oxford, 1986); H. McLeod, 'Building the "Catholic Ghetto": Catholic Organisations, 1870–1914', in Sheils and Wood, *Voluntary Religion*, 411–44; M. Hickman, *Religion, Class and Identity: The State, the Catholic Church and the Education of the Irish in Britain* (Aldershot, 1995); M. McClelland, 'Catholic Education in Victorian Hull', in Swift and Gilley, *The Irish in Victo-rian Britain*, 101–21. For a local study of the role and contribution of Irish women, see M. Kanya-Forstner, 'Defining Womanhood: Irish Women and the Catholic Church in Victo-rian Liverpool', in MacRaild, *The Great Famine and Beyond*, 168–88.

described in Barrow (**Doc. 16.9**) united the appeal of religion with nationalism. Irish priests visited English towns, and Irish news was included in new Catholic newspapers such as *The Universe* and *The Universal News*, which themselves testified to the fact that Irish communities were taking on a well-defined character.

Thus Irish migrants found both a national and a religious identity within the Roman Catholic Church and were drawn in various ways and on various levels – as in late Victorian Leicester (**Doc. 16.10**) – into a highly religious popular culture on their arrival from Ireland. Two kinds of Irish Catholic emerged; at one end, those who might get drunk, live disorganized lives and seldom attend church, but who believed in Faith and Fatherland, would give money to the priests, have their children baptised and sent to Catholic schools, and at the very least expect the last rites; and at the other end the more devout and disciplined, more women than men, who formed the backbone of the parochial devotional associations, guilds and societies in which every Catholic parish abounded. Moreover, beyond the sectarian redoubts of Merseyside and Clydeside, Irish Catholics formed a viable and distinct culture which was intrinsically dynamic in that being Irish, Catholic and working class forced individuals to reconcile different demands and particular identities. Yet, as Robert Roberts observed in Salford at the turn of the century, the Irish Catholic working class was far from homogeneous: relations between the Irish-born and the culturally Irish were not always amicable; there was sometimes animosity between long-established emigrant families and new arrivals; and Irishness was itself a contested concept, with those who lived outside Ireland often perceived as distinct from, and inferior to, those who remained (**Doc. 17.1**).[8] Moreover, the persistent failure of some Irish Catholics to pass on their faith to a generation born in England, Scotland and Wales (the so-called process of 'leakage', variously influenced by working-class attitudes, social distinctions, poverty, mixed marriages, irreligious parents, and Protestant schools) continued to inhibit the strenuous efforts of the Roman Catholic Church to re-evangelize the Irish in Britain completely.

Nevertheless, Irish Catholic identity in Victorian Britain was reinforced by manifestations of anti-Catholicism, both covert and overt.[9] The English, Scots and Welsh were overwhelmingly Protestant by tradition and there had been a distrust of Roman Catholicism in Britain since the Reformation.

---

[8] R. Roberts, *The Classic Slum: Salford Life in the First Quarter of the Century*, 6–9; 84–5.
[9] G.F.A. Best, 'Popular Protestantism in Victorian Britain', in R. Robson (ed.), *Ideas and Institutions of Victorian Britain* (London, 1967), 115–42; E.R. Norman, *Anti-Catholicism in Victorian England* (London, 1968); D.G. Paz, *Popular Anti-Catholicism in Mid-Victorian England* (Stanford, 1992).

Anti-Catholic feeling in England was rooted in an historic hatred of France and Spain, Catholic powers and England's traditional enemies; in scriptural and theological arguments against Roman Catholicism; in the Settlement of 1688, which ensured the Protestant Succession of William and Mary; in the fact that the Church of England imparted a religious dimension into political life and had therefore to be protected; and in the belief that Roman Catholicism, with its legacy of the Inquisition, was a persecuting sect. Thus, by the end of the eighteenth century, English Protestants held that the Roman Catholic Church was both theologically unsound and politically subversive; that it was intolerant and persecuting; that it was a hindrance to the moral, intellectual and economic development of its flock; and that it should be excluded from political power. In this context, Irish Catholics were particularly vulnerable because their allegiance was to a foreigner rather than to the Crown (the head of the Protestant Church and State), hence they were also regarded as potentially, if not actually, politically subversive, a perception which Irish nationalist activity consequent upon the Act of Union of 1800 appeared to confirm.

The strength of popular Protestantism was greatly reinforced by the Evangelical Revival, and religious issues provided a vital ingredient in determining Anglo-Irish relations on a local level during the Victorian period, although Victorian 'No Popery' was much more than simply anti-Irishness. Nevertheless, the terms 'Irish' and 'Catholic' were virtually synonymous in British eyes and, although anti-Irish sentiment was more diffuse than anti-Catholicism, the resurgence of popular Protestantism in the wake of the Tractarian controversy, large-scale Irish immigration during the Famine years, and the re-establishment of the Roman Catholic hierarchy in 1850, which prompted Lord John Russell's letter to the Bishop of Durham (**Doc. 17.2**), provided an additional cutting-edge to Anglo-Irish tensions during the mid-Victorian years, when anti-Catholic sentiment contributed to numerous clashes between the English and the Irish.

One of the most serious of these disorders occurred at Stockport in 1852, when the Irish Catholic community in Rock Row was besieged by a Protestant mob and the Roman Catholic Church of Saints Philip and James at Edgeley was desecrated (**Doc. 17.3**),[10] but there were also violent disturbances at Oldham in 1861[11] and London in 1862.[12] More widespread were the so-called Murphy Riots which resulted from anti-Catholic lectures delivered between 1867 and 1871 by William Murphy, a member of the Protestant Evangelical Mission and Electoral Union, in industrial towns

---

[10] P. Millward, 'The Stockport Riots of 1852: A Study of Anti-Catholic and Anti-Irish Sentiment', in Swift and Gilley, *The Irish in the Victorian City*, 207–24.

[11] J. Foster, *Class Struggle and the Industrial Revolution* (London, 1974), 243–6.

[12] S. Gilley, 'The Garibaldi Riots of 1862', *Historical Journal*, 16, 4 (1973), 697–732.

with significant Irish Catholic populations.[13] These lectures, the focal point of which was a talk on 'The Confessional Unmasked: Showing the Depravity of the Romish Priesthood, the Inquiry of the Confessional, and the Questions put to Females in Confession', often provoked a violent Irish Catholic backlash, as in Wolverhampton (**Doc. 17.4**), where Murphy spoke on 'Romanism and Puseyism unmasked', and North Shields (**Doc. 17.5**). The most serious outburst of anti-Irish violence during the period occurred in Wales in July 1882 at Tredegar. Here, economic rivalries between Irish and Welsh workers, exacerbated by the activities of local Salvationists and compounded by the anti-Irish feeling which had been aroused by the Phoenix Park murders in Dublin in May, resulted in several days of rioting which culminated in the eviction from the town of some four hundred Irish men, women and children (**Doc. 17.6**). Yet closer analysis of these and other disorders suggests that more often than not they were, at root, the reflection of deeper strains and stresses within local communities and that religion was sometimes a cloak which concealed wider communal grievances.

Anti-Catholic feeling was exacerbated by the presence of Irish Protestants, largely from Ulster, in those British towns and cities also populated by Irish Catholic migrants, particularly on Clydeside and Merseyside. The experience of the Protestant Irish in nineteenth-century Britain is in many respects opaque and their story is certainly worthy of further attention from historians. Their numbers are difficult to quantify, since census records did not distinguish Irish migrants by religion, although estimates suggest that perhaps one-quarter of all Irish migrants were non-Catholic, and evidence of their religious and associational culture is patchy and sometimes difficult to penetrate. Relatively more is known about Irish Protestants in Scotland than in England and Wales.[14] About one-third of all Irish immigrants in Scotland were Ulster Protestants, many from Presbyterian backgrounds, and they entered the Scottish labour market under conditions rather different from those of Irish Catholics. Although some were unskilled and poor, many were skilled or semi-skilled workers who had been recruited by advertisements in the Belfast newspapers for jobs in the mines and iron and steel works of Lanarkshire.

The labour migration of Irish Protestants from Ulster to the West of Scotland and North-West England was linked directly to the development

---

[13] See W.L. Arnstein, 'The Murphy Riots: A Victorian Dilemma', *Victorian Studies*, XIX (1975), 55–71; R. Swift, 'Anti-Catholicism and Irish Disturbances: Public Order in Mid-Victorian Wolverhampton', *Midland History*, IX (1984), 87–108; D.M. MacRaild, 'William Murphy, the Orange Order and Communal Violence: The Irish in West Cumberland, 1871–84', in Panayi, *Racial Violence in Britain*, 44–64.

[14] G. Walker, *Intimate Strangers: Political and Cultural Interaction Between Scotland and Ulster in Modern Times* (Edinburgh, 1995), 1–16.

of the Orange Order in these regions,[15] although it should be emphasized that not all Irish Protestants were Orangemen. The Irish Orange Order[16] had emerged as a Protestant response to a perceived threat from Roman Catholics in Ulster during the late eighteenth century, when there were a number of attacks on Protestants as the Penal Laws were relaxed. The Order, which originated in 1795 following a clash between Catholics and Protestants in Armagh (the so-called 'Battle of the Diamond'), had support from some of the gentry as well as tenant farmers, shopkeepers and sections of the working classes, and it adopted the Freemasons' organizational structure of lodges and offices, including Grand Masters, and had its own rules and ceremonies (**Doc. 18.1**). By 1800 Orangeism had spread throughout Ireland (although strongest in the northern counties) and the early decades of the nineteenth century witnessed the gradual development of the Order in Scotland and England. By 1835 there were some 44 local lodges in the West of Scotland, some of which had been established by Ulstermen, with a total membership of about 500.[17] The English Orange Order was formally established at Manchester in 1807, but the focus of the movement soon shifted to Liverpool, where it remained. The English Order was based on the Irish model, its membership was largely working class, and by 1830 there were 235 civilian lodges and 30 military lodges, predominating in the North-West, with a total membership of about 6,000.[18]

During the 1820s and early 1830s Orange clubs provided an indication of anti-Catholic feeling in those parts of the country most affected by Irish immigration, especially in Lancashire and the West of Scotland. The organization of processions on the 12th of July to celebrate the Battle of the Boyne caused disturbances in England as early as 1819 when an Orange procession in Liverpool, organized with the usual insignia of 'the lamb, the ark, the Bible, men dressed in ermine, pontifical robes, leopard skins, etc', was attacked by Irishmen armed with brickbats and stones, who tore down the banners and injured several of the participants. In Scotland, Airdrie, where a lodge was first established in 1824, acquired an unenviable reputation for sectarian violence (**Doc. 18.2**).

In 1835 the Whig Government initiated an inquiry into the nature and extent of Orange Institutions in Great Britain and the Colonies. This followed the exposure of the so-called 'Fairman plot', in which Lt. Colonel W.C. Fairman, Grand Secretary of the Orange Movement in Britain, was alleged to have plotted to place the English Grand Master, the Duke of

---

[15] E. McFarland, *Protestants First: Orangeism in Nineteenth-Century Scotland* (Edinburgh, 1990), 95–114.

[16] The standard study of the origins of the Orange Order is H. Senior, *Orangeism in Ireland and Britain, 1795–1836* (London, 1966).

[17] McFarland, *Protestants First*, 56–7.

[18] F. Neal, 'Manchester Origins of the English Orange Order', *Manchester Region History Review* (Autumn 1990), 12–24.

Cumberland (the King's brother), on the throne in place of the then Princess Victoria. *The Report of the Select Committee on Orange Institutions in Great Britain*, published in September 1835, revealed for the first time the character, organization and extent of Orange institutions, including lists of officers and meeting places in Great Britain, and materials relating to terrorist activities attributed to Orangemen. The Select Committee concluded that Orange societies threatened both discipline within the army and public order, and recommended their immediate suppression (**Doc. 18.3**).

The Order was duly proscribed, but reappeared in Lancashire in 1836 as the Loyal Protestant Association. Most Orange branches were located in Liverpool, where the 1840s and 1850s witnessed persistent clashes between Catholics and Protestants against the background of the local activities of the Ancient Order of Hibernians, Irish migration during the Famine period, competition between Catholics and Protestants for unskilled and semi-skilled jobs in a weakly unionised economy, the restoration of the Catholic hierarchy, and the question of rate-aided educational provisions in the city. John Denvir's *Memoirs of an Old Parliamentarian* give some indication of the flavour of these clashes between the Orange and the Green during the 1840s (**Doc. 19.1**). Indeed, the strength of Orangeism in Liverpool – where there were 17,000 lodge members by 1900 – ensured Tory hegemony in local politics (see Part 8), and Orange marches became an important element in Protestant working-class culture, frequently accompanied by violence between Catholics and Protestants well into the twentieth century. These included the disorders arising from the anti-Ritualist campaigns of anti-Catholic zealots such as George Wise and John Kensit during the Edwardian period.[19] Even in smaller centres of Irish settlement, such as Barrow in Cumbria (**Doc. 19.2**),[20] these more visible manifestations of sectarianism continued to disfigure community relations.

In Scotland, the late nineteenth century witnessed the expansion and consolidation of Orangeism, with some 25,000 lodge members by the turn of the century, including 8,000 in Glasgow. Moreover, there is evidence of a considerable Ulster involvement in the Order, in terms of both lodge membership and epithets.[21] By contrast, the relationship between Orangeism and the Scottish Churches is problematic: some Scottish Presbyterians were hostile to Orangeism and while some Ulstermen and

---

[19] For Liverpool, see P.J. Waller, *Democracy and Sectarianism: A Political and Social History of Liverpool, 1868–1939* (Liverpool, 1981), 172–6, 188–92, 249–51; F. Neal, *Sectarian Violence: The Liverpool Experience, 1819–1914* (Manchester, 1987), 196–246; J.C. Belchem (ed.), *Popular Politics, Riot and Labour: Essays in Liverpool History, 1790–1940* (Liverpool, 1992). For Glasgow, see especially T. Gallagher, *Glasgow: The Uneasy Peace – Religious Tension in Modern Scotland, 1819–1940* (Manchester, 1987).

[20] MacRaild, *Culture, Conflict and Migration: The Irish in Victorian Cumbria*, 170–202.

[21] McFarland, *Protestants First*, 105–6.

their descendants were members of the Orange Order and of Scottish Protestant churches, their exact number is difficult to ascertain.[22] Nevertheless, in the West of Scotland in particular the growth of Orangeism was stimulated by the Home Rule crises from 1886 onwards (see Part 8) and, later, by the infusion of Ulster Protestant workers following the establishment of the Harland and Wolff shipyard at Govan in 1912. Indeed, there were parallels between the Orangeism and craft-consciousness of the skilled shipyard workers of Belfast and those on the Clyde.[23] As in Liverpool, Orange Day parades attracted large audiences in Glasgow, providing an outlet for anti-Catholic and anti-Home Rule sentiment, but perhaps one of the most enduring manifestations of sectarian traditions and conflicts at a plebeian level is provided in the sphere of popular culture, by the endemic rivalry between the city's leading football clubs, Rangers (founded in 1872) and Celtic (1887). Celtic – 'the Greens' – was founded for and by Catholics (**Doc. 19.3**); it recognized Ireland as its spiritual home, and it was closely associated with the fight for Home Rule in its early days. Rangers – 'the Blues' – was a Protestant club which had some links with Orangeism, drew support from Ulster Protestants, identified with the Union, and unofficially operated a 'No Catholics' policy on the playing staff. Although both great clubs enjoyed wider support within Scotland and beyond (and continue to do so), matches between them were sometimes attended by 'bad blood' both on and off the field,[24] as the *Scottish Sport* noted in 1896 (**Doc. 19.4**).

CATHOLIC DEVOTIONS

Doc. 16.1: A London Priest

Henry Mayhew, *London Labour and the London Poor* (1861).

Everywhere the people ran out to meet him. He had just returned to them, I found, and the news spread round, and women crowded to their doorsteps, and came creeping up from the cellars through the trap-doors, merely to curtsey to him. One old crone, as he passed, cried 'You're a good father, Heaven comfort you', and the boys playing about stood still to watch him. A lad, in a man's tail coat and a shirt-collar that nearly covered in his head – like the paper round a bouquet – was fortunate enough to be noticed, and his eyes sparkled, as he touched his hair at each word he

---

[22] ibid., 115–38.

[23] G.Walker, 'The Protestant Irish in Scotland', in T. M. Devine, *Irish Immigrants and Scottish Society* (Edinburgh, 1991), 44–66.

[24] See especially B. Murray, *The Old Firm: Sectarianism, Sport and Society in Scotland* (Edinburgh, 1984), 60–61.

spoke in answer. At a conversation that took place between the priest and a woman who kept a dry fish-stall, the dame excused herself for not having been up to take tea 'with his rivirince's mother lately, for thrade had been so busy, and night was the fullest time'. Even as the priest walked along the street, boys running at full speed would pull up to touch their hair, and the stall-women would rise from their baskets; while all noise – even a quarrel – ceased until he had passed by. Still there was no look of fear in the people. He called them all by their names, and asked after their families, and once or twice the 'father' was taken aside and held by the button while some point that required his advice was whispered in his ear.

Doc. 16.2: Secular and Religious Instruction of Irish Navvies in Scotland, 1846

Report of the Select Committee on Railway Labourers, Parliamentary Papers (1846), 86–7, Evidence of Mr. A.J.List, 1480–1493.

[Q] Have they [the Caledonian Company] done anything for the instruction of the men or their children?

[A] The Caledonian Company have been very liberal in that respect; they have voted 300*l*. to provide instruction for the southern half of the line, a distance of between 40 and 50 miles. They have put down 300*l*., and the contractors, Messrs. Stephenson and Company, have agreed to do as much; so that 600*l*. a year are to be expended in the religious and secular instruction of the men.

[Q] How has that sum been appropriated?

[A] There is an English clergyman for the Moffat district, where the men are all English.

[Q] Does he give his whole time to the men?

[A] His whole time . . . At Lockerby the directors and contractor have made an arrangement with the parish schoolmaster, by which his school is to be opened in the evening, after work hours, for the men and their children; that school is now attended by between 80 and 90 of the men.

[Q] Of the adults?

[A] Generally all adults; very few of the men have children; they are mostly unmarried men; these men are learning to read, and some of them, who had never been able to read before, are making great progress, and great progress in writing.

[Q] What are they?

[A] Mostly Irish; the Scotch already read and write.

[Q] Do they manifest much anxiety to get instructed?

[A] They are uncommonly anxious; I saw rather an elderly man and his son learning to read from the same book, sitting on the same form.

[Q] Has it been long enough at work to enable you to judge whether that anxiety is a permanent anxiety?

[A] There have been a good many changes; very few of them remain long enough to profit greatly from it, but some of them from the very commencement have been making great progress.

[Q] How long has that school been opened?

[A] From the commencement of the works.

[Q] They shift about a good deal?

[A] Yes. There is also a Scripture reader from the Irish Society, who was sent in order to read the Scriptures to them.

[Q] Paid by the Company?

[A] Yes, paid by the Company. It was intended that he should read the Scriptures to them in the Irish language; but it was found that very few of the men, when he came, spoke the Irish language; and, besides, the most of them were Catholics.

[Q] Had these Roman Catholics any priests among them?

[A] Yes; one from Dumfries visits them regularly, whom they pay themselves.

[Q] Do they pay him liberally?

[A] Very liberally; and they presented him lately with a gold watch and a purse.

[Q] Are those Irish of the same class as those who come shearing into Scotland?

[A] No, I think a different class.

[Q] Where do they come from; north or south?

[A] Mostly from the north.

Doc. 16.3: Father Mathew, the Apostle of Temperance

The Observer, 6 August 1843.

At 10 o'clock Father Mathew faced a Metropolitan auditory for the first time, and he was received with loud plaudits by the assembled thousands, while the banner, on which was written 'The holy guild of St Joseph and our blessed lady' was waved over his head . . . There were a number of gilt crosses and other insignia of the Roman Catholic religion somewhat ostentatiously paraded about the ground, and a number of young Irish women were industriously collecting pence all day long, towards the expenses of building a new Roman Catholic church intended to be erected on the site. They asked every person on the ground for a penny, and when they obtained one picked a hole in cards, with which they were provided, for the purpose of returning it to their priests and proving they had not misappropriated any portion of the subscriptions . . . Father Mathew then entered on the proceedings by delivering an address upon the blessings of abstinence from intoxicating drinks, and the evils attendant upon intemperance. He then descended from the platform, and called upon those who wished to take the 'pledge' to kneel down, the Rev. gentleman saying it was not a pledge for a day, a month, or a year, but a pledge for life . . . At twelve o'clock Earl Stanhope arrived and was loudly cheered by the people. At this time not less than 30,000 persons were assembled, and the Commercial-Road was nearly impassable. Earl Stanhope and Father Mathew shook hands, and the noble lord addressed the multitude for nearly an hour, saying that he had been a teetotaller for many years, inviting all to follow his example, and declared his intention of taking the pledge from Father Mathew, who then called upon those who were anxious to take the pledge with Earl Stanhope, to come forward and do so. A semicircle was formed, and 400 men and women knelt down and received the pledge. Earl Stan-hope, who laboured under considerable agitation, was directly afterwards embraced by Father Mathew, who, in the enthusiasm of the moment, kissed his cheek. The noble earl smiled and grasped Father Mathew's hands, exclaiming 'God bless you, Sir'. Speeches and administration of the pledge continued till dusk, when Father Mathew left the ground, announc-ing that he should attend at the same place every day this week. A more amiable man was never met with. He appeared nearly exhausted upon leaving the ground, and was very warmly greeted. About 3,000 persons took the pledge during the day, one half of whom were Irish. From the appearance of many of them, we should say the total abstinence pledge was very necessary. All the persons who visited the scene of Father Mathew's labours, however, were anything but teetotallers, for the consumption of beer and spirituous liquors at the George Inn was immense, and the landlord said he did not care how long Father Mathew prolonged his stay in the east. On the ground the consumption of ginger-beer, the staple beverage of the teetotallers, was very great, and a continual cry of 'Gingerbeer, a penny a bottle', was kept up . . .

Doc. 16.4: An Irish Temperance Meeting in London

The Graphic, 19 October 1872.

It is well known that, while there are some special virtues which belong to the poor Irish in London, who are nearly all Roman Catholics, they must be credited also with one vice in which they surpass their English Brethren, and that is intemperance . . . It is by drink more than anything else that the poor Irish increase the bad effects of their own improvident habits, and seal their own doom as 'hewers of wood and drawers of water' in this metrop-olis. Some twenty or thirty years ago, Father Mathew thought that this ought not to be the case, and by the preaching of a crusade against drunk-enness both in London, Liverpool, and Ireland, he effected a sudden revolution in the habits of his fellow-countrymen. But the Irish are impul-sive, not steady and persevering; and the present generation has grown up almost entirely since his time. Since, however, Dr. Manning has resided in London as Archbishop, he has done his best, both by precept and example, to induce the poor Irish to abandon whisky-drinking, and, indeed, all strong liquors. And within the last few weeks Father Lockhart, of Kingsland ... has practically revived Father Mathew's work in London, by holding, on almost every Sunday afternoon, open-air temperance meetings in the neighbourhoods where the Irish 'most do congregate'. At these meetings he has eloquently declaimed, with all the force of honest indignation, against this national vice of the Irish poor, and has succeeded in winning hundreds of converts, not only at Kingsland, Stratford, and Dalston, but at Fulham, in Marylebone, and in Clerkenwell; and last Sunday we believe that he held a similar meeting in the Isle of Dogs for the poor Roman Catholics in the Far East. In all these meetings he appeals to his hearers, not merely as Catholics, but as men and women, with regard not only to their souls, but to their bodies, their homes, and their children, to forswear the 'demon of drink' and to take the temperance pledge – on this point at all events agreeing and shaking hands with the 'Cow Cross Mission' of his Protestant neighbours. On Sunday week perhaps the most important of these open-air meetings was held on Clerkenwell Green ... The day was fine and the crowd was immense; the larger because it had been announced that Archbishop Manning would be present to give the movement his sanction. At the conclusion of Father Lockhart's address, Dr. Manning – who wore his plain black dress with the pectoral cross of a Bishop – spoke to his 'children' as he termed them, and urged them, if they valued their homes and families, and wished to save their souls, to lose no time in taking the pledge. As he spoke of God and the Saviour almost every hat was raised, and every head bared, and the poor Irish seemed very deeply impressed. It should be added that Father Lockhart stated, on the authority of a Roman Catholic Priest at Liverpool, an Irishman by birth, that while the Catholics of Liverpool are only a third of the population of that town they contribute one-half of the criminals to the gaols; and that nine-tenths of all the crimes for which they are brought under the lash of the law are attributable to the 'demon of drink'.

Doc. 16.5: An Irish Wake in Mountain Ash, South Wales, in the 1870s

Joseph Keating, *My Struggle for Life* (London, 1916), cited by P. O'Leary, *Immigration and Integration: The Irish in Wales, 1798–1922* (Cardiff, 2000), 228–9.

At the wake we played games and told tales of enchantments. When an Irish Catholic died in The Barracks (the Irish district) – either a natural death at home or a violent death in the mines – all who could attended the wake. Our kitchen was crowded with men and women, young and old, till three o'clock in the morning. Two lighted candles were at my grandmother's head and another at her feet. On a table near her were saucers of red snuff and tobacco, and a dozen short and long clay pipes. We played

Cock in the Corner, Hunt the Button, and told or listened to tales of leprechauns, giants and old hags – wonderful stories that had never been written or printed. The characters in them often arrived at lonely mountain tops, so bleak and far from anywhere else that in those places the cock never crew, the wind never blew and the 'divil' never stopped to put on his morning gown. The tales enthralled me. A few of the people on coming in would kneel beside the corpse. As soon as their prayers were finished they joined heartily in the games. We talked of everything except the dead. Good humour, humanity and religion were mixed together and the wakes brought relief and consolation to sorrow.

Doc. 16.6: Father Carroll in Merthyr

Glamorgan Record Office, D/Dxha, 4/1, Papers of Fr J.M. Cronin.

One Monday when coming home to Glebeland Place, he [Fr Carroll] was passing through Old Arch in Castle Street when a Welshman spat upon him. He spoke to a passer-by in Irish: 'Are you an Irishman?' 'Yes, Father,' was the reply, 'don't you see that man spitting upon you?' 'Yes', replied Fr. Carroll, 'but by this time tomorrow he won't do so.' This man then walked home with Fr. Carroll for protection from the jeering man who followed him. The following day at about the same hour in the afternoon, a procession up Castle Street brought the dead body of the man who had spat upon Fr. Carroll the day before. He had been killed in the works. Fr. Carroll's remark to the Irishman was town's talk for some time afterwards.

Doc. 16.7: The Order of Our Lady of Mercy, 1862

Anon. (Fanny Taylor), *Religious Orders or Sketches of Some of the Orders and Congregations of Women* (London, 1862), 305–7.

The duties of the Sisters of Mercy are most minutely defined by their holy Rule. They are taught by it how to act in their schools, how to instruct the children, how to visit the sick, and how to guide and instruct those who are inmates of the 'House of Mercy'. The Sisters are also taught to observe strictly the vow of Poverty, remembering His example who 'in His own person consecrated this virtue, and bequeathed it as a most valuable patrimony to His followers'. They are told also to obey 'rather through love than by servile fear'; and 'they shall never murmur; but with humility and spiritual joy carry the sweet yoke of Jesus Christ'. They are also instructed how to say their Office with 'attention and devotion', and how to practise mental prayer; to 'seek it in their comfort and refreshment from the labours and fatigues of the Institute'. They are to have 'the tenderest and most affectionate devotion to the Passion of our Lord and Saviour Jesus Christ; they shall therefore offer the labours and fatigues of their state, the mortifications they undergo, and all their pains and minds of body, in

union with the sufferings of their Crucified Spouse'; 'in all their fears, afflic-
tions, and temptations, they shall seek comfort and consolation at the foot
of the altar'; 'they shall be devout to the sacred heart of Jesus'. They are bid
to remember that their congregation is under the especial protection of the
Mother of God, and that they look on her 'as their Mother, and the greater
Model they are obliged to imitate'; they shall have 'unlimited confidence in
her, have recourse to her in all their difficulties or spiritual wants'; and on
the Feast of our Lady of Mercy they make a solemn act of consecration to
her love and service. The interior spirit of the Order is most beautiful, and is
founded on a deep humility and perfect charity; they are told to strive after
the perfection of their ordinary actions, and to attain great recollection. No
one could observe the Rule of this Order without making sure and rapid
progress in the ways of sanctity. It is governed, as we have said, by the
Bishop, or a priest delegated by him, and the Bishop or his substitute shall
make the visitation of the convent once a year. The Mother Superior must
be thirty years of age, and must have been professed for five years (except
in the case of a new foundation). She is elected by the votes of the Sisters;
she can only govern for three years, but may be re-elected for three more.

Doc. 16.8: St Bridget's Confraternity, 1881

Father Sheridan, *About St Bridget's Confraternity* (1881).

Monday 31.1.81 – Medals and cards procured of Sisters. Feast of St Bridget
for February 1st to be observed. Read story of the pranks of Irish fairies
Carleton's Poor Sch. and other tales com. p.214. Said Rosary; but did not
speak on any religious topic. Present about 60.

Monday 7.2.81 – Read . . . the story of Fin Mac Coul, and a giant from
Carleton. They were amused, but did not laugh to my satisfaction, for, I fear,
their tastes had been vitiated by the excrutiatingly (from Miss Ruffe's
collection of words), funny tales read to them at other sittings . . . We said
the Rosary & asked the assistance of our dear Saint Bridget. Very good
attendance, notwithstanding the heavy downpour. Dispersed at 9.30.

Monday 28.2.81 – . . . read to them a chapter from A.M. Sullivan's 'New
Ireland' about F. Mathew which seemingly pleased. Mem. Always read
beforehand for subject for evening; withdraw the jawbreakers & skip
French and other quotations. Then said Rosary.

Monday 3.10.81 – This evening fair attendance filling hall. Read for them a
few anecdotes concerning Newfoundland dogs taken from Lamp followed
by a laughable & entertaining Irish skit entitled Nell Hegarty's visit to Cork
from October ('80) no of Lamp. Rosary . . . N.B. the bete noire of our
meeting Mrs. Mahoney was present with her snuff, coughing & disturbance.

Monday 24.10.81 – This evening we read one of Lover's comic sketches – the Curse of Roshogue. There was a great deal of laughing and would have been much more had I carefully prepared the reading of the piece. The attendance was extremely large and I believe the largest yet. Rosary as usual.

Monday 7.11.81 – . . . This evening having previously read the account of Guy Fawkes Day in the Clifton Tract series I chatted to those present about it. It took, I fancy, pretty well. As large a number as usual were present though I noticed strange faces which were their proprietors to bring them often might add a little respectability to proceedings.

Monday 14.11.81 – . . . This evening very large attendance so much so that the babies gallery was taken possession by benign matres who couldn't sit elsewhere. Reading was choice as the new 'Irish Pleasantry & Fun' furnish some excellent pieces. 'Shemus O'Brien' & 'The Donnybrook Spree' seemed to excite the risible qualities wonderfully.

Monday 12.12.81 – . . . The evening being cold & wet and having been disappointed the two previous evenings the number of people did not exceed forty. Was not up to much myself but as proceeded reading the 'Waiver of Duleck Gate' (?) (Irish Pleasantry and Fun) our spirits rose and we had a few good roaring laughs. Rosary & a few words wishing a happy Xmas.

Monday 2.1.81 – Our first meeting of 1882 was not brilliantly attended. Something like 56 put in an appearance & all of them listened with apparent satisfaction to the veracious narration of 'Puss in Brogues' (Irish Pleasantry and Fun' p.3). Then Rosary & a few words wishing them a happy New Year.

Doc. 16.9: Irish Concert on St Patrick's Day, 1885

The Barrow Herald, 21 March 1885.

On Tuesday evening last, being St Patrick's Day, a grand Irish ballad concert took place at the Town Hall; most of the performers being connected with the Catholic Church in this town. The Rev. Father Caffrey presided, and amongst those present were the Revs. Father Gordon, Father Collinson, and Father Monaghan; Mr Palmer, and others. There was also a large attendance.

The following was the programme:– Selection of Irish airs, St Mary's Band; quartette, 'The young May moon', Mdles Logan and Craven, and Messrs Ennis and Wyer; original ballad (written for the occasion), 'Pat's Boys', Mr G.B. Harcourt; song, 'Farewell', with flute obligato, Mr L. Wyer and Mr P. Coyne; old melody, 'Soggarth Aroon', Miss M. Craven; harp solo, 'Sounds from the Emerald Isle', Mr Fred Haslam; ballad, 'Dear little shamrock', Mrs Harcourt; song, 'Thinking of home', Mr J.F. Ennis; serio–comic song, 'The gap in the hedge at Kilmare', Miss Logan; impersonation ditty, 'Bridget Muldoon', Mr T.R. Clithero; song with harp, 'The Wolf', Mr Fred Haslam; quartet, 'Let Erin remember', Mdles Logan and Craven, and Messrs Ennis and Wyer; comic song, 'Molly, I can't say ye're honest', Mr G.B. Harcourt; song, 'The meeting of the Waters', Miss M. Craven; duet (selected), Messrs Ennis and Wyer; Irish air, 'Colleen dhas Cruthen na moe', Mrs Harcourt; harp solo, 'Beauties of Irish melody', Mr Fred Haslam; new ballad, 'Barney', Miss M. Logan; song, 'Dublin Bay', Mr J.L. Wyer; character song, 'Brave Captain Magann', Mr T.R. Clitheroe; melody, 'The minstrel boy', Mr J.F. Ennis; humorous sketch, 'I'm a married man myself', Mr and Mrs Harcourt; Irish selection, 'St Patrick's Day', St Mary's Band.

In the interval between the parts, the Rev. Father Caffrey briefly addressed the meeting. As a rule he remarked he had plenty to say on occasions such as that, but unfortunately for him Father Gordon had covered the whole ground at his talk to them in the morning. He had pointed out to them the advantages of education, and he (the speaker), suffering as he was from bronchitis, would not trouble them further. They were celebrating that night the day dedicated to their patron saint. Just at the present time the Irish were the most envied and admired race on the face of the globe, and the further they went from home the more they were admired. Irishmen everywhere were assembled to celebrate St Patrick's Day - in America, Australia, India, and England, as well as in Ireland. Wherever they went the Irish always got themselves into good positions – from the Mayor of New York to the shoeblacks of Brooklyn. (Laughter) They looked round that night, and they could sympathise with their race throughout the world; with Lord Wolseley, Lord Charles Beresford, and others fighting in Egypt; with the Mayors of Sydney and New York, and hosts of others. (Cheers) He hoped that they were well pleased with the entertainment that night, and that they would come to church on Sunday evening next, and hear a little more about St Patrick's Day.

Doc. 16.10: St Patrick's Church, Leicester, 1900

'Round the Churches', *The Leicester Guardian*, 26 May 1900.

In the heart of Leicester slumdom you will find St Patrick's Church. Like the neighbourhood in which it stands, it is a seedy-looking place, but for years it has performed a splendid mission, particularly amongst the Irish and foreign element of the town. It is round this little temple of the church of their native land that the Hibernian section of our community loves to live, and it is within the walls of this little place that you find them there foregathered in considerable numbers any Sunday morning . . . The people who trooped into St Patrick's last Sunday morning were for the most part very poor. There was a distinctly Irish look about the whole congregation . . . Most of those present had made themselves smart before coming to worship, but there were those who, not having the wedding garment, still did not absent themselves from the worship of the great Bridegroom . . . It was very pretty to see these poor people, waifs of society many of them looked, bowing reverently to the altar as they entered the church, and again as they entered their seats; very impressive to see them devoutly kneel down in prayer for several minutes before seating themselves . . . St Patrick's is only an epitome of a church. Everything is on a small scale. The place is only about as big as a couple of good sized drawing rooms joined together, and with the hundred and fifty or so worshippers that assembled on Sunday morning, it looked quite full. Although it is probably the very poorest church in Leicester, much money has evidently been spent on decoration, on pictures, effigies, &c., to make the place attractive, and this has been achieved, though, of course, the whole looks cheap and tawdry compared with the grandeur of wealthy Catholic churches in this and other countries . . . Considering the neighbourhood in which St Patrick is, the poverty of its finances, and the difficulty of rendering the best musical settings of the Mass, it was surprising to find a very creditable performance given by the organ and choir . . . At the usual break in the middle of the Mass, the officiating priest, a young man with a very devout and pleasant manner, stepped into the pulpit and made a few announcements. He has a brogue which distinctly proclaims his nationality, but he spoke in pretty and musical tones.

ANTI-POPERY

Doc. 17.1: Intra-Communal Tensions in Edwardian Salford

R. Roberts, *The Classic Slum: Salford Life in the First Quarter of the Century* (1971), 6–7; 9; 84–5

Many of the women and girls in the district worked in some branch of the textile industry. Of these, we accepted weavers as 'top' in their class, followed by winders and drawers-in. Then came spinners. They lacked standing on several counts: first, the trade contained a strong Irish Catholic element, and wages generally were lower than in other sections. Again, because of the heat and slippery floors, women worked barefoot, dressed in little more than calico shifts. These garments, the respectable believed, induced in female spinners a certain moral carelessness. They came home, too, covered in dust and fluff; all things which combined to depress their social prestige. Women employees of dye works, however, filled the lowest bracket: their work was dirty, wet and heavy and they paid due penalty for it.

Drunkenness, rowing or fighting in the streets could leave a stigma on a family already registered as 'decent' for a long time afterwards. Another household, for all its clean curtains and impeccable conduct, would remain uneasily aware that its rating had slumped since Grandma died in the work-house or Cousin Alf did time. Still another family would be scorned loudly in a drunken tiff for marrying off its daughter to some 'low Mick from the Bog'. With us, of course, as with many cities in the north, until the coming of the coloured people Irish Roman Catholic immigrants, mostly illiterate, formed the lowest socio-economic stratum. A slum Protestant marrying into the milieu suffered a severe loss of face. Such unions seldom occurred.

In the poorest households, through a lack of knowledge and utensils, little cooking of any kind went on, except for the grilling on a fork before the kitchen fire of bits of bacon and fish. Many never cooked vegetables, not even potatoes. Irish families, however, were ridiculed for their Sunday habit of boiling cabbage, pork ribs and 'murphies' all in one iron pan, then letting the mess serve for every meal far into the following week. But even this, our local xenophobes sneered, was for the 'Micks' a cultural step forward – 'Before coming to England they didn't know food had to be cooked'. Irish families long established in the neighbourhood and figuring, if only modestly, on our social register, disliked the influx of raw compatri-ots whose poverty and ignorance of local mores might again raise doubts about their own standing. In the shop they would, at times, apologise for or try to condone the habits of those who were 'just off the bog' or had 'come over with the cattle'.

Doc. 17.2: Papal Aggression, 1850

Lord John Russell's letter to the Bishop of Durham on papal aggression, November 1850, cited in Spencer Walpole, *Life of Lord John Russell* (1889), II, 120.

My Dear Lord – I agree with you in considering 'the late aggression on the Pope upon our Protestantism' as 'insolent and insidious', and I therefore feel as indignant as you can do upon the subject.

I not only promoted to the utmost of my power the claims of the Roman Catholics to all civil rights, but I thought it right and even desirable that the eccesiastical system of the Roman Catholics should be the means of giving instruction to the numerous Irish immigrants in London and elsewhere, who without such help would have been left in heathen ignorance. This might have been done, however, without any such innovation as that which we have now seen.

It is impossible to confound the recent measures of the Pope with the division of Scotland into dioceses by the Episcopal Church, or the arrange-ment of districts by the Wesleyan Conference.

There is an assumption of power in all the documents which have come from Rome; a pretension of supremacy over the realm of England, and a claim to sole and undivided sway, which is inconsistent with the Queen's supremacy, with the rights of our bishops and clergy, and with the spiritual independence of the nation, as asserted in even Roman Catholic times.

I confess, however, that my alarm is not equal to my indignation. Even if it shall appear that the ministers and servants of the Pope in this country have not transgressed the law, I feel persuaded that we are strong enough to repel any outwards attacks. The liberty of Protestantism has been enjoyed too long in England to allow of any successful attempt to impose a foreign yoke upon our minds and consciences. No foreign prince or potentate will be at liberty to fasten his fetters upon a nation which has so long and so nobly vindicated its right to freedom of opinion, civil, political, and religious . . .

I have little doubt that the propounders and framers of these innovations will desist from their insidious course. But I rely with confidence on the people of England; and I will not bate a jot of heart or hope so long as the glorious principles and the immortal martyrs of the Reformation shall be held in reverence by the great mass of a nation which looks with contempt on the mummeries of superstition, and with scorn at the laborious endeavours which are now making to confine the intellect and enslave the soul.

Doc. 17.3: The Stockport Riots, 1852

The Annual Register (1852), 90–93.

A scene of shameful disturbance arose in the town of Stockport which continued for three days and was accompanied by some loss of life, many injustices to persons, and great destruction of property. The riots which seem to bring us back to the days of the Gordon riots, arose from an old feud existing between the English operatives and the Irish who have become settled in that town in large numbers, and had incurred the hatred of the natives by the effect of their competition in the labour market. This feud had assumed the character of a religious war – Protestants against Roman Catholics. The immediate occasions of the riots were the parades of the latter through the streets of the town and the recent proclamation of the Queen against Roman Catholic processions.

It has been the custom of the Roman Catholics of Stockport to have a procession of the children of their charity schools at this season of the year – not a party or sectarian demonstration but a display of the results of the educational zeal of the Roman Catholics. When the Royal proclamation appeared, the lower classes of Protestants hailed it as a sectarian triumph and boasted that they would see the proclamation enforced in the case of the 'Young red-necked scholars'– as they term the Roman Catholic children. The Romanists held that the meeting of the scholars was not a procession of the sort interdicted, and they published their resolves to make their demonstration as usual. There was great excitement upon the subject and it is said that the authorities thought of preventing the school-gathering but when the day came (Sunday last) the Protestants seemed less excited, and the schools were allowed to make their procession without interruptions. There was a studious avoidance of any sort of Catholic insignia, and the priests appeared in their plain attire.

On Monday a few casual fights, such as not uncommonly occur at Stockport on the Monday afternoon, took an international and religious character. Englishmen and Irishmen happened to be engaged, and the seconders of the combatants got into conflicts, which the police stopped with difficulty. On Tuesday afternoon, the fights were renewed in several places at once; the fights were so fierce, and so many combatants engaged in them, that the police could not repress them. Great anxiety was felt by the Roman Catholic priests, and warnings were given by them to the mayor: and, in consequence, some preparation was made to increase the small police force, which consists only of ten men, by a staff of assistant constables. With this the Chief Constable sallied out to controlling points; but by the time that he got his men into action, the various detached fights had merged in a general battle between the Roman Catholic and Protestant lower orders. The Protestant gained the upper hand, and drove their opponents first into their houses and the Roman Catholic Chapels. By great efforts the police managed to hold the chief body of rioters in check till the mayor and magistrates had assembled and sworn in some hundreds of special constables, and entered into co-operation with them. The civil power had just gained the upper hand, when a body of military also turned out, and the rioters were quelled. A great many persons engaged on either side were arrested. The next day it appeared how serious the conflict had been.

The first attack on persons, on Tuesday, was made by the Irish; it would seem that this ended in an assault on St Peter's Protestant School; and that it was in retaliation for this last outrage that the English turned the fight into an attack in the houses and chapels of the Catholics. The Protestant School where the damage began, was not much damaged but all windows, and those of the master's house were smashed in. An alehouse was first attacked by the Protestants, who broke in the windows, and furniture and reduced them to complete wrecks. Down Bridge Street, a row of houses three stories high in front and two behind were next attacked. The ruffians first made entry into a house where Mrs Ann Bradley was lying having only a week before been confined of a child, disregarding the woman's weak condition the ruffians broke and destroyed everything in the house: they even destroyed the roof over her head, allowing the debris to fall upon her. The furniture was destroyed and the house gutted. The other houses in the row were wrecked in succession. It was while demolishing the windows and furniture of these houses that the signal was given by one of the leaders of the mob 'to the Catholic chapels.' Immediately a considerable proportion of the mob rushed off to Edgeley chapel half a mile distant; and, forcing an entrance, they broke the altars, and carried out the furniture and pews, the pictures, chalices, surplices, and vestments and heaped them in a pile before the house of the priest. The mob completely destroyed every-thing in the chapel and then attacked the priest's house. They carried out the furniture of his house out of doors, and, heaping it on that of the chapel, lighted it for a bonfire. An organ worth £400 was broken to atoms, and the chapel and minister's house were reduced to a wreck.

Doc. 17.4: The Murphy Riots in Wolverhampton, 1867

Wolverhampton Chronicle, 27 February 1867

In last week's *Chronicle* We gave an account of the disturbances which occurred in this town on Monday and Tuesday evenings, consequent upon addresses on Romanism by Mr. W. Murphy, an agent of the Protestant Evangelical Mission Electoral Union . . . Owing to the violence of a portion of the crowd on Tuesday evening and threats that still further violence would be resorted to, unless the lectures were discontinued, the Magis-trates met to consult as to the advisability of still further increasing the means for the protection of the public peace. A rumour had gained currency that a meeting of Roman Catholics, chiefly those resident in Stafford Street, had been held, and that emissaries had been despatched to various parts of the Black Country to rouse up their religion out of the town . . . The latter supposition was borne out by anonymous letters received by the Chief Constable and by residents in the town and neighbourhood, warning them that violence was intended . . .

From the following statistics it will be seen that the force at the disposal of the authorities was more than double that of any previous evening . . . It was as follows: 8th Hussars, 70 men; the Wolverhampton troop of Yeomanry, 40 men; the Borough Police, upwards of 60 men; County Constabulary, 120 men. There were 300 special constables . . . Meanwhile the crowds in the streets had increased to such an extent that locomotion was almost impossible, the number congregated being estimated at upwards of fifteen thousand. A large proportion were youths and young girls of the lower class, with a fair sprinkling of the more respectable portion of the community, and it was also stated that a large influx of strangers were present, it is supposed, from the surrounding district . . .

The subject of this evening's (Friday) lecture was 'The Teaching of Maynooth, and the Confessional Unmasked', and the number present amounted to between 3,000 and 4,000 persons, all male adults, females and boys being excluded, in consequence of the indelicacy of the revelations which the Lecturer was about to make . . . Mr. Murphy then commenced his lecture, which consisted of extracts from (as he stated) Roman Catholic books. Some of the extracts were, perhaps, the most indecent ever read before a public meeting, and elicited frequent expressions of astonishment . . . He complained of the conduct of the Magistrates. The Magistrates had written to the Home Secretary to see if they could not stop him, but the Home Secretary could not do it. Dr Pusey and his followers were endeavouring to introduce the Confessional into the Church of England, but he warned Protestants to beware of them, for they were only Popish priests in disguise . . . The lecture was well received, and it was not interrupted during his address, which was much shorter than that of any previous evening, not occupying more than thirty or forty minutes . . . Constabulary and special constables were formed in two lines from each side of the entrance door down below the cannon. Simultaneously the Hussars on duty in the square began to wheel round into column and then opened files right and left, to the great consternation of the dense masses who filled the streets, but who were gradually driven back in to the footpaths . . . The lecturer had, however, made his exit by the side door and escorted only by Inspector Thomas, was taken to his lodgings.

Doc. 17.5: Murphy Disturbances at North Shields, 1869

Shields Daily News, 22 March 1869.

Mr Murphy resumed his no-Popery lectures in the Oddfellows Hall, North Shields, on Saturday. In the afternoon, he addressed a large company of women on the 'Confessional Unmasked', and in the evening he spoke to a crowded audience of men on the same subject. At the close of the lecture Murphy stated that he had paid about £14 to the trustees of the hall, the cost of repairing the damage which had been done on Friday night; and he trusted the audience would not allow him to be that amount out of pocket. The 'hat' was sent round, and the sum of £2. 8s was collected and handed over to Murphy. A second attack on the hall was threatened by the Irish Catholics, and the steamboats and the railway brought a good few persons down from Jarrow, Willington Quay, and Walker, but the preparations made by the authorities to quell any disturbance which might be made seem to have completely cowed them. Saville Street, in which the Oddfellows Hall is situated, was crowded from end to end by excited people until ten o'clock on Saturday night but there was no rioting or disorder. The town was quiet at 10, and the military returned to the barracks. Murphy and his audience were permitted to leave the hall unmolested. The lecturer proceeded by cab to Tynemouth, and took the train at that place for Durham. The authorities at North Shields had made the most ample preparations for keeping the peace on Saturday night. They had about a hundred of the First Northumberland Artillery Volunteers sworn in as special constables, who were placed under the charge of Mr J.F. Spence, borough magistrate, and they patrolled the streets for the protection of the public. A strong detachment of the 40th Regiment was also brought from Tynemouth Garrison to the Town Hall, where they were held in readiness for an outbreak. The following is an extract from a despatch from the Home Office, which the Mayor received yesterday in answer to a communication which had been forwarded to the Home Secretary with regard to Murphy's lectures:– 'I am to inform you that the magistrates have not the power to stop lectures on a subject not illegal, delivered in a private hall hired for the purpose; or to prevent people meeting to hear such lectures. Were it not [so] any meeting called for the discussion of questions of public interest might be stopped, if those who took an opposite side threatened to disturb the meeting.' On Sunday, Murphy made his appearance at Durham, but all passed off quietly. The authorities were prepared to meet any emergency.

Doc. 17.6: The Tredegar Riots, 1882

John Denvir, *The Irish in Britain* (1892), 302–12.

If you leave out the Irish in the seaports of Newport, Cardiff and Swansea, the densest mass of our people in South Wales and Monmouth is to be found in and about the towns and among the hills within a radius of little more than ten miles east, south and west of Tredegar, which may be said to be the centre of the iron and steel working district. Besides Tredegar, the Irish are most numerous in Merthyr, Dowlais, Aberdare, Mountain Ash, Blaenavon, Brynmawr, Abersychan, Pontypool and Cwmbran. In the vicinity of most of these places are immense heaps of cinders, the refuse from the mines and other works. These smoulder for a long time, and at night the flamelets of various hues, bursting forth here and there, present a singular appearance. Then, as in the Black Country in the Midlands, the whole district is lit up by the weird-like glare of the blast furnaces, which work night and day . . . At the ironworks the Irish are at the hardest labour, which neither Englishman nor Welshman can nor will do, and if you go into the works you cannot but admire the strength and dexterity with which they draw out the huge bars at white heat into the rollers which shape them into iron and steel rails.

The jealousy against the Irish which culminated in the terrible riots at Tredegar was greatly increased because many of the native population had been thrown out of employment, for in the making of rails iron was becoming superseded by steel, which was being rapidly turned out in large quantities by the Bessemer process. There being less hands required to work the new system, some one must go, and the Welsh were determined that, so far as in them lay, it was the Irish who must suffer. The correspondent of the *South Wales Daily News*, speaking of the aversion with which the Irish were regarded previous to the Tredegar riots, said – 'The Phoenix Park and other outrages intensified this feeling, and it had been an open secret for some days that an outbreak was contemplated and inevitable.'

The impending outbreak was not entirely unknown to the Irish. Many of them, particularly the younger generation, knew sufficient of the Welsh tongue to catch the muttered threats of vengeance let fall in public-houses and elsewhere by the native population, when none but themselves were supposed to be near. The special correspondent of the *Freeman* said:– 'On Friday night there were ominous knots of Welsh and Irish in the streets, and in the evening, when the Salvationists were holding a service in the "Paddy Quarter", as it was called . . . A little hooting and the throwing of some flour over the converted one gave a pretext for the next night's attack.' It was not until the following evening, Saturday July 8th, 1882, when the week's work was done, and men's passions were inflamed by drink, that the Civil War – for it was no less – broke out. Hostilities commenced by the smashing of the glass in many of the Irish houses. Then a large mob proceeded to attack one of the places in which they lived – Red Lion Square. At this time there do not appear to have been many Irishmen present to defend their homes, for one who was amongst the defenders states that when the mob attempted to enter the square it was held against them by but a couple of men and four women, and that these would actually have succeeded in keeping out their assailants until more help arrived, but that the police broke through, by way of affording protection to the people of the square, and let the mob in to do their work of pillage and destruction.

By the time this is said to have occurred there were some five thousand Welshmen in and about Red Lion Square, and the houses of the Irish were attacked with the utmost fury. They made a resolute stand for their homes and their families. But what could they do against such overwhelming odds? Doors and windows were broken in, furniture and bedding were tossed out into the square and a bonfire made of them; while the unfortunate people, after being brutally treated and rendered homeless, had to fly to seek shelter wherever they could. Some found it for the night about the coal-pits or out on the bleak, open hills, where they remained huddled together under severe showers of rain. A number made their way to Cardiff, Newport, and elsewhere, and some families even found their way to Ireland. Nothing less than the immediate clearing out of the whole Irish population would now seem to satisfy the mob, and the attacks on Irish houses and their inhabitants were carried on during the second day of the rioting – Sunday. The fury of the mob made no distinction between those who had come from Ireland and those of Irish parentage, who were actually natives of the place.

At length it seemed as if the mob had nothing left to exhaust its fury upon, for the Irish who had not been previously driven out, finding the authorities gave them no protection, left the place almost en masse, so that out of a population estimated at from 1500 to 2000, there were only about 100 of them left. Such was the reign of terror, that the benevolent Welsh people who assisted the destitute Irish families were threatened with attack also. It was feared too that the Irish in the other towns among the hills would suffer, so that many left these places to seek safety elsewhere. Although the bulk of them were able to return when the storm of passion had subsided, the uprising against them materially checked whatever progress they were making; particularly in connection with the younger people who were learning trades.

It was only on the Monday, when all the damage had been done, that the police, who had not been able to cope with the rioting, were sufficiently reinforced, and the military arrived on the scene. In the House of Commons, Sir William Harcourt was severely brought to task by Mr. Parnell and Mr. T. P. O'Connor as to why the rioting was allowed to go on unchecked, and why the additional police and military were so late in arriving on the scene.

ORANGEISM

Doc. 18.1: The Obligation of an Orangeman

Report of the Select Committee on Orange Institutions in Great Britain and the Colonies, Parliamentary Papers, XVII (1835), vi.

I, A.B., do solemnly and sincerely swear, of my own free will and accord, that I will, to the utmost of my power, support and defend the present King George the Third, his heirs and successors, so long as he and they support the Protestant ascendancy, the constitution and laws of these kingdoms, and that I will ever hold sacred the name of our glorious deliverer, William the Third, Prince of Orange; and I do further swear, that I am not, nor ever was a Roman Catholic or Papist; that I was not, am not, nor ever will be a United Irishman; and that I never took the oath of secrecy to that or any other Treasonable Society; and I do further swear, in the presence of Almighty God, that I will always conceal, and never will reveal either part or parts of what is now to be privately communicated to me, until I shall be authorized to do so by the proper authorities of the Orange Institution; that I will neither write it nor indite it, stamp, stain or engrave it, nor cause it so to be done, on Paper, Parchment, Leaf, Bark, Stick, Stone, or any thing, so that it may be known; and I do further swear, that I have not, to my knowledge or belief, been proposed and rejected in, or expelled from any other Orange Lodge; and that I now become an Orangeman without fear, bribery or corruption. So help me God.

Doc. 18.2: Orangeism and Disorder in Scotland

Select Committee on Orange Institutions (1835), xxiv–xxv.

To show the tendency of Orange Lodges in the West of Scotland, the whole of Mr. Innes's evidence must be read. Mr. Innes was deputed by the Lord Advocate of Scotland, the law officer of the Crown, to proceed to Airdrie,

Glasgow and other places in the west part of Scotland, to inquire into the nature and extent of the riots, that had taken place in July last in several parts of that country, and their causes; he stated to the Committee, that the existence of Orange Lodges had been the cause of those riots, some of which had been attended with loss of life, and the subsequent execution of the offender; and that some of the late rioters were now waiting their trial. It will be seen that the meeting and procession of the Orangemen, at one time, led to the riot and breach of the peace; that, at another time, the Catholics became the aggressors, having met and proceeded in great numbers with the determination of preventing any Orange procession which they expected to take place; and, on another occasion, the inhabitants of the town were brought forth to put down the riot between those two parties, and to drive them from the town . . . Mr. Innes states, an authority on which Your Committee place confidence, that the existence of the Orange Lodges, their meetings, processions, and proceedings, have roused an opposition on the part of the Catholics to protect themselves from the insults offered by the Orangemen; and, that secret societies have been formed for that purpose, by which the members can be called forth at any time when occasion shall require their meeting to protect themselves against the insults of the Orangemen or to be revenged upon them; that the meeting of Catholics on the Green at Glasgow before they marched to Airdrie, where they expected the Orangemen to walk in procession, was assembled by that means; and, from the proofs already mentioned . . . he is satisfied that the delegates of no less than 24 of these societies, which he calls Riband Societies, having secret oaths and signs, previously met together to arrange the meeting and procession to Airdrie. The opinion of Mr. Innes, after all the information he has become officially possessed of, is, that it will not be possible to restore the west of Scotland to tranquillity, and to prevent breaches of the peace occurring occasionally, unless measures are taken to put down the Orange Lodges and Ribandmen and every other secret society.

Doc. 18.3: The Need to Suppress Orangeism

Select Committee on Orange Institutions (1835), xxvii.

The number of Orangemen in Ireland is 220,000, as stated by the deputy grand secretary for that country, and these chiefly with arms in their possession; and, if the Orangemen in Great Britain and the Colonies amount only to half that number, The House will judge how dangerous such an association, bound together by religious ceremony and sanction, almost equal to that of an oath, might become under possible circumstances of the country. A great political body thus organized in the ranks of the army, and in every part of the British empire, is a formidable power at any time and under any circumstances; but when Your Committee look to the political tendency of the measures of the Orange Societies in England and in Ireland, and particularly in the language contained in addresses to the public, and in the correspondence with the grand officers of the Institution, and consider the possible use that might be made of such an organized power, its suppression becomes, in their opinion, imperatively necessary.

SECTARIAN RIVALRIES

Doc. 19.1: Sectarian Rivalries in Liverpool

John Denvir, *The Life Story of an Old Rebel* (1910),15–23.

I had an aunt – my mother's sister – married to a good patriotic Irishman, Hugh Roney, who kept a public house in Crosbie Street . . . Nearly all in Crosbie Street were from the West of Ireland, and, amongst them, there was scarcely but Irish spoken . . . After a time Hughey Roney retired, and the house was carried on by his daughter and her husband, John McArdle, a good, decent patriotic Irishman, much respected by his Connaught neighbours, though he was from 'Black North'. So popular was John McArdle's house, that it was used as one of the lodges of the Ancient Order of Hibernians – then very strong in Liverpool, and stout champions of country and creed . . . These were the qualifications laid down: Members must be Catholic and Irish, or of Irish descent. They must be of good moral character, and were not to join in any secret secieties contrary to the laws of the Catholic Church . . .

Our country sent over to Liverpool, besides sterling Nationalists, as bitter a colony of Irishmen – I suppose we can scarcely deny the name to men born in Ireland – as were, perhaps, to be found anywhere in the world. These were the Orangemen. If there was one place more obnoxious to them than another it was the club room of the Hibernians in Crosbie Street. But though in their frequent conflicts with the 'Papishes' they wrecked houses and even killed several Irishmen – for they frequently used deadly weapons against unarmed Catholics – they were never able to make a successful attack on McArdle's. One of my earliest experiences was being on the spot on the occasion of a contemplated assault on the Hibernian club room on the day of an Orange anniversary. This was in 1843.

Parallel to Crosbie Street, where the club room was situated, was Blundell Street, where my uncle, Hughey Roney, lived in a house immediately behind McArdle's . . . There we were in the first-floor front room of my Uncle Hughey's. Every room, from cellar to garret, was crowded with stalwart dock labourers – at that time these were almost to a man Irish – prepared to support another contingent of Hibernians who garrisoned McArdle's in a similar manner. Hearing outside the cry – 'The Orangemen'

– I looked out of the window and up the street, and there, sure enough, was a strong body of them, marching down, armed with guns, swords, and ship carpenter's hatchets. At once the word was passed to the contingent in Crosbie Street to be prepared to meet the threatened attack. Nearer and nearer the Orangemen came. They had got within some thirty yards of Roneys when, between them and the object of their attack, out of Simpson Street, which at this point crosses Blundell Street at right angles, there intervened the head of a column of police, under the Liverpool Chief Constable, an Irishman, Michael James Whitty. There was a desperate engagement, but, notwithstanding their murderous weapons, the Orangemen were utterly routed, flying before the disciplined charge of the police, who freely used their batons on the retreating opponents . . .

In my boyhood a great feature in Liverpool was the annual procession of one or other of the local societies. The great Irish and Catholic procession of which the Hibernians formed the largest contingent, was, of course, on St Patrick's Day. A considerable portion of the processionists were dock labourers . . . The Orange processions in Liverpool were often the occasion of bloodshed, for in them they carried guns, hatchets, and other deadly weapons, as if they were always prepared for deeds of violence. The ship carpenters were the most numerous body in the Orange processions. Indeed, they formed such a large proportion that, by many, the 12th of July was called 'Carpenter's Day'. Ship-building used to flourish in Liverpool, and, as none of the firms engaged in it would take a Catholic apprentice, it was quite an Orange preserve. This became changed when the Chaloners, an English Catholic family, who were already extensive timber merchants, commenced ship-building, and, of course, took Catholic apprentices. The Orange ring was thus gradually broken up, and as iron ships superseded wooden ones, ultimately the ship-building trade almost vanished from Liverpool.

Doc. 19.2: An Orange Demonstration in Barrow, 1881

The Barrow Herald, 16 July 1881.

RIOTING IN THE STREETS: On Tuesday last the Orangemen of Barrow and the surrounding neighbourhood held two distinct celebrations – one at Fleetwood and a second one at Lake Side. Every provision was made by the committee of each contingent for the accommodation of their followers, and at an early hour the sound of drums awakened many sleepers.

The Fleetwood party were the first to show their presence, as it was advertised they would leave in the steamer *Roses* from the dock entrance at nine o'clock prompt. The members and friends going with the order were all to the front opposite the Junction Hotel about a quarter of an hour previous to that time. The following lodges made a good turnout:– 365, 427, 482, and 576. When the procession was formed they were led by Gradwell's, St George's, St Paul's, and St Mark's bands down to the boat, and on board during the passage enlivened the company with music. Both the outward and inward voyages were good, which added largely to the pleasure of all concerned. On reaching Fleetwood the Barrow party were met by two lodges from Fleetwood, who gave them a hearty greeting. After landing, the united brethren formed themselves in order for procession in Victoria Terrace, after which they paraded the principal streets of the town, and adjourned to a field specially engaged for the day where sports of various kinds were indulged in. Dinner was provided at the Queen's Hotel, where the chair was taken by Mr James Kennedy, of Barrow, the vice-chair being occupied by Mr James McClatchey, of Fleetwood. The usual loyal and patriotic toasts were duly honoured, in most cases with Kentish fire. The proceedings were varied by selections of vocal and instrumental music. On the homeward journey, owing to the tide, the party were unable to land before ten o'clock, and they reached Ramsden and Church-streets in an orderly manner about half-past ten.

The second contingent, who secured the services of the Earl of Beaconsfield's Band from Belfast, had arranged to go to Lake Side, but before doing so paraded the streets. The lodges in question were 539 and 563. A good muster was made of members from both lodges and their friends, and the Belfast Band added to the attraction of the proceedings. The Sun Hotel was the place selected for the Belfast Band, and on their arrival at the Station they were loyally greeted by their friends, who accompanied them to the hotel. After refreshment, the fife and drum band from the Robin Hood arrived and the order of procession formed, when the principal streets of the town were paraded. During the parade in Church Street, a man, whether through drink or the excitement that prevailed, got knocked amongst the processionists. Blow for blow was exchanged and the man was locked up by the police. No further disturbance took place, and the party proceeded to the station, where the arrangements made by the railway officials reflect the highest credit on the Company. At Lake Side both a hall and field had been engaged; in the latter a large tent was erected and owing to the fine day the hall was not called into requisition. Speeches were made by several of the leaders present at the luncheon, and everything passed off in an enjoyable and jubilant manner. The excursionists returned home about half-past seven, a large crowd of people congregating at the station awaiting the arrival of the train. A large party of police were in attendance in the event of any disturbance breaking out.

The Orangemen formed in procession immediately on leaving the station, but they had not proceeded far when they were charged by about 20 or 30 men, which brought all to a standstill. The large drums were beaten with full vigour to rally the followers. The police were to the front in every instance, who used their sticks freely over the heads of the combatants. A start was again made, the police leading until opposite the Ship Inn, a man rushed at one of the standard-bearers, and striking amongst them in every direction, he was immediately surrounded, and was being severely handled until rescued by the police, who evidently thought he had received sufficient punishment. On reaching the Buccleuch Arms there was some slight skirmishing, but the heaviest hand to hand contest took place off Market Street. Sticks and staves were freely used and stones and bricks thrown amongst the processionists, who returned the attack with vigour. A severe *mêlée* occurred for some time, and the disturbance was assuming serious proportions, when fortunately the presence of a large force of police somewhat subdued the combatants. Nevertheless, several men and youths were severely hurt in the crowd. The procession marched up Cornwallis Street followed by a large crowd and slight disturbances occurred along the whole line of route. Passing through the Church-street Extension the party separated, each led by a band, one going in the direction of the Robin Hood Inn, and the other marching to the Sun Hotel. At each place a large company assembled, who spent an enjoyable evening. When indoors the opposition party desisted from any further annoyance and everything afterwards passed off quietly. A number of people taking part in the disturbances were apprehended by the police and brought before the magistrates and fined. The Beaconsfield Band left Barrow on Wednesday. Before leaving the town they played through the streets of the town several selections of music.

Doc. 19.3: Circular Announcing the Formation of Celtic Football Club, 1888

Circular announcing the formation of Celtic, January 1888, cited by W. Maley, *The Story of the Celtic* (Bishopbriggs, 1939), 7–8.

CELTIC PARK, PARKHEAD
(Corner of Dalmarnock and Janefield Streets)

His Grace the Archbishop of Glasgow and the Clergy of St Mary's, Sacred Heart, and St Michael's Missions, and the principal Catholic laymen of the East End:

The above Club was formed in November 1887 by a number of the Catholics of the East End of the City.

The main object of the club is to supply the East End conferences of the St Vincent de Paul Society with funds for the maintenance of the 'Dinner Tables' of our needy children in the Missions of St Mary's, Sacred Heart, and St Michael's. Many cases of sheer poverty are left unaided through lack of means. It is therefore with this principal object that we have set afloat the 'Celtic', and we invite you as one of our ever-ready friends to assist in putting our new Park in proper working order for the coming football season.

We have already several of the leading Catholic football players of the West of Scotland on our membership list. They have most thoughtfully offered to assist in the good work.

We are fully aware that the 'elite' of football players belong to this City and suburbs, and we know that from there we can select a team which will be able to do credit to the Catholics of the West of Scotland as the Hibernians have been doing in the East.

Again there is also the desire to have a large recreation ground where our Catholic young men will be able to enjoy the various sports which will build them up physically, and we feel sure we will have many supporters with us in this laudable object.

Any subscriptions may be handed to any of the Clergy of the three Missions or to the President, Mr. John Glass, 60 Marlborough Street, Glasgow, Dr. John Conway, 14 Abercromby Street, Glasgow, or to J. O'Hara, 77 East Rose Street, Glasgow, or to any member of the Committee, and the same will be gratefully acknowledged in due course.

Doc. 19.4: 'Bad Blood' between Rangers and Celtic, 1896

Scottish Sport, 13 October 1896.

None of the bad blood which unfortunately disgraced more than one of the recent meetings of the two clubs, and even threatened the amenity of a good paying fixture, came to the surface, and it is therefore all the more regrettable that a handful of fools should have sought to cast reproach upon the proceedings by an outbreak of disorder at the close. It was well, however, that they tackled those so capable of dealing with them as the police.

Part 6

Radical and Labour Movements

James Bronterre O'Brien (1804–1864)
By courtesy of the National Portrait Gallery, London.
Artist Unknown.

INTRODUCTION

Irish migrants have sometimes been presented by historians as an 'out-group' marginalised by the control of the Roman Catholic Church and the distractions of Irish nationalism from participation in British labour and radical organizations. Moreover, it has been argued that the participation of Irish migrants in a range of indigenous Irish organizations served also to limit their involvement in British radical and labour politics. These organizations were many and varied. The Catholic Church promoted a range of benevolent organizations dedicated to the dispensation of charity and moral and social improvement, including the St Vincent de Paul Society, benefit societies such as the United Order of Catholic Brethren, and temperance organizations such as the Catholic Total Abstinence League and the League of the Cross. Ribbonism was also an important ingredient of Irish Catholic political and associational culture, particularly in Lancashire, and provided a vehicle for entry into communal networks and employment opportunities for some migrants. Orangeism served a similar function for Irish Protestants, particularly in Glasgow and Liverpool.[1]

The participation of Irish migrants in British labour organizations was further compounded by the fact that during the 1830s and 1840s many English workers believed, rightly or wrongly, that Irish migrants helped to undermine working-class trade union activity by undercutting wages. In South Wales, for example, the belief that the Irish presence led to competition for jobs in industries where casual labour was significant and that the Irish lowered wages in the docks, mines and ironworks resulted in anti-Irish feeling and instances of communal violence.[2] Antipathy towards Irish labourers was exacerbated by their occasional use by employers as strike-breakers: in 1844 Lord Londonderry tried to break the Durham colliers by importing men from his Irish estates, whilst in 1854 the cotton manufacturers used blackleg Irish labour to defeat the Preston cotton strike, an event which subsequently formed the backcloth for Charles Dickens's *Hard Times*.[3]

Yet the attitudes of Irish workers to labour organizations were in many respects ambivalent. Some Irish migrants, notably from Dublin and Cork, possessed previous trade union experience in Ireland which they put to good use in Britain during the 1820s and 1830s, when several Irishmen emerged as prominent trade union leaders. John Doherty, Irish Catholic leader of Manchester's cotton spinners, editor of the visionary *Voice of the People* and *The Poor Man's Advocate*, and one of the greatest trade union

---

[1] For further discussion of this theme, see MacRaild, *Irish Migrants in Modern Britain*, 123–54.

[2] P. O'Leary, *Immigration and Integration: The Irish in Wales, 1798–1922* (Cardiff, 2000), 134–52.

[3] Swift, *The Irish in Britain, 1815–1914: Perspectives and Sources*, 19.

pioneers, was born and bred in Donegal.[4] Doherty, popularly referred to as 'the little Hibernian', first came to prominence in 1825 during the agitation for the repeal of the Combination Acts, which placed restrictions on trade union activity. Later, in December 1829, he organized a conference at Ramsay, Isle of Man, attended by delegates from Ireland, England and Scotland, at which the Grand Union of all the Operative Spinners in the United Kingdom was set up. In addition to protecting the interests of the spinners, the Union (the English branch broke up in 1831, but the Scottish one survived until 1837) sought also to advance the cause of factory reform, as Doherty later explained in his evidence to the Select Committee on Combinations of Workmen (**Doc. 20.1**).[5]

In June 1830 Doherty established the National Association for the Protection of Labour in Manchester. Its main aim was to encourage and organise trade unions and to provide support in times of trouble (**Doc. 20.2**), but it also became associated with the work of the Short Time Committees in their agitation for factory legislation which culminated in the Factory Act of 1833. Elsewhere in England, other prominent Irishmen within the pre-Chartist trade union movement included John Allison and Christopher Doyle of the Lancashire powerloom weavers, and Peter Hoey, Arthur Collins and William Ashton of the Barnsley linen weavers. The Irish were active in these industries, in part due to the decline of Irish textile industry and the emigration of Irish textile workers to Britain during the 1820s.[6]

Handloom weavers, cotton spinners, miners and colliers, both Catholic and Protestant, also participated in trade unions and strikes in the West of Scotland in the first half of the nineteenth century. Patrick McGowan, an Irish Catholic, was a prominent figure within the Glasgow Cotton Spinners' Association during the early 1830s and helped to promote Doherty's National Association of United Trades for the Protection of Labour. He later participated in the campaign for Factory Reform and the Reform Bill,[7] as the report on his speech from the hustings at a reform demonstration in Glasgow in May 1832 at the height of the Reform Agitation illustrates (**Doc. 20.3**).

The careers of Doherty, McGowan and others suggest that Irish migrants were not necessarily isolated from the social and economic

---

[4] For Doherty (1798–1854), see especially R.J. Kirby and A.E. Musson, *The Voice of the People: A Biography of John Doherty, 1798–1854* (Manchester, 1975).

[5] G.D.H. Cole and A.W. Filson, *British Working Class Movements: Select Documents, 1789–1875* (London, 1967), 241–94.

[6] D. Thompson, 'Ireland and the Irish in English Radicalism before 1850', in J. Epstein and D. Thompson (eds), *The Chartist Experience: Studies in Working-Class Radicalism and Culture, 1830–1860* (London, 1982), 130–3.

[7] M. Mitchell, *The Irish in the West of Scotland, 1797–1848* (Edinburgh, 1998, 26–8; see also John F. McCaffrey, 'Irish Immigrants and Radical Movements in the West of Scotland in the Early Nineteenth Century', *Innes Review*, 29, 1 (1988).

context in which they found themselves, and illustrate how Irish support for radical causes – parliamentary reform, factory reform, and opposition to the Poor Law – and trade unionism could be combined with loyalty to Catholicism and support for Irish nationalism. These were not mutually exclusive objectives. Indeed, there is some evidence that co-operation among workers transcended differences of nationality, as the *Weavers' Journal* noted in 1837 (**Doc. 20.4**).

Moreover, the British radical movement had real concerns about Ireland and Irish issues after 1815 – the Repeal of the Union was implicit in the agenda of the National Union of the Working Classes – and went to considerable lengths to both secure and welcome Irish support, particularly during the Reform Bill agitation.[8] Under the leadership of Daniel O'Connell, 'The Irish Liberator', the dominant aims of Irish nationalists were Catholic Emancipation and, after 1829, the Repeal of the Act of Union. Although the subsequent activities of O'Connell's Repeal Association were confined largely to Ireland, the cause of Irish nationalism found strong echoes within British radicalism, most notably within the Chartist movement between 1838 and 1848.[9]

Although Chartism belonged to an older radical tradition, its immediate origins lay in working-class disillusion with the terms of the 1832 Reform Act. The People's Charter, prepared largely by Francis Place and William Lovett, was published on 8 May 1838. Its six-point programme for political reform demanded universal male suffrage, secret ballot, annual parliaments, equal electoral districts, payment of MPs, and the abolition of the property qualification for MPs (**Doc. 21.1**). But the Charter also concealed wider working-class social and economic grievances, some of which had been exacerbated by Whig legislation of the 1830s, including the New Poor Law of 1834. Between 1838 and 1848 Chartism engendered tremendous support and loyalty within working-class communities, and, although Chartist petitions in support of the 'Six Points' were defeated in Parliament in 1839, 1842 and 1848, the movement marked a critical stage in the development of working-class consciousness and working-class political activity and organization.[10]

---

[8] J. Belchem, 'English Working-Class Radicalism and the Irish, 1815–50', in Swift and Gilley, *The Irish in the Victorian City*, 85–97.

[9] For the relationship between Irish nationalism and British radicalism, see especially E. Strauss, *Irish Nationalism and British Democracy* (London, 1951); R. O'Higgins, 'The Irish Influence in the Chartist Movement', *Past and Present*, 20 (1961), 83–96; Davis, *The Irish in Britain, 1815–1914*, 159–90; MacRaild, *Irish Migrants in Modern Britain*, 131–8.

[10] Chartism is the subject of an extensive historiography, for which readers should consult O. Ashton, R. Fyson and S. Roberts (eds), *The Chartist Movement: A New Annotated Bibliography* (London, 1995). The most important studies of Chartism include A. Briggs (ed.), *Chartist Studies* (London, 1959); J.T.Ward, *The Chartists* (London, 1973); D. Jones, *Chartism and the Chartists* (London, 1975); E. Royle, *Chartism* (London, 1980); Epstein and Thompson, *The Chartist Experience*; D. Thompson, *The Chartists* (London, 1984); John Saville, *1848: The British State and the Chartist Movement* (Cambridge, 1987); O. Ashton, R. Fyson and S. Roberts (eds), *The Chartist Legacy* (Rendlesham, 1999).

From the outset, the movement displayed some distinctive Irish influences, for two Irish MPs were signatories to the Charter: Daniel O'Connell, MP for County Clare, and leader of the movement for the repeal of the Act of Union; and William Sharman Crawford, an Ulster Protestant landowner and MP for Dundalk. Many Irish subsequently played significant roles in the Chartist movement, most notably Feargus O'Connor.[11] O'Connor was a Repeal MP for his native County Cork between 1832 and 1835 but then quarrelled with Daniel O'Connell. In 1837 O'Connor founded the *Northern Star*, the chief organ of the National Charter Association, and subsequently became the best-known Chartist leader, the architect of 'physical force' and the mass platform, and the chief proponent of the Chartist Land Plan (**Doc. 21.2**). Another major figure in the movement was James Bronterre O'Brien, a native of County Longford.[12] O'Brien, perhaps the greatest romantic and intellectual figure within the national leadership of the movement, saw Chartism as a social as well as a political movement and advocated 'moral force', which contributed to his quarrel with O'Connor in 1841 (**Doc. 21.3**).

Apart from these well-known national leaders, Irish people were also evident within the local Chartist rank-and-file, although their exact number is difficult to discern. Many of these Irish Chartists were quite outside O'Connell's sphere of influence because they favoured radical republicanism rather than O'Connell's constitutionalist approach (which derived from his belief in the continued rule of Ireland by the British crown), and their political experience was duly extended by the development of informal associations between the Chartists and Irish organizations in the manufacturing districts, particularly Lancashire, where Irish operatives took part in the Chartist General Strike of 1842. This co-operation sheds some doubt on the view that English workers automatically reacted with hostility to Irish competition in the labour market, and the *Northern Star* claimed that many workers 'had taken the very competition by the hand and treated them (the Irish) not as aliens but as brethren'. Moreover, and contrary to some historical interpretations,[13] for many Irish immigrants there was no contradiction

---

[11] For O'Connor, see especially D. Read and E. Glasgow, *Fergus O'Connor: Irishman and Chartist* (London, 1961); T.M. Kemnitz, 'Approaches to the Chartist Movement: Feargus O'Connor and Chartist Strategy', *Albion*, 5 (1973), 67–73; J. Epstein, *The Lion of Freedom: Feargus O'Connor and the Chartist Movement, 1832–42* (London, 1982); J. Belchem, '1848: Feargus O'Connor and the Collapse of the Mass Platform', in Epstein and Thompson, *The Chartist Experience*; S. Roberts, 'Feargus O'Connor in the House of Commons', in Ashton, Fyson and Roberts, *The Chartist Legacy*, 102–18.

[12] See A. Plummer, *Bronterre: A Political Biography of Bronterre O'Brien, 1804–1864* (London, 1971); T. Koseki, 'Chartism and Irish Nationalism, 1829–48: Bronterre O'Brien, the London Irish and Attempts at a Chartist-Irish Alliance' (University Birmingham M.Phil thesis, 1988).

[13] See, for example, J.H. Treble, 'O'Connor, O'Connell and the Attitudes of Irish Immigrants towards Chartism in the North of England, 1838–48', in J. Butt and I.F. Clarke (eds), *The Victorians and Social Protest: A Symposium* (Newton Abbot, 1973).

between support for Chartism and support for Irish nationalism; even John Doherty, described by Anthony Trollope as 'an Irishman, a Roman Catholic, and a furious radical, but a very clever man',[14] retained, as an Irish nationalist, his admiration for O'Connell.

Nevertheless, and until his death in 1847, O'Connell saw Chartism as an unwelcome distraction from the Repeal cause and actively discouraged Irishmen from involvement in the movement (**Doc. 21.4**). In south Lancashire, for example, the relatively cordial relationship between the Chartists and the Repeal Association was badly damaged by the events of 1841, when some Chartist meetings were broken up by Repealers, and anti-corn Law Leaguers and Chartists and Irish supporters of O'Connell clashed on the streets of Manchester, Stockport, Hyde and Stalybridge (**Doc. 21.5**). Despite the hostility of O'Connell and the Catholic hierarchy, Chartism also made minor inroads in Ireland; a Chartist Association was established in Dublin in 1839, which built on trade union activity in the city, and Chartist groups in Belfast, Newry, Drogheda and Dublin were coordinated within the Irish Universal Suffrage Association in 1841. Subsequently, under the leadership of Patrick O'Higgins, the Association organized several petitions to Parliament in favour of the People's Charter and Repeal of the Union between 1841 and 1844.[15]

The alliance between English and Irish radicals, coupled with the convictions of Feargus O'Connor, forced 'the Irish question' on English Chartists. Devotion to Ireland and the cause of Irish nationalism was common to all Irish Chartists in England, but they differed from Irish nationalists largely in their opposition to the existing class structure of society which, they argued, had to be altered in order to enable the masses to enjoy the benefits of self-government. Hence the reform of the franchise, the urgency of which was noted by O'Brien (**Doc. 21.6**), had to precede Repeal of the Union. Significantly, as early as 1839 O'Connor urged the Chartist Convention to consider the best means of enlisting the support of the Irish people in the furtherance of the People's Charter. In 1847, when he was elected MP for Nottingham, O'Connor supported Irish demands for Repeal in the House of Commons, a stance which was approved by a considerable section of the Irish Confederation, formed in Dublin in January 1847 under the leadership of Smith O'Brien for the purpose of achieving independence for the Irish nation by revolutionary means. In January 1847 a joint meeting of Irish Confederates and Chartists was held in Dublin, and in the spring of 1848 Chartist propaganda included appeals to the Irish in Britain (**Doc. 21.7**), whilst Confederates played a significant role in the sequence of events culminating in the Chartist rally at Kennington Common on 10 April 1848,

---

[14] Kirby and Musson, *The Voice of the People*, 1.
[15] For O'Higgins, see T. Koseki, 'Patrick O'Higgins and Irish Chartism', *Ireland-Japan Papers*, 2 (Hosei University, 1988).

prior to the fiasco that attended the presentation of the third Chartist petition to Parliament (**Doc. 21.8**).

Indeed, as the *Weekly Despatch* observed (**Doc. 21.9**), the Irish ingredient in this final phase of Chartism compounded the fears of the British establishment that Chartism constituted a revolutionary threat to the state, and Irish issues did much to sustain Chartism in London and the manufacturing districts during the summer of 1848.[16] Events in Ireland, including the arrest of John Mitchel, the suspension of Habeas Corpus, and the abortive rising of the Young Irelanders in Tipperary, provoked Chartist demonstrations at Clerkenwell Green in May, at Bradford in June, and at Birmingham, Manchester and Bolton in July. In August 1848 there were preparations by some Chartists and Confederates for insurrectionary activity in Manchester, but these were crushed by an exhaustive police round-up of Chartist and Confederate activists in South Lancashire, effectively marking the end of Chartism in the North. These events suggest that the Irish provided Chartism with a militant and revolutionary edge which contrasted with the largely constitutionalist methods which the movement had generally employed. Yet the 'Irish connection' also weakened the Chartist cause because it projected the Chartists as dangerous revolutionaries rather than constitutional reformers; thus the government was able to mobilise anti-Chartist opinion and, in April 1848, to pass the Crown and Government Security Act, which replaced the capital charge of treason with that of sedition, a mere misdemeanour, and made it easier for the authorities in the manufacturing districts to restrain the Chartist platform. Finally, the failure of Chartism in 1848 had a decided effect on the increasing social and political isolation of the Irish in Britain during the 1850s, when post-Famine immigration and the restoration of the Catholic hierarchy enabled Tory politicians to stir up anti-Irish feeling.[17]

Nevertheless, the Irish in Britain continued to participate in radical and labour movements during the second half of the nineteenth century. In particular, first and second-generation Irishmen played a prominent role in the 'New Unionism' – the unionisation of unskilled workers – in the 1880s and 1890s. Will Thorne, a member of the Social Democratic Federation, became leader of the Gasworkers' and General Labourers Union and secured shorter shifts and pay increases for gasworkers employed by the South Metropolitan Gas Company following a strike in 1889. Most notably,

---

[16] See especially J. Belchem, 'The Year of Revolutions: The Political and Associational Culture of the Irish Immigrant Community in 1848', in Belchem (ed.), *Popular Politics, Riot and Labour* (Liverpool, 1992), 68–97; J. Belchem, 'Nationalism, Republicanism and Exile: Irish Emigrants and the Revolutions of 1848', *Past and Present*, 146 (1995), 103–135.

[17] See, for example, N. Kirk, 'Ethnicity, Class and Popular Toryism, 1850–1870', in K. Lunn (ed.), *Hosts, Immigrants and Minorities: Historical Responses to Newcomers in British Society, 1870–1914*, 64–106, and the relevant sections in N. Kirk, *The Growth of Working-Class Reformism in Mid-Victorian England* (London, 1985).

Ben Tillett led the London dockers, who included many Irish labourers, to victory in the famous London Dock Strike of 1889.[18] The dockers sought a pay increase from 5d. an hour to 6d. (the so-called 'Dockers' Tanner'), overtime pay, the abolition of piece-work, and better working conditions. The strike commenced on 12 August and the dockers received support from all the various dock trades, including stevedores. The stevedores, who were skilled workers, were members of the Amalgamated Stevedores Union, founded in 1871 by Patrick Hennessey, an Irish trade unionist. Although they had a strong Irish Catholic connection, some had been reluctant to assist unorganized dock labourers even though many of these were also of Irish Catholic descent, as Charles Booth observed (**Doc. 22.1**). Nevertheless, once the strike began, Tom McCarthy, the Secretary of the Stevedores Union, pledged the support of his 5,000 members to Tillett.[19] The strike lasted for five weeks until Cardinal Manning, the Archbishop of Westminster, and the Lord Mayor of London arranged a conciliation meeting at the Mansion House (**Doc. 22.2**). Manning's support for the dockers' cause stemmed in part from his sympathy for the estimated 40,000 Roman Catholics variously employed in London's poorly paid and demoralising East End trades, including dockers, and Ben Tillett later claimed that the Cardinal's intervention was crucial to the dockers' ultimate victory (they secured the 'tanner' and 8d. per hour for overtime).[20] Throughout the strike the dockers were sustained by donations from all over the world, including an impressive £30,000 from Australian trade unionists who had already won the eight-hour day and whose ranks contained a large number of Irish members; this undoubtedly influenced the staunch support they gave to their compatriots in the London docks (**Doc. 22.3**). In the aftermath of the strike, the Dock, Wharf, Riverside and General Labourers' Union was formed under the leadership of Ben Tillett and Tom Mann, reaching a membership of 30,000 men within two months.

Irish workers also contributed to the 'New Unionism' in South Wales. The National Amalgamated Labourers' Union of Great Britain, which included dock workers, was established by Albert Kenny at Newport before the great London Dock Strike. Kenny had previously helped to organise the Seamen's Union at Dublin and Cork. The NALU was established in Cardiff in June 1889. Some Irishmen played prominent roles within this union. Irish workers also participated in the South Wales Miners' Federation and the Mineworkers' Federation of Great Britain, with which it was affiliated, and some local iron companies actually advertised for labourers in southern Ireland and brought them from Cork and Waterford. Subsequently, Irish workers established a strong position during the industrial

---

[18] For the career of Tillett, see J. Saville and A.J. Topham, 'Ben Tillett', in J.M. Bellamy and J. Saville (eds), *Dictionary of Labour Biography* (London, 1977), vol. 4, 177–85.

[19] T. McCarthy, *The Great Dock Strike, 1889* (London, 1988), 84–5.

[20] B. Tillet, *Memories and Reflections* (London, 1931), 145–7.

unrest of 1910–11 in the district, leading the fight against the importation of blackleg labour from London.[21]

James Connolly and James Larkin, both brought up in Irish communities in Britain, and both revolutionary socialists, were influential figures in labour organizations during the Edwardian period. Connolly was born of Irish immigrant parents in Edinburgh's Cowgate district. After working as a carter he became active in socialist and trade union affairs, later founding *The Workers' Republic*, the first Irish socialist paper. He became the organiser in Ulster for the Irish Transport Workers' Union and led the Dublin workers during the lock-out of 1913.[22] Larkin was born in Liverpool of Irish parents, becoming a foreman on the Liverpool docks and then an organiser for the National Union of Dockers, organising sympathetic strikes during the Belfast disputes of 1907 and founding the Irish Transport and General Workers' Union in Dublin in 1909.[23]

The careers of Connolly and Larkin are illustrative of the interplay between the growth of 'New Unionism' in Britain and Ireland, as well as raising the broader question of the extent to which the Irish in Britain were influenced by socialist ideas and, indeed, supported the emerging Labour Party. This latter subject is particularly worthy of further research. In Glasgow, for example, it appears that because Irish politics in the city were dominated by religion and nationalism, it was difficult for labour organizations to attract the support of the Irish without the acquiescence of the United Irish League and the Catholic Church. Since the former urged the Irish in Britain to vote Liberal because the Liberals were pledged to Home Rule, the prospect of the Independent Labour Party (from 1893) and the Labour Party (from 1906) attracting significant Irish support was minimal. Nevertheless, some Irish Catholics developed a commitment to socialism, most notably Irish-born John Wheatley, who became president of the Shettleston branch of the United Irish League in 1898 and joined the Independent Labour Party in 1907.[24] In 1906 Wheatley founded the Catholic Socialist Society, which survived until 1920. Membership of the Society, which was confined to Catholic communicants, never exceeded 100 and Wheatley faced considerable hostility from the Catholic Church in Glasgow, being regarded in some quarters as little more than a heretic – 'a mal-content Catholic', as a report of the Diocesan Committee on Socialism noted in 1908 (**Doc. 22.4**). Yet in the longer term Wheatley played a vital role in reconciling Catholicism and Labour, ultimately becoming a

---

[21] O'Leary, *Immigration and Integration,* 152–60.

[22] For Connolly (1868–1916), see especially C.D. Greaves, *The Life and Times of James Connolly* (New York, 1972).

[23] For Larkin (1876–1947), see especially E. Larkin, *James Larkin: Irish Labour Leader, 1876–1946* (London, 1965).

[24] For John Wheatley, see S. Gilley's biography of him in *Dictionary of Labour Biography* (London, 1984), vol. 7, 251–5.

Labour MP in 1922 and Minister of Health in 1924, by which time Irish Catholic participation in Labour politics was considerable, not only in Glasgow but also in many other British towns and cities.[25]

RADICALISM

Doc. 20.1: John Doherty's Grand Union of Operative Spinners, 1829

First Report of the Select Committee on Combinations of Workmen, Parliamentary Papers (1838), 257.

There were several objects of the Spinners' association; the main object was to prevent reductions of wages; and next, if it be possible, and we hope it will be certain, to procure an Act of Parliament to lessen the hours of labour in factories. That point, I believe, in fact I know, during the whole of my connection with the spinners of Manchester, has been one that has never changed. Our society has been abandoned at different periods, and our meetings given up, but we have never abandoned the hope and attempt to lessen the hours of labour by Act of Parliament . . . The other object of combination would be in endeavouring to prevent certain harsh treatment, to which we find we are gradually becoming more and more subjected.

Doc. 20.2: Aims of the National Association for the Protection of Labour, 1830

United Trades Co-operative Journal, 10 July 1830.

1. That the miserable conditions to which, by repeated and unnecessary reductions of wages, the working people of this country are reduced, urges upon this meeting the imperative necessity of adopting some effectual means for preventing such reductions and securing to the industrious workman a just and adequate remuneration for his labour.
2. That to accomplish this necessary object a Society shall be formed consisting of the various Trades throughout the kingdom.
3. That this Society be called 'The National Association for the Protection of Labour'.

---

[25] S. Gilley, 'Catholics and Socialists in Scotland, 1900–30', in Swift and Gilley, *The Irish in Britain*, 280–323; J.F. McCaffrey, 'Irish Issues in the Nineteenth and Twentieth Century: Radicalism in a Scottish Context', in Devine, *Irish Immigrants and Scottish Society*, 116–37; Fielding, *Class and Ethnicity*, chap. 6, 'Labour and the Church', 105–26.

4. That the general laws and government of this Society be formed and conducted by a general Committee, consisting of one delegate from every 1000 members.
5. That such general Committee shall meet every six months, and decide upon all subjects affecting the interests of the Association.

Doc. 20.3: Patrick McGowan on Parliamentary Reform, 1832

Glasgow Free Press, 16 May 1832.

[McGowan said] that although the meeting viewed with surprise and indignation the artifices of the House of Lords in attempting to dupe the people, the recent resolution of the Peers, instead of disorganising the country, had tended rather to unite more firmly all classes of society in their exertions for Reform. He believed he delivered the sentiments of 100,000 well organised operatives in this part of the country, when he stated that they were now determined to support the upper and middle classes in recovering their just rights and privileges . . . The extension of the elective franchise was the only way to raise the operatives from their present degraded political position. It was to low wages, high rates of provisions, and to political misrule that they attributed all their sufferings, and for the removal of which, every class in society must apply all their strength, and be determined in obtaining their object.

Doc. 20.4: Working-Class Interests, 1837

Weavers' Journal, 1 February 1837.

Fellow operatives, it is time we were laying all our petty differences aside. We have a common enemy to oppose. Let us unite in common to oppose them. Let their rule of tactics be the example which we will follow. Do they pay any deference to the nationality of a man, or the predominance of a political party? Do they refuse giving a man the twist sent to his web, because he is an Irishman? Or do they charge a man one-third more carriage than what they give the carrier because he is a Radical? No. Then why let such interference with the social intercourse of the operatives of this place? Why let the poisonous influence of the bigots of party interfere with the energies of your minds, that when called upon by the most pressing emergency to bring them into active operation, they are sapped and powerless?

CHARTISM

21.1: The People's Charter, 1838

Chartist broadsheet, 1838, cited in F.C. Mather, *Chartism and Society* (London, 1980), 47–8.

THE SIX POINTS OF THE PEOPLE'S CHARTER

1. A VOTE for every man twenty-one years of age, of sound mind, and not undergoing punishment for crime.
2. THE BALLOT – To protect the elector in the exercise of his vote.
3. NO PROPERTY QUALIFICATION for Members of Parliament – thus enabling the constituencies to return the man of their choice, be he rich or poor.
4. PAYMENT OF MEMBERS, thus enabling an honest tradesman, working man, or other person, to serve a constituency, when taken from his business to attend in the interests of the Country.
5. EQUAL CONSTITUENCIES, securing the same amount of representation for the same number of electors, instead of allowing small constituencies to swamp the votes of large ones.
6. ANNUAL PARLIAMENTS, thus presenting the most effectual check to bribery and intimidation, since though a constituency might be bought once in seven years (even with the ballot), no purse could buy a constituency (under a system of universal suffrage) in each ensuing twelve-month; and since members, when elected for a year, would not be able to defy and betray their constituents as now.

Subjoined are the names of the gentlemen who embodied these principles into the document called the 'People's Charter' at an influential meeting held at the British Coffee House, London, on the 7th of June 1837:

Daniel O'Connell, Esq., MP	Mr Henry Heatherington.
John Arthur Roebuck, Esq., MP	Mr John Cleave.
John Temple Leader, Esq., MP	Mr James Watson.
Charles Hindley, Esq., MP	Mr Richard Moore.
Thomas Perronet Thompson, Esq., MP	Mr William Lovett.
William Sharman Crawford, Esq., MP	Mr Henry Vincent.

Doc. 21.2: Reflections on Feargus O'Connor

R.C. Gammage, *History of the Chartist Movement, 1837–54* (1854), 45.

[a]   Upwards of six feet in height, stout and athletic, and in spite of his opinions invested with a sort of aristocratic bearing, the sight of his person was calculated to inspire the masses with a solemn awe . . . O'Connor however did not depend alone upon physical strength for the involuntary respect in which he was held by the multitude. His broad massive forehead,

very full in those parts where phrenologists place the organs of perception, though considerably deficient in the faculties of reflection, bore evidence, in spite of these defects, of great intellectual force. To assert that he possessed a mind solid and steady were to say too much, no man with an equal amount of intellect was ever more erratic. Had the solidity of his judgment been equal to his quickness of perception he would intellectually have been a great man, but this essential quality of greatness he lacked, hence his life presents a series of mistakes and contradictions, which, as men reflected more lowered him in their estimation. No man in the movement was so certain of popularity as O'Connor. No man was so certain to lose it after its attainment. It was not till he proceeded to speak that his full influence was felt. This however depended upon circumstances. With an indoor assembly Vincent was by far his superior. Out of doors O'Connor was the almost universal idol, for the thunder of his voice would reach the ears of the most careless, and put to silence the most noisy of his audience.

W. Lovett, *The Life and Struggles of William Lovett* (1876), 294–7.

[b]   I regard Feargus O'Connor as the chief marplot of our movement . . . a man who, by his personal conduct joined to his malignant influence in the *Northern Star*, has been the blight of democracy from the first moment he opened his mouth as its *professed advocate* . . . Not possessing a nature to appreciate intellectual exertions, he began his career by ridiculing our '*moral force humbuggery!*' . . . By his great professions, by trickery and deceit, he got the aid of the working classes to establish an organ to promulgate their principles, which he soon converted into an instrument for destroying everything intellectual and moral in our movement.

R. Balmforth, *Some Social and Political Pioneers of the Nineteenth Century* (1900), 189.

[c]   Its [Chartism's] 'moral force' was largely neutralised, and its adherents deluded and misled, by one or two inordinately vain and self-seeking agitators. Of these, perhaps, the most culpable was Feargus O'Connor. O'Connor was the editor and chief proprietor of the *Northern Star*, the principal working-class newspaper of the time, and, through its pages, wielded great influence. Possessing lungs of brass and a voice like a trumpet, he was the most effective outdoor orator of his time, and the idol of the immense assemblages which were often brought together in those days. Unfortunately, both for the movement and for himself, he was a man of unbounded conceit and egotism, extremely jealous of precedence, and regarding himself as a sort of uncrowned king of the working classes.

W.E. Adams, *Memoirs of a Social Atom* (1903), 203–5.

[d]   Quarrelling was almost inevitable when not one man, but many men, desired to become dictators. It was almost equally inevitable when such a man as Feargus O'Connor, who had few of the qualities of a powerful leader save extraordinary force of character, had acquired absolute dominion over

the cause. The ascendancy of Feargus O'Connor would have been unac-countable but for the fact that he owned the *Northern Star*. Through it Feargus every week addressed a letter to his followers – 'the blistered hands and unshorn chins of the working classes'. The letter was generally as full of claptrap as it was bestrewn with words and sentences in capital type. But the turgid claptrap took. The people of that period seemed to relish denun-ciation, and O'Connor gave them plenty of it. Blatant in print, he was equally blatant on the platform. More of a demagogue than a democrat, he was fond of posing as the descendant of Irish kings. 'Never a man of my order,' he was in the habit of declaring, 'has devoted himself as I have done to the working classes'. It was his delight, too, to boast that he had 'never travelled a mile or eaten a meal at the people's expense' . . . The common notion of O'Connor outside the ranks of his personal followers was that he was a charlatan and a humbug – an adventurer who traded on the passions of the people for his own profit and advantage. A correcter notion would have been that he was a victim of his own delusions.

Doc. 21.3: An Appreciation of Bronterre O'Brien, 1854

R.C. Gammage, *History of the Chartist Movement, 1837–54* (1854), 76–7, 103–4.

There was one man who wielded more of the real democratic mind than any other man in the movement; and who, with the single exception of O'Con-nor, was also more generally popular. Yet this man had been but little accustomed to the labours and honours of the platform. It was through the medium of the press that his influence had been principally felt. The name of the gentleman was James Bronterre O'Brien. There was no man more fascinating. In stature he was considerably above the middle size, of fine figure, though rather inclined to the stooping posture of the profound student . . . He was undoubtedly the man with the greatest breadth of mind. In the Chartist ranks he was universally known as the schoolmaster, a title bestowed on him by O'Connor . . . When reasoning a point he was deliber-ate to admiration. No other speaker was capable of rising to such a height, or of so impressing an audience with the strength and intensity of his feel-ings, while no orator could outrival him in action and flexibility of voice. In handling the weapon of satire, he enjoyed an immeasurable superiority over all his compeers. There was no flippancy in his wit. It was grand and solid . . . A man who was possessed of such capabilities was an orator of no ordinary power, and he must have been a master, not only of words, but of ideas.

He had but little sympathy with the class of landlords whom he looked upon as the hereditary enemies of society. But there was another class whom he regarded with greater dread, viz., the great monied class, which had risen to immense importance, and whose power was on the increase. He saw in that class a multitude of persons who were living on fixed incomes. The natural tendency of Free Trade, the economists themselves admitted, would be to cheapen commodities, and O'Brien argued that this would enable the usurer, the tax eater, the parson, and all other classes whose incomes were fixed, to command, with the same amount of money, an increase of those commodities, just in proportion to their cheapness, and in that proportion their incomes would thus be virtually raised. He contended then, that if those parties were thus enabled to command a larger share of wealth, they could obtain it only at the expense of others, those others being the labouring class, who are the source of all the wealth produced.

Doc. 21.4: Daniel O'Connell Opposes Irish Involvement in Chartism, 1839

The Merlin, 14 December 1839

In the manufacturing towns in England, the mass of the poor population – not more poor than active – everyone of them subsisting on small means – in every one of these towns there was a large garrison of Irishmen. Did they join the Chartists? Did they join the insurrection ?

Oh, blessed be God, no. Not only the Irish in Ireland refused to gain any advantage by force, but the Irish in England joined not the Chartists but opposed them, for they only looked for justice by turning the hearts of those who opposed them. Take the town of Cardiff alone. In that town there were a considerable number of Irish, poor people, who went there to earn their wages in this world, and who endeavoured to procure the means of having a clergyman . . . What did they do in respect of the Chartist insurrection ? Why! 100 of the Irish who had come into the town of Cardiff were sworn in as special constables.

Doc. 21.5: Co-operation between Irish Repealers and the Anti-Corn Law League, 1841

Extract from the diary of Edward Watkin, organiser of the Manchester Operative Anti-Corn Law Association, 23 May 1841, from E.W. Watkin, *Alderman Cobden of Manchester* (1891), 68–9.

On Monday evening last the Chartists held a meeting in Carpenters' Hall for the purpose of continuing McDowall as a member of the Convention a fortnight longer, and also – but this did not appear in the bills – for that of passing an address to the Chartists of Newry.

Our associates and the Irish and other repealers of the Union and the Corn Laws mustered in full strength, and we had as pretty a row as I ever witnessed. The Chartists were driven out of the hall four times. We regularly thrashed them and passed our own resolutions.

On Tuesday we mustered all up for the meeting in the town hall, where we gained another complete victory.

On Friday a public meeting took place in the town hall, Salford, which we attended, and were victorious also.

On Thursday night there was a tea party in the Corn Exchange, which went off admirably. I was there, but had to leave for near an hour to attend a committee meeting of the Operative Anti-Corn Law Association. We resolved upon a committee to make arrangements for the public meeting to be held in race week.

Doc. 21.6: Bronterre O'Brien on the Parliamentary Franchise, 1839

Charter, 14 April 1839.

What a farce the present system is! The present House of Commons does not represent the people, but only those fellows who live by profits and usury – a rascally crew who have no interest in the real welfare of the country. Pawnbrokers are enfranchised, and two thousand brothel-owners in London all have votes, but honest folk have none. Not a single stock-broker is without a vote, yet there is not a man among them who does not deserve the gallows. Every lawyer in the country can vote – every thief of them – yet when did any one of this gang add a stiver to the wealth of the nation? . . . Votes have been given to all the parsons, who live by explaining those things which they tell us are inexplicable, who preach abnegation of the lusts of the flesh while losing no opportunities of greasing their own rosy gills . . . Then you have those slaughtering, soldier-flogging, billiard-playing creatures called officers of the army, and the cotton-lords who possess all the skill and trickery and daring and effrontery of the pick-pocket, the burglar and the highwayman rolled into one – they all have votes, but not the working people. It is, indeed, disgusting to see how much of the honey is appropriated by the drones, and what a pittance is left to the bees of the hive; and how the parliamentary franchise is monopolised by one-tenth of the population – and that tenth the worst tenth.

Doc. 21.7: Chartist Appeal to the London Irish, 1848

Chartist Convention Placard, 5 April 1848.

Irishmen resident in London, on the part of the democrats in England we extend to you the warm hand of fraternization; your principles are ours, and our principles shall be yours. Remember the aphorisms, that union is strength, and division is weakness; centuries of bitter experience prove to you the truth of the latter, let us now cordially endeavour to test the virtue of the former. Look to your fatherland, the most degraded in the scale of nations. Behold it bleeding at every pore under the horrible lashings of cruel misrule! What an awful spectacle is Ireland, after forty-seven years of the vaunted Union! Her trade ruined, her agriculture paralysed, her people scattered over the four quarters of the globe, and her green fields in the twelve months just past made the dreary grave yards of 1,000,000 of famished human beings. Irishmen, if you love your country, if you detest these monstrous atrocities, unite in heart and soul with those who will struggle with you to exterminate the hell-engendered cause of your country's degradation – beggary and slavery.

Doc. 21.8: Co-operation between Chartists and Irish Confederates, 1848

R.C. Gammage, *History of the Chartist Movement, 1837–54* (1854), 296–9.

Public meetings were held, and the spark of Democracy seemed to light up every breast . . . In Dublin, John Mitchel started a paper, under the title of *The United Irishman*. It breathed a vengeance against the English Government, and gave plain instructions on street warfare, showing that every woman might be a soldier, by throwing bottles and other missiles, and even vitriol on the troops. The Chartist Executive summoned a Convention, to meet in London on the 3rd of April. The following week brought no cessation of agitation. A great meeting was held on Kennington Common, on the 13th of March. There were about twenty thousand persons present. Four thousand police were in attendance; eighty were mounted and armed with sabres and pistols, and amused themselves with riding about the Common. Numbers of the force were scattered through the meeting, dressed in plain clothes. Special constables were sworn in. The gun-makers were requested by the authorities to unscrew the barrels of their fire-arms, and the dealers in powder and shot were ordered to be cautious in the sale of those articles. The tri-colour waved from the hustings on which speakers were assembled.

On Sunday the 12th, Peep Green was visited by thousands of the inhabitants of the West Riding of Yorkshire, who were addressed by Messrs. Kydd, Shaw, of Leeds, and other speakers. The flag of the Republic was exhibited, and resolutions were passed pledging the meeting to stand by the Charter.

On the 17th March, a great gathering took place in the Free-trade Hall, Manchester, to promote a fraternization of the Chartists and the Irish Repealers. Although charges of one shilling, fourpence, and twopence, were made for admission, a dense mass of people crowded the Hall, which was estimated to hold nine thousand persons. Smith O'Brien, MP, and John Mitchel were expected to be present, but did not attend; but the enthusiastic multitude was addressed by J. Leach, G. Archdeacon, F. O'Connor, W.P. Roberts, Michael Doheny, and T.F. Meagher, who spoke to resolutions in favour of the repeal of the union. This meeting was followed on the Saturday evening by a great soirée in the Town Hall, which was decorated with banners, and all the other emblems of Democracy. The most democratic sentiments were responded to, and the meeting broke up, with deafening cheers for the Charter and Repeal . . .

In London the agitation was kept up with vigour. The Irish Confederates nightly enrolled numbers in their clubs, which seemed to be the more augmented in numbers in consequence of news having arrived of the arrest of Smith O'Brien, Meagher and Mitchel. Almost every European country was now in the throes of revolution; and as each post brought news of the risings and triumphs of the people in Austria, Prussia, the minor German, and many of the Italian States, so appeared to increase the determination of the Chartists and Irish Repealers to establish the long cherished principles for which they had struggled.

Doc. 21.9: Irish Confederate Activity, 1848

Weekly Despatch, 2 April 1848

We observe that [Irish Confederates] are endeavouring to organise the Irish, who are either settled or are vagrant in England, to be prepared to create a diversion in their favour whenever their purposes are ripe for execution. From the centre of Confederation Hall the riots of Edinburgh, Glasgow, Manchester and London were worked, and the English Chartists are lending themselves to the same stupid conspiracy against the peace, order and stability of the empire . . . But at such a time as this, when peril threatens us from every side, when the very existence, because the integrity of this great empire is put to hazard, and when internal disorder and financial confusion are aggravating the difficulties of our Government, we know of but one cause, that of our common country, and one way to save it and serve it, by union, fidelity, order and public spirit. Every Englishman who is worthy of such a country will feel that the stability of this majestic fabric is his first care, his chief interest, his primary duty. We want no foreign propaganda to settle our quarrels. We want no revolution of shoplifters and pick pockets.

SOCIALISM AND LABOUR

Doc. 22.1: The Organisation of Labour in the London Docks, 1889

Charles Booth, *Life and Labour of the People in London* (1889–1903), First Series: Poverty, vol. IV, 16–22.

Dock labour in London is, properly speaking, the employment offered by the import trade. In the export trade the shipowners contract directly with a body of skilled men called stevedores, for whose work the dock company are in no way responsible. These men act under master stevedores, and are the only section of dock or waterside workmen who have formed themselves into a trade union . . . At least the docks are free from the reproach of other London industries; they are not overrun with foreigners. The foreign element is conspicuous by its absence – unless we are to persuade ourselves that the Irish are foreigners. For Paddy enjoys more than his proportional share of dock work with its privileges and miseries. He is to be found especially among the irregular hands, disliking as a rule the 'six to six' business for six days of the week. The cockney-born Irishman, as distinguished from the immigrant, is not favourably looked upon by the majority of employers.

Doc. 22.2: The London Dock Strike, 1889: Cardinal Manning's Intervention

Ben Tillett, *Memories and Reflections* (1931), 145–7.

It was precisely at this moment that Cardinal Manning intervened. He sought an interview with the dock directors and he urged them to reconsider their position. Undoubtedly the Cardinal was apprehensive of the possibilities of disorder arising from the strike and he was, of course, aware of the menace implied in the proposal to extend the area of the dispute . . . My respect for the Cardinal was enhanced by the feeling I entertained towards the square-jawed, hard-featured Bishop of London, Dr Temple, who had refused to assist, and answered my appeal with a letter full of the most virulent abuse of the docker and his claim for a higher wage. Dr Temple, as Bishop of London, felt that he could not allow the Catholic Cardinal to obtain all the credit of promoting a settlement of the strike. Accordingly, he hurried back from North Wales, when he learned that the door of negotiation had been gently forced open by the Cardinal, and joined with him in forming, with the Lord Mayor, Mr Sydney Buxton, Lord Brassey, Sir John Lambert, and others what was called the Mansion House Committee to act as mediators between the Joint Committee representing the dock companies, and the General Committee of the strike . . . From the first the Cardinal showed himself to be the dockers' friend, though he had family connections in the shipping interests, represented on the other side. Our demands were too reasonable, too moderate, to be set aside by an intelligence so fine, a spirit so lofty, as that which animated the frail, tall figure with its saintly, emaciated face, and the strangely compelling eyes.

Doc. 22.3: The London Dock Strike, 1889: The Dockers' Victory

The Times, 16 September 1889.

The fourth and last of the strike demonstrations in Hyde Park was held yesterday. A very large number of people attended, and perfect order prevailed. At the first platform Mr T. McCarthy, of the stevedores, presided, and the flag of the Australian colonies waved above and was surrounded by flowers. The flag and its decorations were much cheered, as also was Mr John Burns when he climbed into the crowded wagon with his wife. The chairman said they were there to celebrate the dockers' victory in the great battle they had had for right and justice, and also to thank those who from the outside had given them the assistance which had made the victory secure. He thanked Mr John Burns and Mr Benjamin Tillett, and also the Lord Mayor, Cardinal Manning and Mr Sydney Buxton, MP, who had come in as mediators . . . Mr John Burns, who was received with great cheering, proposed the resolution of the meeting which commenced by giving thanks to those who had assisted in the strike. Special mention was made of Australia, and the resolution pledged the workers to organize a federation of labour. This victory was but the precursor of still greater victories they hoped to secure in the near future (Cheers). It was true that the strike had been helped by benefactors in all parts of Great Britain, France and Belgium, and other places, and the New World – Australia – had given of its bounty to redress the grievances of the Old World. It was strange that most help should have come from across the seas. The fact showed that the internationalization of labour was no longer the myth it was once supposed to be, but was becoming more absolutely a reality from sea to sea and from continent to continent (Cheers). The strike had had great moral effects. It had struck a blow at the selfishness of the rich man and had put straightly the plain fact that a man had a right to live.

Doc. 22.4: Catholic Socialism in Glasgow, 1908

Diocesan Committee on Socialism, Glasgow Archdiocesan Archives, 13 November 1908.

A good many of the Catholic unemployed are drawn to hear the harangues at Socialist meetings, dazzled by the fair promises of work. It has been ascertained on good authority that the interests of labour are the bait, and remain the only connecting link between the workingman and socialism . . . A few individuals here and there, who have been practical Catholics, have given up the Faith and extend the lists of the Socialist party. They are democratic Socialists. A small number of men, and a few women, have joined the so-called *Catholic Socialist party*, which is under the aegis of a mal-content Catholic . . . The people who attend the so-called Catholic

Socialist meetings are in a most dangerous position: as they associate with speakers brought to their meetings, who are agnostics and materialists. They are known to have received addresses from men of the Blatchford Camp and also members of the Fabian Society. The Faith and Priesthood have been decried and denounced by them at meetings attended by the so-called Catholic Socialist party. All are agreed that there is great danger to the faith of our people who attend Socialist meetings, but especially the meetings of 'the Catholic Socialist party'. The qualification *Catholic* is a snare.

Part 7

Nationalism

THE IRISH FRANKENSTEIN.

The Irish Frankenstein, *Punch*, 20 May 1882.

INTRODUCTION

Throughout the nineteenth century, Anglo-Irish political relationships were dominated by 'the Irish Question', central to which was the desire of many Irish people for the repeal of the Act of Union of 1800, by which the United Kingdom of Great Britain and Ireland had been established (**Doc. 23.1**). Thereafter, Irish nationalism, in its various definitions and forms, found expression in both constitutionalist and revolutionary activity.[1] The former, which combined a parliamentary and legalistic approach to Home Rule for Ireland, was very much a majority tradition which found expression in the repeal campaigns orchestrated before 1847 by Daniel O'Connell, 'The Irish Liberator', and, after 1870, by the Home Rule movement. By contrast, the revolutionary and separatist tradition, manifested in the rising of the Young Irelanders in 1848, Fenian activity in the 1860s, and ultimately in the Easter Rising of 1916, was very much a minority tradition. Nevertheless, the tradition of Irish agrarian outrage, of the 'physical force' resort to street violence and armed rebellion, and the recourse to mass defiance provided grounds for British conservative prejudice, not least in regard to the Irish in Britain, many of whom held a romantic and sentimental attachment to the Home Rule cause.[2]

Under the leadership of Daniel O'Connell, an Irish Catholic barrister, the dominant aims of Irish nationalism were Catholic Emancipation and the repeal of the Act of Union. The Irish rebellion of 1798 had convinced O'Connell that Irish violence was counter-productive and that change should be won by legal and constitutional means. O'Connell's leadership of the Catholic Association from 1821 forced the question of Irish Catholic civil rights on to the political agenda, and in 1828 he stood for Parliament and won a by-election in County Clare, although as a Catholic he could not take his seat. Rather than face the threat of civil war in Ireland, Wellington's government introduced the Catholic Relief Act in 1829. With Catholic Emancipation secured, O'Connell's energies focused on the repeal of the Act of Union by constitutional means. However, twelve years of co-operation with the Whigs at Westminster proved futile and in 1842, under pressure from his more militant supporters, O'Connell launched the Loyal National Repeal Association (**Doc. 23.2**), which attempted to repeat the success of the Catholic Association by embarking on a programme of popular agitation in Ireland. However, in 1843 Robert Peel banned a huge

---

[1] Classic studies include E. Strauss, *Irish Nationalism and British Democracy* (London, 1951); D.G. Boyce, *Englishmen and Irish Troubles* (London, 1972); A. O'Day, *The English Face of Irish Nationalism: Parnellite Involvement in British Politics, 1880–1886* (Dublin, 1977); D.G. Boyce, *The Irish Question and British Politics, 1868–1986* (London, 1988); A. O'Day, 'The Irish Problem', in T.R. Gourvish and A. O'Day (eds), *Later Victorian Britain, 1867–1900* (London, 1988); A. O'Day, *Irish Home Rule, 1867–1921* (Manchester, 1998).

[2] Swift, *The Irish in Britain, 1815–1914: Perspectives and Sources*, 24.

repeal meeting at Clontarf; O'Connell was arrested, tried and convicted of sedition, and sentenced to one year in prison, although a legal technicality enabled his release.[3]

By the time of O'Connell's death in 1847 – at the height of the Famine – the effectiveness of the Repeal Association was waning and more radical voices within the broader nationalist movement had coalesced within the Irish Confederation of 'Young Irelanders', formed in Dublin in January 1847 under the leadership of Smith O'Brien, which sought to achieve independence for the Irish nation by revolutionary means. Nevertheless, with thirty-seven MPs, the Loyal National Repeal Association had gained some parliamentary successes, and O'Connell had succeeded in making Catholicism the distinguishing element in Irish nationalism and in applying the political institutions and values of the British parliamentary system to the Irish nationalist cause. Yet much of the repeal agitation was directed at, and encompassed, Irish Catholics in Ireland, and only in 1847–48, with the emergence of the Young Ireland movement and co-operation between Chartists and Irish Confederates, were Irish nationalist issues more explicitly directed towards the Irish in Britain.[4] However, with the failure of the rising of the Young Irelanders in Tipperary in 1848 (which had been disowned by the bulk of the repeal movement) and the arrest and imprisonment of the leading Confederates, Irish nationalism entered a new phase with the growth of Fenianism, which was to have more significant implications for the Irish in Britain.

The Fenian Brotherhood was founded in America on St Patrick's Day 1858 by James Stephens, who had taken part in the 1848 rising and then fled to America, and John O'Mahoney. The term 'Fenian', used to describe this expatriate Irish republican movement, was derived from the Fianna, the military force led by Finn MacCool, heroic warrior of Irish legend. At the same time Stephens founded the Irish Republican Brotherhood in Ireland. Although these were separate organisations, the entire republican movement became popularly known as 'The Fenians'. Their aim was to achieve an Irish republic by force, and the function of the American organisation was to supply the IRB with arms, volunteers and money.[5] The

---

[3] For the repeal movement, see especially J.H. Treble, 'The Irish Agitation', in J.T. Ward (ed.), *Popular Movements, 1830–1850* (London, 1970).

[4] See especially J. Saville, *1848: The British State and the Chartist Movement* (Cambridge, 1987); J. Belchem, 'Nationalism, Republicanism and Exile: Irish Emigrants and the Revolutions of 1848', *Past and Present*, 146 (1995), 103–35.

[5] For Fenianism, see especially P. Quinlivan and P. Rose, *The Fenians in England, 1865–72: A Sense of Insecurity* (London, 1962); P. Rose, *The Manchester Martyrs* (London, 1970); R.V. Comerford, *The Fenians in Context: Irish Politics and Society, 1848–1882* (Dublin, 1985); J. Newsinger, *Fenianism in Mid-Victorian Britain* (London, 1994); P. Quinlivan, 'Hunting the Fenians: Problems in the Historiography of a Secret Organisation', in O'Sullivan, *The Irish World Wide*, vol. 3, *The Creative Migrant* (Leicester, 1994), 133–53; O.P. Rafferty, 'The Church, the State, and the Fenian Threat, 1861–75' (University of Oxford PhD thesis, 1996).

Fenians never attracted widespread support in Ireland, where they faced great opposition from constitutional nationalist politicians and the Roman Catholic Church.

By 1865 Stephens, who had recruited Irish-American veterans of the American Civil War, had decided to stage an armed rebellion in Ireland. For various reasons the decision to act was postponed, but rumours abounded in England of Fenian preparations, and of Fenian strength and arms dumps in Liverpool and Manchester.[6] The Fenians in England, seeing their colleagues in Ireland stymied for the time, hoped to salvage the cause from utter collapse. John McCafferty, one of 'Morgan's Raiders' in the American Civil War, devised a plan for an attack on Chester Castle with a view to capturing the arsenal, followed by the seizure of the train for Holyhead, its harbour to be used as the base for an invasion of Ireland. However, details of the plot were acquired by a police agent who had infiltrated the IRB in Liverpool and were passed on to the police and the Home Office. The ensuing raid in February 1867 was a complete *débâcle*; massive security greeted some 1,200 armed Fenians from South Lancashire when they arrived by train in Chester, and many were arrested (**Doc. 24.1**, **Doc. 24.2**). McCafferty was captured and imprisoned, and the rising in Ireland was crushed within twenty-four hours.[7]

In the summer of 1867 a Fenian terrorist campaign of sabotage and incendiarism in England struck without warning at gasworks, railways and other public facilities. By chance, Thomas Kelly, who had replaced Stephens as Chief Executive of the Fenian Brotherhood and had set up headquarters in Manchester, and another Fenian, Timothy Deasy, were apprehended and imprisoned in Manchester gaol. An attempted rescue was quickly organized by Colonel Richard O'Sullivan Burke. On 18 September a group of thirty armed Fenians waylaid a police van which was transferring Kelly and Deasy to the county gaol. The two Fenians escaped, but the fracas resulted in the death of a policeman, Sergeant Brett (**Doc. 24.3**). Five Fenians were duly apprehended and convicted of murder, of whom three – Larkin, Allen and O'Brien – were executed. Although they had been involved in the rescue, it is not certain that any of them fired the fatal shot. O'Sullivan Burke was also apprehended, charged with being an arms agent, and

---

[6] South Lancashire was the focus for much Fenian activity in England: see W.J. Lowe, 'Lancashire Fenianism, 1846–71', *Transactions of the Historic Society of Lancashire and Cheshire*, 126 (1977), 156–85. See also G. Moran, 'Nationalists in Exile: The Brotherhood of St Patrick in Lancashire, 1861–1865', in Swift and Gilley, *The Irish in Victorian Britain*, 212–35.

[7] For the Chester Raid, see *The Chester Chronicle*, 16 February 1867; F. Turley, 'Centenary of the Fenian Raid', *The Cheshire Sheaf* (Oct. 1967), 45–6; R.W. Durdey, 'The Fenians in Chester: Prelude and Aftermath', Chester College MA dissertation, 1994). Fenian reminiscences of the raid are provided by J. Denvir, *Life Story of an Old Rebel* (Dublin, 1910), 81–5, and J. Devoy, *Recollections of an Irish Rebel* (New York, 1929), 187–9. See also Quinlivan and Rose, *The Fenians in England*, 16–32.

imprisoned in Clerkenwell gaol, London.[8] The executions prompted a wave of sympathy from Irish Catholics in Britain, most of whom were sympathetic to the nationalist ideal, if not Fenian violence. The Irish writer and versifier T.D. Sullivan subsequently immortalised the 'Manchester martyrs' in his ballad *The Smashing of the Van* (**Doc. 24.4**), and in November 1868, on the first anniversary of the executions, Sullivan (who later succeeded his brother, A.M. Sullivan, as proprietor of *The Nation*), produced the ballad *God Save Ireland*, which thereafter became the unofficial anthem of the Irish nationalist movement.

In December 1867 O'Sullivan Burke and others arranged his own breakout from Clerkenwell gaol. Again, Irish intelligence got wind of the plot and informed the Metropolitan police when and how it would be executed. Nevertheless, the authorities failed to prevent a major tragedy on 13 December, when a barrel of explosives placed outside the wall of the prison exercise-yard killed twelve civilians and injured 120. Burke failed to escape. The Clerkenwell explosion resulted in popular outrage and panic, embodied in John Tenniel's *Punch* cartoon of 28 December, *The Fenian Guy Fawkes*, which not only condemned the Fenian dynamiter but also played on old anti-Catholic prejudices in a new version of the gunpowder plot. There were genuine fears of a Fenian rising and rumours proliferated of Fenian plots: arsenals were to be raided in Colchester, Canterbury and Chelmsford; Merthyr mine pit-ropes were to be cut; Lancashire railways dynamited; Shrewsbury railway station to be blown up; and the Queen and Cabinet to be assassinated. Gathorne Hardy, the Home Secretary, took elaborate security preparations in order to protect public buildings in London and the provinces in December 1867 and January 1868. A known Fenian, Michael Barrett, who claimed to have been in Glasgow at the time, was duly convicted of the bombing and was executed in May 1868. Fears of Fenian violence underlay Matt Morgan's illustration of 18 December 1869, 'The Irish Frankenstein', in *The Tomahawk*, which depicted a simianised Fenian monster awaiting Dr Frankenstein's orders to commit terrorist outrages.

Although the Fenian campaign was effectively over, Fenianism threatened the position of the Irish in Britain because violence, and particularly the Clerkenwell bombing with its loss of life, provoked strong anti-Irish feeling, and some employers showed a temporary reluctance to take on Irish labour. Yet *The Times* (12 February 1868) went to great pains to temper public opinion, pointing out that the bulk of the Irish in Britain were not Fenian terrorists but were honest, loyal and law-abiding people, adding that Anglo-Irish disagreements were political rather than a quarrel between races. Irish repudiation of the explosion was prompt, and many Irish communities in Britain publicly disavowed all connections with Fenianism; over 500 Irish Catholics met at Woolwich to denounce Fenian terror,

---

[8] Quinlivan and Rose, *The Fenians in England*, 50–53; Rose, *The Manchester Martyrs*, 53.

whilst an address signed by 22,000 London Irish was sent to the Queen pledging loyalty to the Crown and condemning the outrage.[9] Pope Pius IX denounced the Fenians, as did the Catholic Church in Britain and Ireland.

The events of 1867 brought Irish independence no closer and showed the futility of violent republicanism, although the Fenians became martyrs in the eyes of some Irish nationalists. Moreover, Fenianism had relatively little support among the Irish in Britain, despite Fenian claims to the contrary (**Doc. 24.5**). At most, there were 18,000 British members of the Brotherhood in 1865. Subsequently some Fenians, including John Denvir, turned to legitimate constitutional activities, initially, at least, as part of the Amnesty Movement, founded in London in February 1869 for the release of Fenian convicts. Although Fenian-style violence erupted in Britain during the 1880s, with bombings in Liverpool, Glasgow and London, the campaigns were directed by teams whose leadership, finance and personnel came from two Irish-American and not British Fenian organisations: the 'Skirmishers', led by Jeremiah O' Donovan Rossa, and Clan na Gael, whose leadership included John Devoy.[10] When some members of the latter were apprehended in London in 1887, the event made headline news in the popular press (**Doc. 24.6**).

Fenianism and the amnesty campaign, coupled with the 1867 Reform Act which extended the franchise to some of the Irish in Britain, supplied an impetus for the development of Irish nationalist organisations in Britain. More influential, perhaps, was the new constitutional Home Government Association, founded in Ireland in May 1870 by Isaac Butt, a Protestant lawyer and MP, whose aim was to achieve Home Rule for Ireland by constitutional means, without breaking the connection between Britain and Ireland. In 1873 the movement was renamed the Home Rule League and Home Rule League candidates won 59 seats at the general election of 1874, laying the basis for an independent Irish Parliamentary Party. In this context, Irish nationalists held that the Irish vote in Britain could be decisive in many British constituencies, as *The Nation* observed in 1872 (**Doc. 25.1**).

Between 1870 and 1872 meetings in support of Home Rule were held in several cities, including Glasgow, Liverpool, Manchester, Birmingham and London and a network of clubs and committees was established. In January 1873 twenty provincial organizations were brought together with the establishment of the Home Rule Confederation of Great Britain.[11] Based in

---

[9] O'Day, 'Varieties of Anti-Irish Behaviour in Britain, 1846–1922', 38.
[10] For further details, see especially K.R.M. Short, *The Dynamite War: Irish-American Bombers in Victorian Britain* (Dublin, 1979).
[11] O'Day, 'The Political Organization of the Irish in Britain, 1867–90', 183–211; A. O'Day, 'Irish Diaspora Politics in Perspective: The United Irish Leagues of Great Britain and America, 1900–14', in D.M. MacRaild (ed.), *The Great Famine and Beyond*, 214–39.

Manchester, the first executive of the Confederation included several ex-Fenians, including the secretary, John Denvir, for whom involvement in constitutional nationalism was an acknowledgement that revolution was no longer practicable. The title of the Confederation was several times changed over the next quarter of a century, but its character and functions changed little. In 1881 it was replaced by the National Land League of Great Britain, and in 1883 it became the Irish National League of Great Britain. Throughout this period the movement was largely controlled by the Irish Parliamentary Party: Charles Stewart Parnell, the MP for Meath and Butt's successor as leader of the Irish Parliamentary Party from 1879, was President from 1877–1883, and was succeeded by T.P. O'Connor, the only Irish Nationalist to be elected as a Member of Parliament in Britain (for the Scotland division of Liverpool from 1885 to 1929).[12]

The changes of title of the organization reflected attempts to rectify a number of inherent weaknesses in the movement. First, most Irish Catholics in Britain showed little interest in becoming actively involved; this political apathy was observed by *The Nation* in its 1872 survey and later, in 1892, by John Denvir; thus membership was relatively small, reaching a maximum of 40,000 in 1890, about one-tenth of the adult Irish male population of Britain. By 1909 membership had fallen to 25,000. Second, the League was constantly short of funds: expenditure normally exceeded income and the number of paid officials had to be reduced. Third, internal divisions within the executive and bickerings between branches impeded organizational efficiency. Fourth, the low circulation of nationalist newspapers such as William O'Brien's *United Irishman* and its successor *The Irish People* provided a further indication of the indifference of the Irish in Britain towards organized nationalism.

Between 1879 and 1882 events in Ireland hardened British attitudes to Home Rule. In 1879 Parnell had also become President of the Land League, which aimed at helping tenants to own their own land. Although both the Liberals (in 1881) and the Tories (in 1885) passed Land Acts, which fixed fair rents and provided for government grants to tenants, neither delivered on Home Rule. The violent activities of the Land League, which prompted *Punch* to depict Gladstone wrestling with the forces of anarchy, rebellion, terrorism, sedition, lawlessness, outrage, intimidation and obstruction resulted in Coercion Acts. Moreover, the murder of Lord Frederick Cavendish, the newly appointed Chief Secretary for Ireland, and Thomas Burke, the Under-Secretary (an Irish Catholic), by the 'Irish National Invincibles', a splinter-group of the IRB, in Phoenix Park, Dublin, in 1882 horrified public opinion in Britain, where it was held that Parnell was implicated in the murders.

---

[12] For O'Connor, see especially L.W. Brady, *T.P. O'Connor and the Liverpool Irish* (London, 1983).

On the eve of the 1885 general election, the Irish National League directed Irish voters in England and Scotland to vote against Liberal candidates (**Doc. 25.2**). Although the influence of Irish voters in some British constituencies was, in reality, far from decisive,[13] the eventual outcome of the election produced an interesting situation: the Liberals won 335 seats, the Tories 249, and the Irish Nationalists 86, leaving them holding the balance of power, which Parnell sought to exploit. With Gladstone's subsequent conversion to Home Rule (**Doc. 25.3a, b**), Parnell directed Irish voters in Britain to vote Liberal. The Liberals were duly returned in February 1886 and Gladstone introduced his first Home Rule Bill, proposing the establishment of an Irish Parliament in Dublin which would have control over domestic affairs. However, 93 Liberal Unionists, led by Joseph Chamberlain, voted against the Bill and it was defeated by 341 votes to 311, and the Tories were returned to power in the election of August 1886.

Thereafter, the prospects for Home Rule appeared bleak, for the 1886 election ushered in a period of Conservative hegemony at Westminster which was to last until 1906, apart from the short-lived Liberal Ministry of 1892–94. Gladstone's second Home Rule Bill of 1893 was passed by the Commons but rejected by the Lords, with its inbuilt Tory majority. The limitations of the Irish National League's outlook now became more apparent, and Parnell expressed his disappointment at the failure of the Irish in Britain to provide sufficient support for Home Rule (**Doc. 25.4**). Parnell's political career was ended in 1890 by the O'Shea divorce case, and the Irish Nationalist Party split into pro-Parnellite and anti-Parnellite factions. However, the party was reunited in 1900 under the leadership of John Redmond, MP for Waterford, who saw an alliance between the Irish Nationalists and the Liberals as the best means of securing Home Rule, and in the same year the Irish National League was reformed as the United Irish League of Great Britain under the leadership of T.P. O'Connor, who also favoured co-operation with the Liberals.

The hopes of Irish Nationalists were duly raised by the victory of the Liberals at the General Election of December 1905 and after 1910, when Asquith's Government became dependent for their majority in the Commons on the support of Irish Nationalists, Home Rule was at the forefront of the political agenda. In face of opposition from Ulster Unionists and Conservatives, the Government introduced the third Home Rule Bill in April 1912. During the political crisis which followed (see Part 8), the Bill went back and forth between the Houses at Westminster according to the provisions of the Parliament Act of 1911, which had limited the power of the Lords to counter legislation from the Commons. The Bill was not finally enacted until September 1914, by which time Britain was at war, and its

---

[13] A. O'Day, 'Irish Influence on Parliamentary Elections in London, 1885–1914: A Simple Test', in Swift and Gilley, *The Irish in the Victorian City*, 98–105.

operation was suspended – with an exclusion formula for Ulster still unresolved – until the end of the war.

Despite the flourishing yet immensely varied cultural, political and religious life developed within larger Irish neighbourhoods in British towns and cities, including London (**Doc. 25.5**), the influence of the Irish in Britain on these momentous political developments was marginal. With the exception of T.P. O'Connor's constituents in Liverpool, Irish voters had little impact on the outcome of British elections, due to their lack of concentration in sufficient numbers within parliamentary constituencies and to difficulties associated with registration.[14] Yet within the Irish Catholic districts of some British cities the cause of Home Rule was promoted by the active participation of Irish Nationalists in local politics,[15] as the careers of Dan McCabe and Dan Boyle in Manchester illustrate[16]. McCabe, the owner of a small clothing company and the leading Irish Nationalist in the city before 1914, was active in parochial confraternities in St Patrick's parish and became the city's first Catholic Lord Mayor in 1913, while Boyle, a railway clerk who became registrar of births, deaths and marriages, was the Irish National League's organiser for Lancashire and Cheshire, a correspondent for the *Freeman's Journal*, and elected Irish Nationalist MP for North Mayo in 1910. Both men were also leading Liberals in the city, playing important roles within Liberal divisional associations, and emerge as ethnic leaders and Liberal Radicals with a sincere interest in local government as well as Home Rule. By contrast, while McCabe and Boyle saw an alliance between Irish Nationalists and the Liberals as the best means to secure Home Rule, others supported the ideas of Michael Davitt, the Lancashire-born Fenian, who argued that Home Rule could only be achieved with the support of English working-class voters, and favoured an alliance between nationalist and labour interests.

In Liverpool, where there were around 10,000 members of various Home Rule organizations, forty-eight Irish Nationalists were elected to the Liverpool City Council between 1875 and 1922, although there were, as in Manchester, divisions and disagreements over the best means to achieve Home Rule. During this period the leadership of the local Nationalist movement fell progressively into the hands of more second-generation (Liverpool-born) and upwardly mobile Irishmen who were more interested in serving the needs of Liverpool's Catholic community than in the fate of Ireland. By contrast, the political activist and ex-Fenian John Denvir, the editor of the *Catholic Times*, the *United Irishman*, and the *Nationalist* (all

---

[14] ibid.

[15] See, for example, B.O'Connell, 'Irish Nationalism in Liverpool, 1873–1923', *Eire-Ireland*, 10 (1975), 24–37; P.J. Waller, *Democracy and Sectarianism: A Political and Social History of Liverpool, 1868–1939* (Liverpool, 1981); S.J. Fielding, 'Irish Politics in Manchester, 1890–1914', *International Review of Social History*, 23 (1988), 261–84.

[16] See especially Fielding, *Class and Ethnicity: Irish Catholics in England*, 87–104.

published in Liverpool) and the leading protagonist of Home Rule in the city, dedicated himself to the return of independent Irish Nationalists to the city council, while other nationalists favoured local alliances with either the Liberals, or, more cautiously, with Labour.[17]

Pro-Home Rulers were also active in other towns, including Glasgow, where membership of the United Irish League stood at 2,600 in 1908, Leeds, with 1800 members, and London, with 1500.[18] Moreover, during the Home Rule crisis of 1912–14 Irish Nationalist MPs gave public lectures in towns with substantial Irish populations; John Redmond, for example, sought to allay Protestant fears that 'Home Rule meant Rome Rule' in speeches in Scotland in November 1913 (**Doc. 25.6**). In broad terms, however, by 1914 Irish nationalist movements held little attraction for the majority of Irish men and women as they advanced along the path towards an accommodation in British society and increasingly gravitated towards conventional forms of British political expression. In this context, the rise of Labour ultimately placed the Irish vote and the Liberal alliance under strain, although the full measure of this belonged to the post-1914 period.

UNION AND REPEAL

Doc. 23.1: The Act of Union, 1800

Statutes of the Realm, 39 and 40 George III, C. 67., Articles I–IV.

Article I.   That it be the first Article of the Union of the Kingdoms of Great Britain and Ireland, that the said Kingdoms of Great Britain and Ireland shall, upon the first Day of January which shall be in the Year of our Lord one thousand eight hundred and one, and forever after, be united in one Kingdom, by the name of United Kingdom of Great Britain and Ireland . . .

Article II.   That it be the second Article of Union that the Succession of the Imperial Crown of the said United Kingdoms and of the Dominions thereunto belonging, shall continue limited and settled in the same Manner as the Succession to the Imperial Crown of the said Kingdoms of Great Britain and Ireland now stands limited and settled . . .

Article III.   That it be the third Article of Union, that the said United Kingdom be represented in one and the same Parliament to be styled *The Parliament of the United Kingdom of Great Britain and Ireland.*

Article IV.   That it be the fourth Article of Union, that four Lords Spiritual of Ireland by Rotation of Sessions, and twenty eight-Lords Temporal of

---

[17] Belchem, 'Class, Creed and Country: The Irish Middle Class in Victorian Liverpool', 190–211; Waller, *Democracy and Sectarianism*, 230–47.

[18] MacRaild, *Irish Migrants in Modern Britain*, 150.

Ireland elected for life by the Peers of Ireland, shall be the Number to sit and vote on the Part of Ireland in the House of Lords of the Parliament of the United Kingdom; and one hundred Commoners (two for each County of Ireland, two for the City of Dublin, two for the City of Cork, one for the University of Trinity College, and one for each of the thirty-one most considerable Cities, Towns and Boroughs) be the Number to sit and vote in the House of Commons of the Parliament of the United Kingdom.

Doc. 23.2: The Loyal National Repeal Association, 1842

Report on a public speech by Daniel O'Connell, *The Nation*, 20 May 1843.

Old Ireland and liberty! That is what I am struggling for. If I was to tell the Scotch that they should not have Scotland – if I was to tell the English that they should not have England – if I was to tell the Spaniards that they should not have Spain – or the French that they should not have France, they would have a right to laugh at, to hate, to attack, or to assail me in whatever manner they chose. But I do not say any such thing. What I say is, that as all these people have their own countries, the Irish ought to have Ireland. What numberless advantages would not the Irish enjoy if they possessed their own country! A domestic Parliament would encourage Irish manufactures. The linen trade, and the woollen would spread amongst you. An Irish Parliament would foster Irish commerce, and protect Irish agriculture. The labourer, the artizan and the shopkeeper would be all benefited by repeal of the union; but if I were to describe all the blessings that it would confer, I would detain you here crowding on each other's backs until morning before I would be done . . . They say we want separation from England, but what I want is to prevent separation taking place, and there is not a man in existence more loyally attached to the Queen than I am – God bless her. The present state of Ireland is nearly unendurable and if the people of Ireland had not some person like me to lead them in the paths of peace and constitutional exertion, I am afraid of the result. While I live I will stand by the throne. But what motive could we have to separate if we have all those blessings? They would all serve as golden links of connexion with England. But I would be glad to know what good did the Union do? What I want you to do is, for every one of you to join with me in looking for Repeal . . . But what do I want you to do? Is it to turn out into battle or war? Remember, whoever commits a crime gives strength to the enemy. I want you to do nothing that is not open and legal, but if the people unite with me and follow my advice it is impossible not to get repeal.

FENIANISM

Doc. 24.1: The Chester Raid: A Fenian View

John Devoy, *Recollections of an Irish Rebel* (1929), 187–9.

The Raid on Chester Castle by Captain John McCafferty . . . reawakened the English to the menace of Fenianism, and they were on the *qui vive* to deal with the March outbreak in its initial stages. Yet, if the Chester Raid had succeeded, its effect on the Rising in Ireland would have had a totally different effect.

The Fenians of Northern England answered McCafferty's call to concentrate on Chester on February 11. Michael Davitt, who had lost his right arm, tells of carrying a bag of bullets to Chester, as he couldn't use a weapon. He was not an officer of the organisation, but knew that the order was for the February date and the men in Lancashire, where he lived, obeyed it. Of course, no written record of the meetings was kept. Captain McCafferty had a surprise plan for the capture of Chester Castle which seemed to give promise of success. Several thousand rifles and a large quantity of ammunition were stored in the castle, there was no large body of troops stationed near it, and two or three steamers were anchored in the harbour. The men of the North of England were armed only with revolvers, but they would have been sufficient to enable them to overpower the small military guard in the castle and to take possession of the steamer. Loading the arms on one of the vessels would require some time, but, with the telegraph wires cut, the work could be done before any military force could arrive. McCafferty's plan was to land the arms on the Eastern Coast of Ireland near Dublin.

But the plans were all upset by the spy, John Joseph Corydon, whom nobody suspected at the time. He was trusted by McCafferty and gave the Government timely information, which enabled it to frustrate the project. Troops were rapidly moved to Chester and many of them arrived before the hour set for the attack. The Fenians were at their rendezvous, ready for action, but McCafferty did not arrive on time and they had no commander. They could not fight regular soldiers with revolvers and were puzzled by the absence of McCafferty. When he reached Chester several hours late he doubtless explained his delay satisfactorily, but the rest of the organisation were left in ignorance of it for several years. The awkward and maddening fact to him was that the train on which he was coming from London was sidetracked to allow the troop trains to pass. The North of England men could not return to their homes and would not have got their jobs back if they did, so many of them tried to get to Ireland, as they believed the fight was going on there. Three hundred of them went on a Liverpool steamer to Dublin, but a large force of police was waiting for them on the quay and they were all arrested. The number of Irishmen on the trains in the Chester area had attracted widespread attention and the townspeople were greatly alarmed, but no arrests were made in England. McCafferty made his way to Dublin, but was arrested on landing and later tried and convicted. I met him in Portland Prison and we worked at stone cutting in the same gang.

The Government was greatly alarmed at the danger of fighting in England itself. As the episode developed, Chester was only a demonstration, but its significance was not lost on the Government. There were no warships near Chester or anywhere on the East Coast of Ireland at the time and the arms could have been easily landed if Corydon had not been told of the intended attack on the castle. Then the fight in Ireland would have been begun with several thousand fully armed men, with a desperate fighter at their head. McCafferty would have probably landed in Wicklow where the mountains afford excellent fighting ground. His experience in the Confederate Army was entirely as Guerilla.

Doc. 24.2: The Chester Raid: A Police View

G.L. Fenwick, Chief Constable of Chester, *The Illustrated Times*, 16 February 1867.

In Chester the Irish population at that time was between four and five thousand, who knew of the conspiracy, sympathised with it, and contributed to its funds. On Sunday afternoon, 10 February 1867, the leaders of the movement met in the house of a member in Brickwell Street, Liverpool. Within a very select circle it had been known for several weeks that some important development was imminent, and the 'centres' in all parts of the country had been warned to be in readiness, to proceed with their men without loss of time to some point to be indicated by telegram. The meeting in question was held for the purpose of finally settling the order of procedure and to give the word. That word was 'Chester'.

At that time there were stored in Chester Castle thirty thousand stand of arms and a million rounds of ball-cartridge. The Garrison consisted only of fifty soldiers of the 54th Regiment. And in addition to the arms in the Castle, there were nearly a thousand rifles belonging to the Volunteers in a building known as the Old Cockpit, and entirely unprotected. When the details of the mad project were afterwards made known, the public were astounded by its audacity. The Fenians came provided with a few rounds of ammunition; they were first to seize the rifles in the Cockpit and then to surprise the Castle. A railway train was to be impressed into the desperate service to carry the men and arms to Holyhead, where another party was waiting to take possession of the Royal Mail steamer to carry the conspirators across to the coast of Kerry. In that county all was in readiness for the rising which actually took place a few days later, but which was shorn of much of its power for harm by the failure of the raid at Chester.

The man who conceived this scheme and was entrusted with its execution, so far as it went, was Captain John McCafferty. He had served in a corps known as 'Morgan's Guerillas', which had acquired some notoriety in the United States of America during the Civil War, and for some days he had been at Chester maturing his plans, and lodged at the King's Head Hotel in Grosvenor Street, in the name of Frederick Johnson. McCafferty was present at the meeting at Liverpool and distributed money among the officers there. Fortunately, there was amongst them one John James Corydon, who was in constant communication with the police. As soon as possible after the word 'Chester' had been flashed along the wires to Manchester, Birmingham, Leeds, Sheffield, Wolverhampton, London, and other large towns, he reported the position to the Head Constable of Liverpool, and messengers were promptly despatched to apprise the Chief Constable of Chester, arriving at about eleven o'clock on Sunday 10 February. No time was lost in warning the military and calling out the Volunteers. Late on Sunday night groups of strangers began to arrive by train. They took possession of the public rooms at the Railway Station and their officers, men of smart military bearing, patrolled the platforms in small parties throughout the night, most of them wearing a haversack slung across the shoulder by a green sash. Thanks to the prompt measures taken before daylight, in the morning the Castle and arms were in the possession of the Volunteers under the command of Major Humberston. Several large guns were brought into position, and every possible precaution taken against any attack.

Happily, nothing more was necessary. Corydon's information and the prompt measures taken in consequence saved Chester Castle, and doubtless prevented much bloodshed in Ireland. A little after midday the fifteen or sixteen hundred Fenians who had by this time arrived were hurriedly making their way out of the City in all directions. McCafferty announced at the Railway Station that 'the affair is sold'. In their alarm at the reception which had been prepared for them the fugitives threw away ammunition, pistols, daggers, and other weapons in their flight, and a large collection of these was subsequently recovered from the canal, Flookersbrook Pits, and other places. McCafferty and his lieutenant, Flood, left the City and drove to Warrington in a cab, where they took the train to Fleetwood and crossed to the Isle of Man. A few days later they were arrested while entering Dublin Bay in a collier rig from Whitehaven.

Doc. 24.3: Fenian Activity in Manchester, September 1867

The Times, 19 September 1867

About 3 o'clock the van was drawn up in front of the police court to remove all the prisoners to gaol, and among them the two Fenians. At this time the police noticed two men hanging about whom they suspected to be Fenians, and a policeman made a rush at one of them to arrest him, in which he succeeded, but not till the man had drawn a dagger and attempted to stab him. The blow was avoided. The other suspected person made his escape. In consequence of this Kelly and Deasy were put in irons before being taken to the van. When the van left the city it was drawn by two horses and was guarded behind by seven policemen. The van had proceeded about half a mile up this road when on passing under a viaduct which carries the London and North Western Railway across, with an open field on the right, a volley of shots were fired at it. The policemen, not seeing where the shots came from, dropped off the van and spread themselves out wide. There was a rush of 30 to 40 Irishmen upon the police and upon the van. One man had a hatchet, another a hammer, and a third a bayonet with which they set to work to break open the van. One man took a revolver and fired into the lock. Ultimately, men with large stones – one of them nearly 100 lb. weight – broke through the top of the van and the panels of the door behind, and set all the prisoners including the Fenians at liberty. The policemen collected in a body and made a rush to prevent the prisoners being liberated, but several revolvers were discharged among them, and one constable was shot over one of his eyes, causing his eye to protrude, and was taken to the infirmary. A young man, a bystander, was shot through the head. It is expected the Fenians, being in irons, will be recaptured. The streets of Manchester have been in a state of great excitement all the evening. The officer shot in the head is Sgt. Brett. The ball passed through his head and lodged in his hat. William O'Meara Allen, said to have fired the fatal shot, was chased and taken. Detective Bromley received a shot in one of his thighs. Another policeman was shot in his back, wounded but slightly. Both the horses in the van were shot. The driver was knocked off his box with a stone. A dozen arrests have been made. The two Fenians are at liberty.

Doc. 24.4: The Manchester Martyrs

T.D. Sullivan, *The Smashing of the Van* (1867).

Attend, you gallant Irishmen, and listen for a while:
I'll sing to you the praises of the sons of Erin's Isle.
It's of those gallant heroes who voluntarily ran
To release two Irish Fenians from an English prison van.

Hurrah, my lads, for freedom, let all join heart and hand!
May the Lord have mercy on the boys that helped to smash the van!

On the Eighteenth of September, it was a dreadful year,
When sorrow and excitement ran all through Lancashire.
At a gathering of the Irish boys they volunteered each man
To release those Irish prisoners from out of the prison van.

Kelly and Deasy were their names. I suppose you know them well;
Remanded for a week they were in Belle Vue Gaol to swell.
When taking of the prisoners back, their trial for to stand,
To make a safe deliverance they conveyed them in a van.

William Deasy was a man of good and noted fame
Likewise Michael Larkin, we'll ne'er forget his name;
With young Allen and O'Brien they took a part so grand
In that glorious liberation and the smashing of the van.

In Manchester one morning these heroes did agree
Their leaders, Kelly and Deasy, should have their liberty:
They drank a health to Ireland, and soon made up the plan.
To meet the prisoners on the road and take and smash the van.

With courage bold those heroes went, and soon the van did stop;
They cleared the guards from back and front, and then smashed in the top;
But when blowing open of the lock they chanced to kill a man.
So three must die on the scaffold high for smashing of the van.

One cold November morning in Eighteen Sixty-seven,
These martyrs to their country's cause a sacrifice were given.
'God save Ireland!' was their cry, all through the crowd it ran.
The Lord have mercy on the boys that helped to smash the van!

So now kind friends, I will conclude; I think it would be right
That all true-hearted Irishmen together should unite;
Together should unite, my friends, and do the best we can
To keep the memory ever green of the boys that smashed the van.

Doc. 24.5: Fenian Agitation in England

James Sexton, *The Life of Sir James Sexton, Agitator* (1936), 30.

The Irish Republican Brotherhood, or Fenian agitation, was spreading rapidly in those days, finding support in every corner of the world where Irishmen had settled, and in England even the Army and the police were to some extent affected. It is not surprising that my father, after the bitter experience of his youth, was immediately attracted to the movement, becoming one of its most enthusiastic adherents. Its growth was amazing. Recruiting went on night and day; and new members were enrolled at a rate that was almost staggering. I saw a good deal of this side of the Fenian effort. A railway running from Liverpool through St. Helens to the north was being constructed, and the navvies were mostly Irishmen. My grandfather was the 'boss ganger' and, young though I was, I often accompanied him and my father when they were doing 'missionary work' for the IRB, going to the shanties in which the men were housed and hearing the oath administered. I forget its exact words, but to me it seemed a fearsome pledge, with death swift and sure for the man who broke it, and I shuddered as I tried to imagine the fate of the unfortunate man who, chosen by secret ballot to inflict the penalty, should fail to do so. Members were instructed to join the local volunteer corps for the purpose of becoming efficient in the use of fire-arms, and therefore all the more valuable when the rebellion came ... hundreds of men acted upon this and many rifles were purloined from the local armoury and transported, by some mysterious means, to Ireland for secret storage until the day came when they should be wanted for use against their rightful owners.

Doc. 24.6: Capture of American Fenians, 1887

The Bromyard News and *North Herefordshire and West Worcestershire Gazette*, 24 November 1887.

CAPTURE OF AMERICAN FENIANS: DYNAMITE CONSPIRACY.   At Bowstreet court, London, in the Extradition Court, before Sir James Ingham, two men have been placed in the dock, in the special custody of two constables, to answer a charge of being in possession of dynamite, and with being concerned in a conspiracy likely to endanger life. The Court was occupied by constables and the arrest was regarded as one of the highest importance. The prisoners give the names of Thomas Callan, alias Thomas Scott, aged 46, giving an address at Lowell, Massachusetts, U.S., and 24, Baxter-road, Essex road, Islington, an operative stocking borer; and Michael Harkins, of 1939, North Second-street, Philadelphia, and 9, Alfred-street, Colebrooke-row, Islington, a grocer.

The warrant charged the prisoners with unlawfully and feloniously conspiring together to cause, by an explosive substance, an explosion in the United Kingdom of a nature likely to endanger life or to cause serious injury to property.

Mr. Superintendent Williamson entered the witness-box, and having been sworn, Mr. Alexander, the chief clerk, read over his sworn information upon which the warrants were issued. The information set out that Superintendent Williamson had received information that the two prisoners, under several aliases, had come over to England, and were then in London, and had been for several months, for the purpose of causing an explosion or explosions by means of dynamite. From inquiries which he had immediately caused to be made, he discovered that the prisoner Callan was in possession of a large heavy tin box, which he believed to contain an explosive, and which he had reason to believe he intended to use in causing explosions, by which the lives and properties of her Majesty's subjects would have been endangered. He further stated that Michael Harkins was engaged with Callan in the attempt to carry out this felonious conspiracy. He found upon him a letter signed Thomas Scott, in which reference was made to the destruction of 'tea', which meant, in his opinion, dynamite, or some explosive substance. Both the men were in possession of revolvers marked with the name of an American firm, and had about 25 cartridges fitting the revolvers which they carried. Callan described himself as a stocking-piercer of Lowell, in Massachusetts. The other man was a 'hauler' on a railway, and his home was in Philadelphia. Since their arrival in England they had not done any work, and were living under false names. Upon Harkins being arrested a paragraph cut from a newspaper was found upon him referring to a projected meeting at Birmingham, at which Mr. Balfour, the Chief Secretary, was expected to be present. The men had been seen together on several occasions.

Mr. Superintendent Williamson added since that information was sworn the house in which Callan resided had been searched, and a quantity of a substance had been found which had since been examined by Colonel Majendie and Dr. Dupre, and they had pronounced the substance to be dynamite. That was all he had to say at present, and begged that a remand might be granted. Sir James Ingham asked upon whom the letter referred to was found. Mr. Superintendent Williamson said it was found upon Callan. Sir James Ingham directed the prisoners to be remanded. They were at once removed from the dock by police-constables, and were despatched to prison in the course of the afternoon in the van, guarded by an armed escort of mounted police.

ALARMING DISCLOSURES.   By means of the arrest of Callan and the discovery of dynamite at his lodgings, the police authorities, it is said, have obtained the one piece of evidence which was wanted in order to enable them to institute a prosecution. Harkins, who, it will be remembered, was called as a witness at the inquest held on the body of Cohen, *alias* Brown, who, it has been ascertained, was the paymaster of the Clan-na-Gael gang in London, has since October 26 been under close police surveillance, and letters addressed to him have been seized by the detectives, who have kept observation upon him and Harkins, who, by the death of Cohen, was left without any source from whence he could obtain funds in this country, all the cash being secreted in Cohen's bed, admitted at the inquest that he had written to a Mr. Burchall, in Philadelphia, asking for money. Strange to say a reply to his letter was received signed by Joseph Melville, the man who succeeeded General Millen as the director of the gang, and who is now in America, enclosing £20 in bank notes. This was kept by the police, and then 'from information received', Callan was apprehended. This person has been identified as Cohen's last visitor at 42, Lambeth-road. It is understood he has been in this country about three months. A letter found upon him at the time of his arrest connects him with Millen, Melville, and Cohen. In his possession was discovered 14lb. of dynamite, which had evidently been divided into cakes, but which, through the action of time and the influence of the temperature, had run together into one solid mass. In addition to the two men who have appeared at Bow-street, there is another individual for whom anxious inquiries are being made. About him very little information appears to be in the possession of the authorities. He was a comparatively recent arrival, and it is believed was to fill the position which had been occupied by Millen and Melville. The police, therefore, have succeeded in tracing the following men: General Millen, Joseph Melville, Dennehey (who met Melville in Paris some time in August), Michael Harkins, now under arrest, Callan, also in custody, and Cohen, who is dead. When the magisterial examination is resumed, Mr. Poland will appear on behalf of the Treasury, but no opportunity has yet been given to the prisoners to instruct counsel. Harkins persists in stating that he knows nothing of the matter, but some little time ago he was, without being aware of the fact, photographed, and his portrait had been largely distributed and identified. With respect to the paragraph referred to in the sworn information, it was cut from a daily newspaper, and was in the following terms: 'Mr. A.J.Balfour, the Chief Secretary for Ireland, will address a public meeting at the Town hall, Birmingham, in connection with the Midland Union of Conservative Associations, on November 4.' In the course of inquiries made in connection with this gang of suspected members of the Clan-na-Gael, the police have ascertained the fact that Mr. John J. Breslin, whose death was cabled a few days ago from America, is the person who sent to Daly, the Birmingham dynamiter, the collection of bombs found in the latter's possession, and which were referred to in letters from Breslin as 'Love Apples.'

HOME RULE

Doc. 25.1: The Political Potential of the Irish in England, 1872

The Nation, 3 July 1872.

Between the sybarites of society who squander Irish wealth in the English metropolis, and the poor crushed and heartbroken victims who perish unnoticed by the wayside of life, there is in London, as in nearly all the large towns in England, an immense force of Irish life, energy, and intelligence, which, if organised and united, would constitute a most valuable aid in accomplishing the national regeneration of their native land. Strong in numbers, influential in position, gifted with high intelligence and clear political sagacity, and withal intensely national, there is today an Irish power in England which, if marshalled and led with one desire and one aim, would make the possession of power by any political party inimical to Irish interests or Irish rights an utter impossibility. Practically the urban constituencies are at their disposal, and hence, if so minded, the power of what is known as the great Liberal party is in their hands . . . The patriotism, the will, the power exists – organisation alone is wanting. There are Home Rule Associations and Irish political and literary unions of much promise existing in London, but none whose scope embraces the whole, or whose work could unaided produce the results which the means at the disposal of the Irish people places within their power. The destiny of our country was never more manifestly in the hands of the people than at the present moment, and this is as true of the Irish in England as of their brethren at home.

Doc. 25.2: Address to the Irish in Britain, 1885

Manifesto of the Irish National League, 21 November 1885.

To Our Countrymen in England and Scotland – The Liberal Party are making an appeal to the confidences of the electors at the general election of 1885, as at the general election of 1880, on false pretences. In 1880 the Liberal party promised peace, and it afterwards made unjust war; economy, and its Budget reached the highest point yet attained; justice to aspiring nationalities, and it mercilessly crushed the national movement of Egypt and Arabi Pasha, and murdered thousands of Arabs rightly struggling to be free. To Ireland, more than any other country, it bound itself by most solemn pledges, and these it most flagrantly violated. It denounced coercion, and it practised a system of coercion more brutal than that of any previous Administration, Liberal or Tory . . . Under such circumstances we feel bound to advise our countrymen to place no confidence in the Liberal or Radical party, and so far as in them lies to prevent the government of the empire falling into the hands of a party so perfidious, treacherous and incompetent. In no case ought an Irish Nationalist to give a vote in our opinion to a member of that Liberal or Radical party, except in some few cases in which courageous fealty to the Irish cause in the last Parliament has given a guarantee that the candidate will not belong to the servile, and cowardly, and unprincipled herd that would break every pledge and violate every principle in obedience to the call of the whip and the mandate of the caucus. The Executive of the Irish National League will communicate the names of the candidates whom they think would be excepted from the terms of this manifesto. In every other instance we earnestly advise our countrymen to vote against the men who coerced Ireland, deluged Egypt with blood, menaced religious liberty in the school, freedom of speech in Parliament, and promised to the country generally a repetition of the crimes and follies of the last Liberal Administration.

Doc. 25.3: Gladstone's 'Conversion' to Home Rule, December 1885–January 1886

The Gladstone Diaries, ed. H.C.G. Matthew, vol. XXI, July 1883 – December 1886, [a] p. 451; [b] p. 485.

[a]   Letter from Gladstone to Lord Hartington, 17 December 1885.

The whole stream of public excitement is now turned upon me, and I am pestered with incessant telegrams which there is no defence against but either suicide or Parnell's method of self-concealment.

The truth is I have more or less of opinions and ideas, but no intentions or negotiations.

In these ideas and opinions there is I think little that I have not conveyed in public declarations: in principle, nothing. I will try to lay them before you.

I consider that Ireland has now spoken; and that an effort ought to be made by the Government without delay to meet her demands for the management by an Irish legislative body of Irish as distinct from Imperial affairs.

Only a government can do it and a Tory government can do it more easily and safely than any other. There is first a postulate – that the state of Ireland shall be such as to warrant it. The conditions of an admissable plan I think are

1. Union of the Empire and due supremacy of Parliament.

2. Protection for the minority – a difficult matter, on which I have talked much with Spencer, certain points however remaining to be considered.

3. Fair allocation of Imperial charges.

4. A statutory basis seems to me better and safer than the revival of Grattan's Parliament, but I wish to hear more upon this; as the minds of men are still in so crude a state on the whole subject.

5. Neither as opinions nor as intentions have I to any one alive promulgated those ideas as decided by me.

6. As to intentions, I am determined to have none at present – to leave space to the Government – I should wish to encourage them if I properly could – above all on no account to say or do anything which would enable the Nationalists to establish rival biddings between us.

If this storm of rumours continues to rage, it may be necessary for me to write some new letter to my constituents, but I am desirous to do nothing, simply leaving the field open for the Government, until time makes it necessary to decide . . .

With regard to the letter I sent you, my opinion is that there is a Parnell party and a separation or civil war party, and that the question which is to have the upper hand will have to be decided in a limited time.

My earnest recommendation to everybody is not to commit himself. Upon this rule, under whatever pressure, I shall act as long as I can. There shall be no private negotiation carried on by me but the time may come when I shall be obliged to speak publicly. Meantime I hope you will keep in free and full communication with old colleagues. Pray put questions if this letter seems ambiguous.

[P.S.] Pray remember I am at all times ready for personal communication here should you think it desirable.

[b]   Gladstone's Memorandum on Home Rule of 30 January 1886.

I propose to examine whether it is or is not practicable to comply with the desire widely prevalent in Ireland, and testified by the return of 85 out of her 103 representatives, for the establishment, by Statute, of a Legislative body, to sit in Dublin, and to deal with Irish as distinguished from Imperial affairs; in such a manner, as would be just to each of the three Kingdoms, equitable with reference to every class of the people of Ireland, conducive to the social order and harmony of that country, and calculated to support and consolidate the unity of the Empire on the combined basis of Imperial authority and mutual attachment. W.E.G.

Doc. 25.4: Parnell on Irish Political Organisation in Britain, 1890

The Nation, 24 May 1890.

It is difficult to believe at first sight the truth of the figures which have been placed before me in regard to this matter. But it is undoubtedly true that a very large portion of our strength in this country is wasted and lost, owing to the neglect, and in some cases the inability of those Irishmen who are entitled to a vote to look after their vote and secure it.

Doc. 25.5: Irish Cultural Institutions in London, 1902

C. O'Conor Eccles, 'Scottish, Irish and Welsh London', in George R. Sims (ed.), *Living London* (London, 1902), vol. 3, 100–104.

The Irishman finds in London his own literary, athletic, political and social institutions. He may join the Irish Literary Society, and stroll down to its headquarters, where he can read all the Irish papers, have luncheon, tea, or dinner, and meet his friends, since this organisation combines the advantages of a club with lectures, concerts, and other attractions, and is becoming more and more the chief centre of social intercourse for the Irish in London. It is non-sectarian and non-political, and, as its primary object is the advancement of Irish literature, appeals to all parties. To it belong many literary men and women of Irish nationality. Several of these are members of a kindred association, the Irish Texts Society. This was established to publish, with English translations, glossaries, and notes, the large and interesting body of Irish MSS. which still exists.

The most Irish of the Irish belong to a flourishing young organisation which is friendly in its relations with the Irish Literary Society, though quite independent of it. I allude to the Gaelic League, which attracts a number of the most energetic and practical of the younger generation, and has its headquarters at Duke Street, Adelphi. Its direct object is to extend the living Irish language, and preserve the store of fine Irish songs and traditions that, without such timely help, might die out; indirectly – being based on principles of national self-reliance – it stands for the revival of Irish industries, for all that is at once national and progressive. The visitor to the Athenaeum Hall, Tottenham Court Road, will find on any Monday evening some two hundred young men and women assembled to study Gaelic. There is always a large mixture of Irish speakers who make it a point of honour at these meetings to speak in Gaelic only. Amongst them are some who, though born and bred in London and speaking English without a trace of accent, are well acquainted with the sweet native tongue of their forefathers. The League has fifteen Irish schools in the Metropolis. Recreation, on traditional lines, is not lost sight of. The Irish dancing classes are always popular, and in addition there are in summer pleasant *Seilgi* and *Scoruidheachta*, or excursions and social gatherings, with now and then a *Pleraca* or dance, while an annual music festival is held at the Queen's Hall. This has a large number of Gaelic songs on the programme, and the music is exclusively traditional. This festival is now considered the central event in the Irish musical year. It is distinct from the Irish concert always held at St. James's Hall on St. Patrick's Night, which is on the lines of the popular Scottish concert on St. Andrew's Night, and attracts the same kind of audience. On St. Patrick's Day there is a wonderful sale of so-called 'shamrock' in the London streets – most of it, alas, pure clover that grew probably in Surrey meadows. It is often decorated with sparkling bits of gold foil, and to the uninitiated looks cheap at a penny a bunch. The expert, however, notes the white dot on each leaf and the hairy stems, and prefers to get his button-hole direct from Ireland, where, indeed, there is a considerable export trade in the genuine article about this time. The religious service in honour of St. Patrick at the Roman Catholic Church, Dockhead, is unique, the hymns, sermons, and responses being respectively in Irish and Latin. It attracts a crowded congregation.

The Gaelic Athletic Association possesses some eight or nine clubs, mostly in North London, devoted to hurling, football, and athletics generally, their chief grounds being at Muswell Hill and Lea Bridge. They hold no matches or competitions with English clubs. The 'G.A.A.' has its headquarters in Ireland, and Great Britain ranks as one of its provinces, London being considered a county. There are in the Metropolis a large body of members, of whom over 200 belong to the Hibernian Athletic Club, the oldest of the group, which was founded in 1895. Hurling, as practised by Irish teams, differs in certain respects from hockey, and is a more dashing game; while the Gaelic Athletic Rules for football prohibit handling, pushing, or tripping, which are permitted by Rugby rules. When the grass is very wet, however, some of the players discard boots and stockings. The various G.A.A. clubs in London challenge each other, and then the winning team challenges some other county, as, for example, the Manchester and Liverpool G.A.A. The winner in this latter match is always expected later to play All Ireland for the championship.

In Holborn there is an Irish club, the members of which are civil servants, medical men and others; the medical men having also an association of their own at 11, Chandos Street, one of the objects of which is to secure the recognition of Irish degrees by London hospitals, which in distributing appointments often refuse to accept Irish qualifications, however capable may be the men holding them.

While the various Irish counties have no such societies as the Scottish for bringing natives together, a province, Ulster, has its own association. It owes its origin to the casual encounter of two or three enthusiastic Northerners who lamented that, proud as was the position of their compatriots in London, they had no general meeting place. Its inaugural banquet was held in January, 1897, when many recruits joined the Society, and, thanks to excellent management, the membership has since greatly increased. Balls, concerts, cinderella dances, banquets and a river trip are among the entertainments offered. The headquarters of the association are at the Hotel Cecil.

In the days of Parnell, the Westminster Palace Hotel was a favourite rendezvous of the Irish Nationalist Members of Parliament. Nowadays, however, they have no recognised centre, but hold their meetings sometimes at one place, sometimes at another. Some of them have town houses, others live in apartments, others again chum together and have rooms or chambers in common, whether in localities like Kensington or Chelsea, or on the Surrey side, which, if less fashionable, is within easier reach of the House of Commons. There are, it may be added, many purely political associations for Irishmen in London.

The above may be taken as covering Irish Ireland in London, but there is also fashionable Ireland, which, if the bull may be pardoned, is not Irish at all, since it includes wealthy non-resident Irish landlords who, for the most part, like the Duke of Devonshire and the Marquess of Londonderry, are Englishmen born and bred, but hold estates across the Channel. Many wealthy women, however, in this circle do good work in buying Irish manufactures, and no trousseau of an aristocratic bride is complete unless the dainty stitchery, the fairy-like embroidery, and the costly lace are provided by workers in some Irish convent. The Irish Peasantry Association at Stamford Street, Blackfriars, offers a free education to a certain number of the London-born children of Irish parents, preference being given to those whose fathers were soldiers or sailors. This Association also offers small prizes in Ireland for the best kept cottages. Since the establishment of the Irish Guards by Queen Victoria, in compliment to Irish valour in South Africa, the uniform and the flat cap with its green band have become familiar in the London streets. There is also a well-known Irish Volunteer regiment, the London Irish Rifles . . . Indeed, the Scottish, Irish, and Welsh elements do and have done much towards making London a world city, and in leavening the Anglo-Saxons with Celtic impetuosity and mental alertness have, with other causes, given to metropolitans a width of outlook and a receptivity not to be found in provincial towns where these elements do not bulk as largely or act as potently.

Doc. 25.6: John Redmond on Home Rule and Rome Rule, 1913

Report on Redmond's speech at Alloa, Scotland, 21 November 1913, *The Liberal Magazine*, December 1913, 686.

He could never have been a Home Ruler for one moment unless Home Rule to his mind meant a free Ireland – free for all creeds, free in all secular and religious matters from any spiritual domination, either from Rome or any place else. The truth was – and this was the best of all safeguards , and the history of the world showed it – bigotry could not long live in an atmosphere of freedom, and if there was today any illegitimate exercise of political power in Ireland – and for his own part he did not admit it – such illegitimate exercise of political power never could survive the establishment of a free parliament. Protestants, therefore, might feel secure, first, in the stringent provisions of the Bill, then in the spirit of this great Protestant nation, which would be able, at any moment, to stretch out its arm and prevent religious intolerance or injustice across the Channel. They might rest secure, also, in the commonsense of the mass of the Irish people themselves, who would know – and they were no fools – that injustice done on any ground to any man in Ireland would mean the immediate ruin of their new constitution.

Part 8

Unionism

Ulster to England
Belfast Postcard published during the 1912–14 Home Rule Crisis, from John
Killen, *John Bull's Famous Circus: lster History through the Postcard, 1905–1985*
(Dublin, 1985), 73.

INTRODUCTION

It is notoriously difficult to chart Irish Unionist activity among the Irish in Britain, and the subject has been largely ignored by historians. Most Irish migrants were Roman Catholics, many of whom held a sentimental if not practical attachment to Irish Nationalism. In contrast, Irish Protestants, most of whom were of Ulster descent, and who comprised a significant minority of the Irish-born population – although their precise numbers are difficult to ascertain – merged much more easily into the host society and are proportionately more difficult for historians to trace. This is particularly true in regard to their political activities, for whilst Unionism was in part subsumed within Orangeism (see Part 6), Irish Unionists also found safe havens in mainstream Conservatism and, from 1886, in Liberal Unionism. However, there was a relatively large Irish Protestant presence in two cities, Glasgow and Liverpool, and there is some evidence to suggest that local politics in these cities was influenced, to varying degrees, by Unionist responses to the Home Rule crises between 1885 and 1914, although the nature and extent of Irish Unionist activity in other British cities remains obscure.

In Ireland, the Union initially received strong support from the Catholic hierarchy and Catholic Unionists remained a significant minority throughout Ireland during the nineteenth century and beyond. Non-Catholics were initially divided over the Union, and Presbyterian support for the Union, which was never general, developed gradually until the Home Rule crisis of the 1880s. Most Unionists, including Protestants of Anglo-Irish or Scotch-Irish descent, populated eastern Ulster, which was more prosperous than the rest of Ireland, largely due to the development of the linen and shipbuilding industries. Ulster Protestants championed the Union from a belief that Ireland had prospered under the Union and that socio-economic progress would be undermined within a united Ireland by the relatively backward South, with its poverty and peasantry. They also feared the religious and political consequences of Home Rule, which many believed would result in the confiscation by Catholics of Protestant land, wealth and property. After the dissolution of the Repeal Association following O'Connell's death in 1847, the threat to the Union seemed to be less serious. However, Protestant fears for the Union revived with the formation of the Home Rule League in 1873, the activities of the Land League, and the emergence of a strong Irish Nationalist Party under Parnell, and from 1885 onwards Irish Unionists significantly influenced the course of British and Irish politics, principally by delaying a settlement of the Irish Question.[1]

---

[1] For Ulster Unionism during the period, see especially Patrick Buckland's seminal studies, *Irish Unionism, I: The Anglo-Irish and the New Ireland, 1885–1922* (Dublin, 1972) and *Irish Unionism, II: Ulster Unionism and the Origins of Northern Ireland, 1886–1922.*

In May 1885 the Irish Loyal and Patriotic Union (ILPU) was formed in the three southern provinces, where Protestants comprised one-tenth of the population, to organize resistance to Parnellite Nationalism. This was a non-sectarian and bi-party movement which voiced familiar Unionist concerns (**Doc. 26.1**) but only two anti-Home Rule candidates were elected in southern constituencies in the election of November 1885. In Ulster, Parnell's opponents were divided, fighting the election as anti-Home Rule Tories, Liberals and Orangemen; indeed, the anti-Home Rulers won only 16 of Ulster's 33 seats in November 1885, whilst the Nationalists took 17. However, in the face of this Nationalist success, and with Gladstone's conversion to Home Rule, the anti-Home Rule groups coalesced to form the Ulster Loyalist Anti-Repeal Union (ULARU) in Belfast in January 1886. The Union subsequently linked up with the long-established Orange Order. January 1886 also witnessed the formation of the Irish Unionist Party, led by Col. Edward Saunderson, MP for Cavan, who had joined the Orange Order in 1882 and who warned that it might be necessary to use physical force to resist Home Rule. Thereafter, the Ulster Protestants maintained an impressive front which transcended denominational differences among Presbyterians, members of the Church of Ireland, Methodists and minor sects, and which also cut across class barriers between landlord and tenant, farmer and labourer, and employer and employee.[2]

Unionist organizations were supported by the Conservative Party, who believed not only that Home Rule was a threat to the unity of the British Empire but also that Ireland was incapable of self-government and would descend into anarchy without British supervision, a view well illustrated in Tenniel's classic cartoon 'Two Forces', published in *Punch* in October 1881; this depicted the confrontation between the forces of good (Britannia, with Gladstonian physiognomy, protecting Hibernia) and evil (the Irish anarchist). In February 1886 the ULARU invited Lord Randolph Churchill, a leading Conservative, to Belfast where he promised Tory support for Unionism and uttered the ominous words 'Ulster will fight and Ulster will be right'. Later he confided to a friend that 'I decided some time ago that if Gladstone went for Home Rule, the Orange Card would be the one to play. Please God it may turn out to be the ace of trumps and not the two'.[3] In the midst of this Unionist activity, Gladstone introduced the first Home Rule Bill in April 1886. Whilst acknowledging that a Home Rule settlement should provide reasonable safeguards for the Protestant

---

(Dublin, 1973). See also Peter Gibbon, *The Origins of Ulster Unionism: The Formation of Popular Protestant Politics and Ideology in Nineteenth Century Ireland* (Manchester, 1975). For the historiography of Unionism, see A. Jackson, 'Irish Unionism', in D.G. Boyce and A. O'Day (eds), *The Making of Modern Irish History: Revisionism and the Revisionist Controversy* (London, 1996), 120–40.

[2] P. Buckland, *The Northern Ireland Question, 1886–1986* (London, 1987), 6–10.

[3] G. Morton, *Home Rule and the Irish Question* (London, 1980), 94–5.

minority, especially in Ulster, Gladstone believed that it was wrong for the Protestant minority to dominate the Irish Question when five-sixths of all Irish MPs – Ireland's chosen political representatives – were of one mind on the matter, although a powerful case against Home Rule was articulated by Albert Venn Dicey, Vinerian Professor of English Law at Oxford, who subsequently became one of Unionism's most effective propagandists (**Doc. 26.2**). The defeat of the Bill in June 1886 was greeted with celebrations in Unionist districts of Ulster and was followed by a serious outbreak of sectarian violence in Belfast. At the general election which followed, Ulster Unionists won 17 of the 33 seats in the province, a majority of one over the Nationalists.

The first Home Rule crisis was not without repercussions in areas of Irish settlement in the West of Scotland and South Lancashire. In Scotland, the crisis witnessed the collapse of the Scottish political consensus. In the previous fifty years the Liberals had dominated Scottish politics, but Gladstone's conversion to Home Rule split the Scottish Liberal vote and provided opportunities for Tory politicians to take advantage of Churchill's 'Orange Card', especially in Glasgow where Irish Protestant opinion was mobilised against the first Home Rule Bill. Other factors contributed to these developments, including Glasgow's geographical proximity to Ulster and the existence of a large Ulster Protestant community there; the feeling that any change in the status of Ireland would leave the undefended western coast of Scotland vulnerable to foreign invasion; and the concern that Home Rule would weaken imperial unity and thus jeopardise Scottish trade with the Empire. Glasgow's Irish Protestant community also feared that Home Rule would weaken the Irish economy and result in massive Irish Catholic immigration into Scotland which would threaten their livelihoods.[4] Yet there was some distance between Liberal Unionists, Conservatives and Orangemen over Home Rule, for the former, drawn largely from the business and commercial sectors of the middle class, opposed Home Rule as Liberals and rejected the populist overtones of Orangeism and its Conservative allies. Not until the Home Rule crisis of 1912–14 did Conservative-Liberal Unionist fusion occur, with the formation of the Scottish Conservative and Unionist Party.[5] This said, the political drama rarely spilled over into major communal violence on the streets of Glasgow, despite the activities of the Irish Loyal and Patriotic Union in the city, which, along with the Scottish Protestant Alliance, used anti-Catholic

---

[4] Gallagher, *Glasgow, The Uneasy Peace*, 71–3. See also Gallagher, 'A Tale of Two Cities: Communal Strife in Glasgow and Liverpool before 1914', 106–29; G. Walker, *Intimate Strangers: Political and Cultural Interaction between Scotland and Ulster in Modern Times* (Edinburgh, 1995), especially chap. 2, 'Religion, Nationality and Empire in the Home Rule Era, c.1880–1920', 17–60.

[5] McFarland, *Protestants First: Orangeism in Nineteenth-Century Scotland*, 195–6.

propaganda to rally support for the Unionist cause in 1886.[6]

By contrast, the Home Rule election campaign in Liverpool in July 1886, which coincided with Irish Protestant celebrations of the Battle of the Boyne, resulted in serious sectarian violence between Protestants and Catholics.[7] Indeed, Liverpool responded enthusiastically to the Ulster drama, not simply because of the strength of Orangeism in the city but also because the Ulster drama mirrored Liverpool's municipal quarrels and enabled the rival Tory and Irish machines to reinforce communal allegiances. In Liverpool, the local Tory party was run by a succession of party bosses, the most famous of whom was a brewer, Archibald Salvidge, who controlled Liverpool Toryism from 1890 to 1928. Salvidge's base was the Workingman's Conservative Association which, like the Orange Order, with which it had links, united the political and leisure activities of its members and was confined to Protestants. With the Irish Home Rulers presenting the main opposition on the Liverpool Council, religious sectarianism was openly fanned by Salvidge and others (see Part 6) in order to keep the working-class Tory vote intact.[8]

By 1892 there were 23 Unionist MPs, 19 of them from Ulster, and when Gladstone became Prime Minister again in that year, a number of Unionist Clubs were formed throughout Ulster. The defeat of Gladstone's second Home Rule Bill in 1893 was followed by Unionist celebrations and the tightening of Ulster Unionist control over the Unionist movement. In 1905 the Ulster Unionist Council was established at the Ulster Hall, Belfast, comprising 200 members, drawn from local Unionist organizations, the Orange Order, Ulster Unionist MPs and peers. In the same year Sir Edward Carson, a Dublin lawyer and Unionist MP for Trinity College Dublin, emerged as leader of the Ulster Unionists, and it was he who led Unionist opposition at Westminster to the third Home Rule Bill, introduced into the Commons in 1912 by H.H. Asquith, the Prime Minister and Liberal Leader since 1908.

The prolonged controversy over this Bill underlined the extent of Unionist determination to resist Home Rule.[9] Carson believed that Home Rule would be detrimental to the interests of the whole of Ireland, although

---

[6] Gallagher, *Glasgow, The Uneasy Peace*, 72.

[7] F. Neal, *Sectarian Violence: The Liverpool Experience, 1819–1914* (Manchester, 1987), 198.

[8] For further details, see Waller, *Democracy and Sectarianism*, 166–248.

[9] For the crisis over the third Home Rule Bill, see especially A.T.Q. Stewart, *The Ulster Crisis: Resistance to Home Rule, 1912–14* (London, 1967); P. Jalland, *The Liberals and Ireland: The Ulster Question in British Politics to 1914* (Brighton, 1980); P. Buckland, 'Irish Unionism and the New Ireland' in D.G. Boyce (ed.), *The Revolution in Ireland, 1879–1923* (London, 1988), 71–90; J. Loughlin, *Ulster Unionism and British National Identity since 1885* (London, 1995); Alvin Jackson, *Ireland, 1798–1998: Politics and War* (Oxford, 1999), 142–243.

most of his supporters, including James Craig, MP for East Down, saw the issue as purely an Ulster one and were prepared to see Ireland divided with Ulster remaining outside the control of a Home Rule Parliament in Dublin. With the passing of the Parliament Act, Carson knew that the Home Rule Bill could not be defeated in Parliament but believed that if the Ulster Unionists opposed it strongly enough, the government would be forced to drop the proposal. Thus Unionist resistance challenged basic assumptions about the nature of parliamentary democracy, rejecting the claim of Irish Nationalism, the majority political movement in Ireland, to speak for the whole of Ireland (in 1910 only 21 of the 105 Irish seats in the House of Commons were held by Unionists, 18 of them in Ulster), and challenging the right of a parliamentary majority at Westminster to legislate for the United Kingdom as a whole. Moreover, Ulster Unionists possessed a concept of loyalty which enabled them to proclaim loyalty to the Crown while at the same time defying Westminster, arguing that any government which forced Home Rule on Ireland would be failing in its duty to protect the interests of all its subjects.

Loyalist resistance was condemned by leading Liberals, including Sir John Simon in an address at Widnes in January 1912 (**Doc. 26.3**) while others, such as Herbert Samuel, sought to allay Unionist fears of injustice if Home Rule was granted (**Doc. 26.4**). By contrast, the Conservative opposition threw its weight behind Unionist agitation for a mixture of motives, including sympathy for the Ulster Unionist case (as a majority in Ulster), determination to maintain the integrity of the Empire, and frustration at continued exclusion from office (since the Irish Nationalists, who held the balance of power in the Commons, protected the Liberal position). Such support, and that of well-placed officers in the British army, made the coercion of Ulster into a United Ireland not just morally questionable but also virtually impossible in both political and military terms, a view with which some Liberals concurred. The signing of the Solemn League and Covenant (**Doc. 27.1**) at the Ulster Hall, Belfast, on 28 September 1912 reflected widespread opposition to Home Rule in Ulster from all social groups. The number of signatories to the Ulster Covenant was 218,206 in Ulster and 19,162 elsewhere. In addition, 228,991 Ulsterwomen signed the separate Women's Declaration in Ulster and 5,055 elsewhere. It was also claimed subsequently that two million people had signed the associated British Covenant, organized by the Grand Orange Lodge of England.

The extent to which Irish Protestant migrants and their descendants in British towns and cities sympathised with the Unionist cause in Ulster and participated in supportive campaigns in Britain during the second Home Rule crisis is by no means clear and is surely a subject worthy of further scholarly study.

Nevertheless, events in Ulster had repercussions in Liverpool and Glasgow. Sir Edward Carson visited Liverpool on 29 September 1912 – the day after the signing of the Covenant – to a tumultuous reception at the pier head from 150,000 people (**Doc. 27.2**), appealing to the 'democracy of Liverpool' to support Ulster's determination to resist Home Rule (**Doc. 27.3**), although later, in a speech at the Junior Constitutional Club in London on 22 November, he expressed some concern at the apparent public apathy in England over the Home Rule issue (**Doc. 27.4**). Liverpool Unionists stood staunchly behind Carson throughout the crisis, although Salvidge was concerned that Liverpool (with some 17,000 Orange Lodge members) might turn out to be a second Ulster, and in September 1912 he transferred an anti-Home Rule rally from St. George's Plateau to Sheil Park in order to minimise the possibilities of disorder.[10] The crisis also stimulated considerable pro-Unionist agitation in Glasgow, where 8,000 people turned out to meet Carson in October 1912, and provided local Conservatives with the opportunity to extend their support among the Protestant working classes for whom popular Toryism combined with a spirit of empire loyalism was attractive. Here, the anti-Home Rule campaign was influenced by the work of the Glasgow Ulster Association, founded in the 1880s to provide welfare support to Irish Protestant migrants in Scotland.[11]

Support for Ulster Unionism in Liverpool and Glasgow was further reflected in local recruitment to the Ulster Volunteer Force. Established by the Ulster Unionist Council in January 1913 to resist the imposition of the Third Home Rule Bill in the province, the UVF was financed by Ulster businessmen and by English supporters, including Lord Rothschild, the Duke of Bedford and Rudyard Kipling. The UVF was commanded by Sir George Richardson, a retired Indian officer who became Commander-in-Chief, and was trained by British army officers. A large disciplined force of 100,000 men duly emerged, reflected in the mass UVF parades at Balmoral, Belfast, inspected by Carson, in September 1913. Carson justified the Unionists' right to defend themselves in a series of speeches in Scotland and England in the summer of 1913: Glasgow, 12 June (**Doc. 27.5**), Edinburgh (13 June), Leeds (14 June), Norwich (16 June) and Bristol (20 June). During a further visit to Glasgow in October 1913, which prompted rallies organized by the Conservatives, the Orange Order, the Primrose League, and the Junior Imperialist League, Carson observed, in a speech at St Andrew's Hall, that 8,700 Ulstermen of Glasgow had signed the Covenant on the previous day. The platform included John Ure Primrose, Chairman of Glasgow Rangers, who had joined the Tories from a Liberal Unionist position. A Glasgow contingent of the Ulster Volunteers was duly recruited in Unionist clubs by The Reverend James Brisby, an Ulster-born Presbyterian and a leading figure of the anti-Home Rule rallies in Glasgow, and paraded through the

---

[10] Waller, *Democracy and Sectarianism*, 268.
[11] Walker, 'The Protestant Irish in Scotland', 60–63.

city centre in March 1914.[12] In Liverpool, F.E. Smith (later Lord Birkenhead), Conservative MP for West Derby, a protégé of Salvidge and one of Carson's most loyal supporters, promised Carson 10,000 Liverpudlian recruits for the UVF, although by March 1914 it was rumoured that Liverpool's Ulster Volunteers numbered far fewer – around 1500. Salvidge suggested that if they wished to go to Ulster this should be done discreetly, without stirring up sectarian violence.[13]

The Ulster Unionist Council also authorised the UVF to purchase weaponry. The task of arming the UVF was entrusted to Frederick Crawford, the UVF's Director of Ordnance, who negotiated with the German firm of Bruno Spiro in Berlin and succeeded in running 20,000 rifles and 3 million rounds of ammunition through the ports of Larne, Bangor and Donaghadee on 24 April 1914. These were then transported to secret depots throughout Ulster by methods enshrined in Ulster Unionist folklore within and without Ulster.

Irish Nationalists had responded to the creation of the UVF with the formation of the Irish Volunteer Force (IVF) in Dublin in November 1913 by Eoin MacNeill, Professor of Irish History at University College Dublin, who argued that Nationalists should take similar steps to the Unionists in order to safeguard their interests. The IVF included some Nationalist MPs and attracted members from the Gaelic League, the Gaelic Athletic Association, Sinn Fein and the IRB; it also had representatives of Redmond's Irish Parliamentary Party on its committee. With some 80,000 members by May 1914, including recruits from Glasgow and Liverpool – it was reported in March 1914 that 3,000 Liverpool Nationalists had received military training[14] – the IVF also sent representatives to Germany to purchase weapons, and on 26 July 1914, 900 rifles and 29,000 rounds of ammunition were landed in broad daylight at Howth, near Dublin.

In the midst of the crisis, Andrew Bonar Law, Glaswegian industrialist, Presbyterian from Ulster stock, and Carson's staunchest supporter within the Conservative Party, had called for a general election on the Home Rule issue (**Doc. 27.6**), a call endorsed by *The Daily Telegraph* (**Doc. 27.7**), although, as *The Liberal Magazine* observed, 'This is all very well, but Ulster expressly says that she will not "abide" by the result of a General Election. That is the salient point of the whole situation.'[15] With the threat of civil war in Ireland a distinct possibility (**Doc. 27.8**), the attention of Westminster now focused on the permanent or temporary exclusion of all or part of Ulster from the jurisdiction of a Dublin parliament. Redmond's Nationalists were prepared to accept the temporary exclusion of the most Protestant parts of Ulster (Antrim, Armagh, Down and Londonderry) from

---

[12] Walker, 'The Protestant Irish in Scotland', 61–2.

[13] Waller, *Democracy and Sectarianism*, 267–8.

[14] ibid., 268.

[15] *The Liberal Magazine*, XXI (July 1913), 413.

a Home Rule settlement, but Carson's Unionists sought the permanent exclusion of the whole of Ulster from the jurisdiction of a Dublin parliament. Talks at Buckingham Palace in July 1914 failed to reconcile Nationalist aspirations with Unionist apprehensions, and the outbreak of the First World War in August postponed further discussions. The solution eventually proposed by Lloyd George's Coalition Government in the aftermath of the war was the partition of Ireland, and under the terms of the Government of Ireland Act, which received the Royal Assent in December 1920, the Northern Ireland parliament, representing the six north-east counties of Ulster, was established.

RESISTANCE TO HOME RULE

Doc. 26.1: Union or Separation, 1886

Extract from Irish Loyal and Patriotic Union pamphlet, 1886, from P. Buckland, *Irish Unionism, 1885–1923: A Documentary History* (Belfast, 1973), 20.

Between those Roman Catholic laymen who have the courage to avow their sentiments of loyalty, and the fanatical rabble who rave against England – it is no longer against the 'Saxon' – there is a large mass of opinion, much of which is in favour of the Union, and much, no doubt, hostile to it; but, owing to the terrorism that prevails, it is impossible to say with certainty what proportion is on either side. Of one thing, however, we may be absolutely certain, that all the Roman Catholics of wealth and position, all the men of intelligence and culture, all who give strength and dignity to a cause, are on the side of loyalty and order. Of this we fortunately have evidence that cannot be controverted; we have but to summon Mr. Parnell's Parliamentary phalanx into court, and our case is proved. If the educated intellect, if the business energy, if the wealth of Catholic Ireland are on the side of revolution, why are they not to be found among the members sent to represent that cause in Parliament? . . . The answer is, because they are unanimously opposed to the revolutionary designs of Mr. Parnell and his followers; because they are loyal to the English connection, from which they and their Church have derived so many benefits; because they foresee the condition of chaos and ruin to which their unhappy country would be reduced if it were handed over to be governed by Mr. Parnell and his communistic crew . . . Those politicians in England who think that they are bound to entertain Mr. Parnell's demands, because he makes them in the name of the 'Irish people' should ponder well on these facts. If Mr. Parnell does not speak with the authority of the Protestants of Ireland, who form one-fourth of the population; if he does not speak in the name of the respectable and intelligent Catholics of Ireland, who certainly form at least another fourth of the population, in whose name and by what authority does he speak? . . . Let there be no mistake in this matter. An Irish Parliament will be composed of the same elements as are found among the Irish Members now gathered under the banner unfurled by Mr. Parnell; only its members will be more numerous, more hostile to the friends of England, more unscrupulous if that be possible – and more rapacious, less restrained by decency or prudence than they are now. And there is this further consideration, that then they will have full power to give effect to their hostility. If some eighty or ninety of the six hundred and seventy Members of the United Parliament can set the authority of the rest at defiance, how will they be controlled in an assembly of their own, where they will be in a majority of four to one?

Doc. 26.2: England's Case against Home Rule, 1886

A.V. Dicey, *England's Case against Home Rule* (1886), 28–33, 67–70.

The notion that Ireland or any one part of the United Kingdom ought, or has a claim, to have the same institutions as every other part rests on a confusion of ideas, and is a false deduction from democratic principles. It is founded on the feeling which has caused half the errors of democracy, that a fraction of a nation has a right to speak with the authority of the whole, and that the right of each portion of the people to make its wishes heard involves the right to have them granted. This delusion has once and again made Paris the ruler of France, and the Parisian mob the master of Paris. The sound principle of democratic government – and England must, under the present state of things, be ruled on democratic principles is, that all parts of the country must be governed in the way which the whole of the state as represented by the majority thereof deems expedient for each part, and that while every part should be allowed a voice to make known its wants, the decision how these wants are to be met must be given by the whole State, that is (in the particular instance) by the majority of the electors of Great Britain and Ireland. From this principle it does not follow either that every part of the kingdom should have those institutions which that part prefers (though in so far as this end can be attained its attainment is desirable), or, still less, that every part of the kingdom should have the same institutions as every other part . . . Home Rule does not mean National Independence. This proposition needs no elaboration. Any plan of Home Rule whatever implies that there are spheres of national life in which Ireland is not to act with the freedom of an independent State. Mr Parnell and his followers accept in principle Mr Gladstone's proposals, and therefore are willing to accept for Ireland restrictions on her political liberty absolutely inconsistent with the principle of nationality . . . A *bona fide* Home Ruler cannot be a *bona fide* Nationalist. This point deserves attention, not for the sake of the miserable and ruinous advantage which is obtained by taunting an adversary in controversy with inconsistency till you drive him to improve his logical position by increasing the exactingness of his demands, but because the advocates of Home Rule (honestly enough, no doubt) confuse the matter under discussion by a strange kind of intellectual shuffle. When they wish to minimise the sacrifice to England of establishing a Parliament in Ireland, they bring Home Rule down nearly to the proportions of Local Self-Government; when they wish to maximise – if the word may be allowed – the blessings to Ireland of a separate legislature, they all but identify Home Rule with National Independence. Yet you have no more right to expect from any form of State-rights the new life which sometimes is roused among a people by the spirit and responsibilities of becoming a nation, than you have to suppose that municipal councils will satisfy the feelings which demand an Irish Parliament . . . The vast majority of the United Kingdom, including a million or more of the inhabitants of Ireland, have expressed their will to maintain the Union. Popular government means government in accordance with the will of the majority, and therefore according to all the principles of popular government the majority of the United Kingdom have a right to maintain the Union. Their wish is decisive, and ought to terminate the whole agitation in favour of Home Rule.

Doc. 26.3: Sir John Simon on Ulster Loyalism, 1912

Extract from a speech by Sir John Simon at Widnes, 31 January 1912, *The Liberal Magazine*, XX (February 1912), 4.

We have been appealed to by these gentlemen [Irish 'Loyalists'] in Belfast to remember that they are the loyalists. They have shown themselves within these last ten days to be of all Irishmen the least entitled to that honourable description. They have told us they are afraid of Home Rule because intolerance is so characteristic of the Catholic population; they have shown us that if you want to see intolerance it is to the Orange Lodges of Belfast that you must go. They have pretended that they are attached to British rule. What they mean is that they are attached to Tory rule – to Dublin Castle rule; they are only attached to British rule so long as British rule leaves them to set every thing they like in their own way. They have exhausted themselves in denouncing boycotting. Did you ever hear of such an immense boycott as that they have attempted to perpetrate about the Ulster Hall? They are the self-appointed accusers of crime in Ireland. Is there any crime more dastardly than the crime of a people who, in an attempt to discredit a Government of England, are prepared to ask their own countrymen to risk their heads and their blood? They tell us that they are the party of law and order – Sir Edward Carson and his committee. They stand for law and order as long as they think law and order helps them, and the moment it does not suit their convenience they repudiate the ordinary law under which we all ought to live.

Doc. 26.4: Herbert Samuel on the Protestant Minority in Ireland, 1912

Extract from a speech by Herbert Samuel at Bretton, Yorkshire, 3 September 1912, *The Liberal Magazine*, XX (October 1912), 530.

There was no danger of the Protestants in Ireland suffering any tyranny from Catholics of that country. The Home Rule Bill made it absolutely impossible. The safeguards were ample and complete. Not only that, if an Irish Parliament were to endeavour to commit injustice or wrong, the Protestants in the British Parliament would immediately interfere to protect the Protestants, who would have behind them not only their own strength, but the whole strength of England, Scotland and Wales. The Protestants of Ireland have no fear of injustice.

CARSON AND COVENANT

Doc. 27.1: Ulster's Solemn League and Covenant, 28 September 1912

Ulster's Solemn League and Covenant, 28 September 1912, Northern Ireland Record Office, D 989a/8/23.

Being convinced in our consciences that Home Rule would be disastrous to the material well-being of Ulster as well as of the whole of Ireland, subversive to our civil and religious freedom, destructive of our citizenship and perilous to the unity of Empire, we, whose names are underwritten, men of Ulster, loyal subjects of His Gracious Majesty King George V, humbly relying on the God whom our fathers in days of stress and trial confidently trusted, do hereby pledge ourselves in solemn covenant throughout this time of threatened calamity to stand by one another in defending for ourselves and our children our cherished position of equal citizenship in the United Kingdom and in using all means which may be found necessary to defeat the present conspiracy to set up a Home Rule Parliament in Ireland. And in the event of such a Parliament being forced upon us we further solemnly and mutually pledge ourselves to refuse to recognise its authority. In sure confidence that God will defend the right we hereto subscribe our names. And further, we individually declare that we have not already signed this Covenant.

The above was signed by me at
'Ulster Day', Saturday, 28th September, 1912.
God Save the King

Doc. 27.2: Sir Edward Carson's Arrival in Liverpool, 29 September 1912

The Earl of Birkenhead, *Frederick Earl of Birkenhead: By His Son, The Earl of Birkenhead* (London, 1933), 291.

Fifteen thousand people waited for the ship in a drizzling rain on the dock of Liverpool. They were the English reserves in the fight for Ulster. It was the early hours of Sunday: the wind was in the east; yet the crowd at the docks was only the vanguard of the vast concourse which was massed down Dale Street and Water Street as far as the eye could reach. It was a hundred thousand strong, the greatest crowd that Liverpool had ever seen, men and women of all ages and of all classes. There was in their enthusiasm a religious tinge which showed that Liverpool had consecrated itself in what it believed to be a sacred cause. The meeting was practically spontaneous. There had been little preparation. At ten minutes to eight the Patriotic came into view: the rain ceased, and a struggling sun broke through the clouds. The haze on the river lifted, and the crowd was revealed waiting in a superb marine amphitheatre with the Princes stage below, the upper stage immediately above, and the Princes Parade higher still in the background, all visible from the deck of the steamer. The ship drew alongside; her Union Jacks fluttering, and her siren screaming: there was an immediate thrilling response from the shore: the great crowd broke into a sudden deep-throated cheer: twenty drums were rolled, hats were waved, handkerchieves fluttered. Twenty bands clashed forth defiance and hopes of victory. There were brass bands, and concertina bands, there were waving banners, many woven with the figure of William III, Saviour of British Liberties and Champion of Protestantism. They broke into loud cheers; again, 'O God, our help in ages past' was sung. Archibald Salvidge was ready with an address of welcome – then the party disembarked, crowded into two open brakes and drove off. Soon the brakes were enveloped in the crowd: the horses were taken from the shafts and the brakes were dragged to the Club by the yelling crowd. So far as the eye could see forward or backward the streets were black with people, but all orderly and good tempered.

Doc. 27.3: Appeal by Carson to the Unionists of Liverpool

Extract from a speech by Sir Edward Carson, Liverpool, 29 September 1912, *The Liberal Magazine*, XX (October 1912), 534.

I bring a simple message from the democracy of Belfast to the democracy of Liverpool. They tell you they were born fellow-citizens in the same community that you were, and all they ask in their own simple way is that they should stay with you. And they tell you that so certain are they that the whole interests of their country and their civil and religious liberty are bound up with the maintenance of the connection between you and them, that they have solemnly pledged themselves that under no circumstances will they ever accept a Home Rule Parliament in Dublin to govern them.

Doc. 27.4: Carson on Apathy in England on Irish Home Rule, December 1912

Report on a speech by Sir Edward Carson at the Junior Constitutional Club, London, 22 November 1912, *The Liberal Magazine*, XX (December 1912), 650.

The one thing which more than all others filled him with despair was that he met so many men in this country who cared about nothing, who did not seem to think that the British Constitution was worth a thought, or a consideration, or a sacrifice. He came across men who said, 'Why do you bother about all this? You could go on making plenty of money by your profession. You could go on living a life, at your age, of ease and comfort'. That was in the upper stratum of society. It might be a shame, but it was prevalent; it was the apathy of men who were well off. Coming to a lower stratum, there were men who asked, 'How does it affect me?' He became almost hopeless when he heard these things said.

Doc. 27.5: Carson Affirms Unionist Resistance to Home Rule, June 1913

Extract from a speech by Sir Edward Carson, Glasgow, 12 June 1913, *The Liberal Magazine*, XXI (July 1913), 348.

We are determined under no circumstances, under no conditions, regardless of consequences and regardless of sufferings, even for one moment to submit to a Home Rule Parliament in Dublin. We have signed our Covenant; we will stick to the letter and the spirit of it. So far as I am concerned, I advise my fellow-countrymen to resist to the end, even if it comes to the necessity of using violence. I advise my fellow-countrymen, even although it may never be necessary – and please God it never will be necessary to use them – to arm themselves as well as they can to beat back any body who dares to filch from them the elementary rights of their citizenship. I have been told sometimes that I ought to remember the Oath I took as a Privy Councillor. Mr Chairman, I have taken it more than once, and I never forget it, My Oath of Allegiance was to King George. I know no other one to whom I have any allegiance. If I break my Oath as a Privy Councillor, well, I have something more I value – highly as I value it – than being a Privy Councillor; I value my honour, and I value my conscience.

Doc. 27.6: Bonar Law Supports Ulster Resistance, 1913

A conversation with Asquith, October 1913, from R. Blake, *The Unknown Prime Minister: The Life and Times of Andrew Bonar Law* (London, 1955), 162.

I pointed out to him that in our opinion the real way out was in a General Election . . . We then discussed what would happen if they went straight on with their present programme. He said that what would happen in that case was purely speculative, that no one could tell what the effect on public opinion would be if they resolutely carried out what they believed to be the law. I agreed that nobody could know in advance; but I told him that in my opinion, at bottom one of the strongest feelings in England and Scotland was Protestantism, or dislike of Roman Catholicism, and that if Protestants of Belfast were actually killed, then in my belief, the effect in Great Britain would be not only that the Government would be beaten but that they would be snowed under . . . I then said to him that of course the prospect before us was not attractive. We should have to try by all means to force an Election, and to be successful we should have to take means which would be distasteful to all of us, and in saying that, I hinted at the possibility of disorder in the House of Commons, of using the letter of the Parliament Act, and as a result of all this of his finding that the Army would not obey orders. He very mildly expressed surprise that we had pledged ourselves so definitely to support Ulster in resistance.

27.7: A Call for a General Election, 1913

The Daily Telegraph, 9 June 1913.

The Unionist Party in England may shortly have to face some momentous decisions in respect of Ulster. But there will be no difficulty and no hesitation so long as the Government refuse to allow the country to have an opportunity of saying whether it consents to Home Rule or not. If Ulster is to be cast out of the Union, let the people say so! If she is to be dragooned into subjection to the Nationalists, let the people assume full responsibility for the decision! The people can only speak by means of a General Election. For that, in their name, we call, and by their decision, and that alone, we will and they abide.

Doc. 27.8: The Threat of Civil War in Ireland

The Times, 27 July 1914.

Grave News from Ireland . . . The grave news which we publish this morning from the European capitals is accompanied, we are sorry to say, by very serious intelligence from Ireland. An attempt at gun-running by the National Volunteers near Dublin yesterday morning resulted in collisions between the Volunteers, the public, the police, and the military. Four persons were killed and some sixty injured, of whom several are not expected to live. The excitement in Dublin is intense. The incident is from every point of view deplorable; but it is emphatic testimony to the true position of affairs across the Irish Channel. The nation to which a Liberal Administration was to bring a message of peace is mobilised for internal war. The past week has seen one more hope of a settlement vanish in thin air. One spark, struck from such a momentary collision as that in Dublin yesterday, may serve, when and where we least expect it, to set in train the long-dreaded conflagration . . . There can no longer be the slightest doubt that the country is now confronted with one of the greatest crises in the history of the British race. The issue was not present in the minds of the electorate at the last election; it is thoroughly present now . . . It is not clear that the Government could go to the country on the single question of Home Rule. It is clear beyond dispute that they ought to consult the electorate before taking steps which must manifestly end in civil war.

A Note on Primary Sources

As the extracts included in this collection perhaps illustrate, the nature, extent and quality of primary source materials for the study of the Irish in Britain during the nineteenth century is variable in the extreme, but there are some essential general sources which provide various insights into the experiences of Irish migrants during the period. They are deposited in most national repositories, university libraries and county and city record offices.

CENSUS ABSTRACTS AND SCHEDULES, 1801–1911, are an essential source for the study of Irish migration and settlement. From 1841 onwards they recorded the place of birth of all persons listed in the census, hence it is possible to calculate the number of Irish-born on local, regional and national levels and to abstract a range of demographic data relating to the origins and distribution of Irish-born, age and sex ratios, familial and household structures, employment patterns, in- and out-migration, and residential and social mobility. However, the census returns do not provide a reliable indication of the true size of ethnic Irish communities in that the children of Irish-born immigrants were variously classified as English, Scottish or Welsh. The census returns also miss inter-censal changes, which were of significance in the case of the Irish, who contained a transient element.

PARLIAMENTARY PAPERS (or 'Blue Books'), comprising the reports of the Royal Commissions and Select Committees of Parliament which examined a range of contemporary social, economic, political and cultural issues during the nineteenth century, contain a wealth of disparate material pertaining to the Irish in Britain, as illustrated in the *Catalogue of British Parliamentary Papers, 1801–1900* published by Irish Academic Press (Dublin, 1977). The most important of these is unquestionably *The Report of the Royal Commission on the Condition of the Poorer Classes in Ireland*, Appendix G, *Report into the State of the Irish Poor in Great Britain* (1836), which constitutes a seminal source for the study of the Irish in Britain, and attitudes towards them, during the early nineteenth century. Popularly referred to as the Cornewall Lewis Report, it contains detailed testimony from factory-owners, poor law officials, clergymen and policemen on the social and economic consequences of Irish settlement and employment in the industrial and manufacturing districts of the Midlands, South Lancashire and Scotland.

The process and consequences of migration from Ireland during the Famine is examined in several 'Blue Books'. *The Report of the Select*

Committee on Emigration (1826–7) argued that the precarious position of hand-loom weavers had been exacerbated by Irish immigration to Scotland and Northern England, lowering wages and undercutting local employment. The witnesses included Thomas Malthus, who argued that emigration from Ireland to Britain should be proscribed and that Irish landlords should encourage their tenants to emigrate to North America. The *Famine (Ireland) Reports: Correspondence on Relief Measures* (1847) contains a wealth of material on the nature and scale of Irish migration to Liverpool at the height of the Famine, and on the reception of Irish paupers at the port. The *Report of the Select Committee on Poor Removal* (1854) documents the plight of Irish paupers, many of whom were subsequently repatriated, in Liverpool, Manchester, Cardiff, Glasgow and Edinburgh during the Famine period, and provides statistical information on the number of Irish pauper immigrants and the number and cost of removals. Irish immigration was also the major issue examined in the *Reports of the Select Committees on Poor Removal and the Irremovable Poor* (1854–5, 1857–8 and 1859), which described the problems faced by the Irish populations of Bradford, Birmingham, Manchester and Newcastle, whilst the *Reports of the Select Committee on Emigrant Ships* (1854) contain horrendous descriptions of the conditions faced by Famine emigrants on some of the vessels that sailed from Ireland to Britain, and from Britain to North America.

The social condition of Irish migrants in the towns and cities of early Victorian Britain, including London, Liverpool, Manchester, Birmingham, Glasgow and Edinburgh, is described in the various *Reports on the State of Large Towns and Populous Districts* (1844–5), more commonly referred to as the 'Health of Towns' series, which are particularly useful sources for the study of public health and housing. Similarly, the *Local Reports to the General Board of Health on the Sanitary Condition of Large Towns and Populous Districts* (1848–54) include specific references to the insanitary condition of poor Irish districts and also illustrate the impact of mass Irish migration during the Famine period on already overcrowded and insanitary urban slums. By contrast, the *Report of the Select Committee on Public Houses* (1852–3) received evidence on the operation of the licensing laws in the provinces and contains some interesting references to Irish pub culture in several towns, including Wolverhampton and Birmingham, while the *Religious Census: England and Wales* (1852–3) and the *Education Census: England and Wales* (1852–3) illustrate in part the efforts made by the Roman Catholic Church to meet the spiritual and educational needs of Irish migrants.

Insights into the employment of Irish migrants are provided by the *Report of the Select Committee on Combinations of Workmen* (1837–8), which contains some material relating to the role of Irish migrants in early trade unionism in the textile industry, notably in Manchester, Glasgow, Dublin and Belfast. It also includes evidence from John Doherty. The plight of Irish weavers is also touched on in the *Report of the Royal Commission on Hand-loom Weavers* (1841), which investigated the condition of hand-loom workers in the West Riding and Scotland, with particular reference to their impoverished state, the irregularity of their work, and the employment of women and children. By contrast, the *First Report from the Royal Commission on Labour* (1892), which dealt with the question of shipping and dockland labour in London's East End in the aftermath of the 1889 Dock Strike, is of relevance to the study of casual Irish dock labour. It contains information on methods of hiring, unemployment, labour disputes, conflicts between unionists and non-unionists, and dockers' homes, and includes evidence from Ben Tillett.

Finally, two 'Blue Books' provide some insights into Irish political culture in Britain. *The Report of the Select Committee on Orange Institutions in Great Britain* (1835) revealed for the first time the character and extent of Orange institutions, which had spread far beyond Ireland since their foundation in 1795, and provided evidence of the rules and rituals of Orange lodges, lists of officers and meeting-places in Britain, and material relating to terrorist activities attributed to Orangemen. The Select Committee concluded that Orange societies threatened army discipline and public order and recommended their suppression. By contrast, the *Reports relating to Treason-Felony Prisoners* (1866 and 1871) deal with the treatment in prison of leading Fenians apprehended and convicted during the period, including Jeremiah O'Donovan Rossa, James Stephens and Daniel O'Sullivan. They also record Stephens's escape from Richmond Gaol as well as complaints about the treatment of Fenian prisoners in Pentonville, Chatham and Woking prisons.

CONTEMPORARY NEWSPAPERS such as *The Times*, *The Observer* and *The Manchester Guardian* are a valuable source for examining contemporary attitudes towards the Irish on specific issues, including the Famine, the Catholic Revival, Fenianism, and Home Rule, whilst alternative perspectives are provided by *The Tablet*, *The Catholic Herald*, and *The Nation*. Periodicals such as *Punch* and *The Illustrated London News* perform a similar function: the former through the publication of a range of satirical and stereotypically anti-Irish political cartoons; the latter through some of its featured articles from special correspondents, most notably on Irish emigration during the 1850s.

CONTEMPORARY PAMPHLETS AND SURVEYS, some of which are in a sense both primary and secondary sources, shed some light on the experience of the Irish in urban Britain during the period. These include the relevant sections in Thomas Carlyle's *Chartism* (1839); the chapters on 'The Great Towns' and 'The Irish Immigration' in Frederick Engels, *The Condition of the Working Class in England* (1845); Henry Mayhew's *London Labour and the London Poor* (1861–2); and Charles Booth's *Life and Labour of the People in London* (1902–3). In essence, these sources offer non-Irish perceptions of the Irish migrant experience. By contrast, the series of articles written by Hugh Heinrick, a Wexford-born schoolteacher in Birmingham, which were published in *The Nation*, an Irish nationalist newspaper printed in Dublin, between July and November 1872, provide an Irish perspective on the experiences of Irish migrants in England. The survey, edited by Alan O'Day and published as *A Survey of the Irish in England in 1872* (1990), had some obvious weaknesses. It was limited to England and *The Nation* did not commission a further series on the Irish in either Wales or Scotland. Moreover, the coverage is patchy, for Heinrick did not visit all of the places described in the text, hence the most valuable sections are the largely first-hand accounts of the Irish settlement and employment in Leicester, Birmingham, the Black Country, Lancashire, Yorkshire and the North-East. Yet this unique survey illustrated just how difficult it was for the Irish to preserve a separate identity in the long-term, for although they were located disproportionately among the labouring poor, there was a degree of Irish upward mobility within the labour market, demonstrating differences in Irish employment patterns over space and generations and placing occupational profiles and differential wage-rates in their local and regional contexts. Likewise, the chapters on 'The Irish in Various Districts of Great Britain' in John Denvir's *The Irish in Britain from the Earliest Times to the Fall and Death of Parnell* (1892), which draw on personal observation, anecdotal evidence, and information gathered from the Census of 1881 and 1891, also provide an Irish Nationalist perspective on the condition of the Irish in late Victorian Britain.

PERSONAL REMINISCENCES of Irish migrants themselves are relatively thin on the ground, although there is some useful material in John Denvir's *Life Story of an Old Rebel* (1910), including descriptions of his early life in Liverpool; Patrick MacGill's autobiographical novel, *Children of the Dead End: The Autobiography of a Navvy* (1914), which covers his life from infancy in Donegal to his move to London and includes detailed descriptions of the poverty he encountered in casual employments en route; John Devoy's *Recollections of an Irish Rebel* (1929); Tom Barclay's *Memories and Medleys: The Autobiography of a Bottlewasher* (1934), which describes Barclay's upbringing in Victorian Leicester; and Pat O'Mara's *The Autobiography of a Liverpool Irish Slummy* (1934), which contains some vivid descriptions of the author's childhood in Edwardian Liverpool; whilst Robert Roberts's *The Classic Slum* (1971) contains some interesting reflections on attitudes to Irish migrants in Edwardian Salford. Clearly, as the collection of reminiscences edited by Lennon, McAdam and O'Brien, *Across the Water: Irish Women's Lives in Britain* (1988) indicates, oral evidence could illuminate our understanding of the experience of Irish migrants in early twentieth-century Britain, and there is considerable potential for further research in this area.

LETTERS written to family and friends in Ireland by Irish men and women who emigrated during the nineteenth century constitute an invaluable resource for the study of the Irish Diaspora, as David

Fitzpatrick's majestic study, *Oceans of Consolation: Personal Accounts of Irish Migration to Australia* (Cork, 1994), well illustrates. By contrast, few Irish migrants in Britain wrote letters to each other, and even fewer survive, thus denying historians a potentially rich resource for exploring the more personal and private side of Irish migrant life. However, some Irish migrants wrote letters to relatives abroad and these included members of the Reynolds family of Manchester, who migrated to the city from Mohill, County Leitrim, during the Great Famine, and whose correspondence with their relatives in Chicago has been edited by Lawrence McBride and published by Cork University Press as *The Reynolds Letters: An Irish Emigrant Family in Late Victorian Manchester* (1999). As these letters show, not all Irish migrants were doomed to a life of poverty in Britain, for the Reynolds family subsequently acquired wealth and respectability in Manchester as the dyeing and cleaning works of William Reynolds – one of six children who had left Ireland with their widowed mother – prospered.

LOCAL SOURCES: The general sources alluded to above contain much local evidence which, though disparate, can be synthesized in order to provide a framework for further local research. The range of local sources deposited in county and city record offices and other archives is also broad, although the quality and quantity of the evidence may vary from one locale to another and the historian often faces a time-consuming task in sifting through a mass of documentary material in the search for references to themes associated with Irish migration and settlement during the period. Nevertheless, Board of Health Reports, Sanitary Committee Minutes and Lodging House Committee Minutes can shed light on Irish living conditions and issues relating to public health and housing. Poor Law Board of Guardians Minute and Letter Books, Out-Relief Registers, and Workhouse records, are invaluable sources for the study of Irish poverty. School Log Books and, from 1870, School Board Minutes can provide insights into the educational provisions for Irish children and the children of the Irish-born, whilst Roman Catholic Diocesan Archives also contain statistics and reports in regard to Catholic education and religious practice, plus a wealth of miscellaneous material, including the records of Catholic Friendly and Benefit societies. Quarter Sessions and Assize Calendars, Petty Sessions Registers, Watch Committee Minutes and the Annual Reports of Chief Constables are essential sources for the study of the nature and patterns of Irish criminality, while Home Office Disturbance Papers (located in the Public Records Office), which contain correspondence between the Home Office and provincial magistrates and chief constables during popular disorders, are particularly useful in the examination of disturbances such as the Stockport Riots or the Murphy Riots which contained an Irish dimension. Of course, the information contained in these essentially qualitative forms of evidence may be complemented by material gleaned from local newspapers, which are of considerable value in the examination and analysis of attitudes towards the Irish on a whole range of local social, economic, political and cultural issues and, occasionally, on national issues with an Irish dimension.

Thus there are plenty of opportunities for students to conduct research on their own Irish community's history during the nineteenth century, and these sources can help them to do so. First, it is necessary to discover how many people born in Ireland were living locally by looking at the 1841 census, and this also provides the opportunity to conduct a simple demographic study of the local Irish by determining where the Irish-born lived, by examining their familial and household structures, and by recording their occupations. Sophisticated quantitative analysis on this and later census schedules, particularly on a comparative basis, can indicate who the Irish were and how they lived, and how their experience changed in time, although this requires the use of specialist techniques, a great deal of time and a computer. Second, and using the census data as a base, it is possible for students to use a range of qualitative sources in order to develop thematic studies – on topics such as public health, housing, poverty, employment, crime, education and religion – of the social history of local Irish communities. Moreover, these are precisely the kind of sources which will enable students to address some of the major issues related to the Irish experience in nineteenth-century Britain and will help them to discover just how far the Irish were the 'outcasts' of society or whether they lived in peace, as an increasingly accepted and acceptable part of the local social landscape.

Bibliography

Primary Sources

Anon., 'The London Irish', *Blackwood's Edinburgh Magazine*, vol.170 (July 1901), 124–34.

Barclay, T., *Memories and Medleys: The Autobiography of a Bottlewasher* (Leicester, 1934).

Booth, C., *Life and Labour of the People of London*, Series 1, *Poverty*, 4 vols; Series 2, *Industry*, 5 vols.; Series 3, *Religious Influences*, 7 vols. (London, 1902–3).

Carlyle, T., *Chartism* (London, 1839).

Denvir, J., *The Irish in Britain from the Earliest Times to the Fall and Death of Parnell* (London, 1892).

——, *Life Story of an Old Rebel* (Dublin, 1910).

Devoy, J., *Recollections of an Irish Rebel* (New York, 1929).

Engels, F., *The Condition of the Working Class in England* (1844 trans. and ed. Henderson, W.O. and Chaloner, W.H., Oxford, 1958).

Gainsforce, R.J., 'English and Irish Crime', *Dublin Review*, 42 (March 1857), 142–56.

Gallagher, P., *My Story. By Paddy the Cope* (London, 1939).

Garratt, S., 'The Irish in London', in *Motives for Missions* (London, 1852).

Heinrick, H., *A Survey of the Irish in England in 1872* (Dublin, 1872; edited by Alan O'Day, London, 1990).

Kay, J.P., *The Moral and Physical Condition of the Working Classes Employed in the Cotton Manufacture in Manchester* (Manchester, 1832).

Lennon, M., McAdam, M., and O'Brien, J., *Across the Water: Irish Women's Lives in Britain* (London, 1988).

MacGill, P., *Children of the Dead End: The Autobiography of a Navvy* (London, 1914).

Mayhew, H., *The Morning Chronicle Survey of Labour and the Poor: The Metropolitan Districts*, 6 vols. (London, 1849–50; reprinted Firle, 1980, with an introduction by P. Razzell).

——, *London Labour and the London Poor*, 4 vols. (London, 1861–2; reprinted New York, 1968).

——, and Binny, J., *The Criminal Prisons of London* (London, 1862).

McBride, L.W. (ed.), *The Reynolds Letters: An Irish Emigrant Family in Late Victorian Manchester* (Cork, 1999).

O'Connor, T.P., *Memoirs of an Old Parliamentarian* (2 vols., London, 1929).

O'Day, A., *A Survey of the Irish in Britain, 1872* (London, 1990).

O'Neill, J., 'Fifty Years Experience as an Irish Shoemaker in London', *St. Crispin*, nos. 1 and 2 (1869).

O'Mara, P., *The Autobiography of a Liverpool Irish Slummy* (London, 1934; rev. ed., Liverpool, 1998).

Roberts, R., *The Classic Slum: Salford Life in the First Quarter of the Century* (London, 1971).

Royal Commission on the Conditions of the Poorer Classes in Ireland, Appendix G, The State of the Irish Poor in Great Britain, Parliamentary Papers (1836), XXXIV.

Sexton, J., *Sir James Sexton: The Life Story of an Agitator* (London, 1936).
Thackeray, W.M., *The Irish Sketchbook* (1843).
Thompson, F., *Lark Rise to Candleford* (London, 1930).
Tillett, B., *Memories and Reflections* (London, 1931).
Todd, W.G., 'The Irish in England', *Dublin Review*, 41 (September 1856), 470–521.
Waugh, N., *These, My Little Ones* (London, 1911).

Secondary Sources

A.   BOOKS AND CONTRIBUTIONS TO BOOKS

Akenson, D.H, *The Irish Diaspora: A Primer* (Belfast, 1996), chap. 8, 'Great Britain: The Place Nearest Home', 189–216.
Arnstein, W.L., *Protestant versus Catholic in Mid-Victorian England: Mr. Newdegate and the Nuns* (Columbia and London, 1982).
Aspinwall, B., 'The Catholic Irish and Wealth in Glasgow', in Devine,T.M., *Irish Immigrants and Scottish Society in the Nineteenth and Twentieth Centuries* (Edinburgh, 1991), 91–115.
——, 'A Long Journey: The Irish in Scotland', in O'Sullivan, P. (ed.), *The Irish World Wide*, vol. 5, *Religion and Identity* (Leicester, 1996), 146–82.
Aspinwall, B. and McCaffrey, J., 'A Comparative View of the Irish in Edinburgh in the Nineteenth Century', in Swift, R. and Gilley, S. (eds), *The Irish in the Victorian City* (London, 1985), 130–57.
Bartlett, A., 'From Strength to Strength: Roman Catholicism in Bermondsey up to 1939', in Fielding, S.J. (ed.), *The Church and the People: Catholics and their Church in Britain, 1880–1939* (University of Warwick, 1988), 29–47.
Beck, G.A. (ed.), *The English Catholics* (London, 1951).
Belchem, J.C., '1848: Feargus O'Connor and the Collapse of the Mass Platform', in Epstein, J. and Thompson, D. (eds), *The Chartist Experience* (London, 1982).
——, 'English Working-Class Radicalism and the Irish, 1815–50', in Swift, R. and Gilley, S. (eds), *The Irish in the Victorian City* (London, 1985), 85–97.
——, *Industrialization and the Working Class: The English Experience, 1750–1900*, (Aldershot, 1990).
—— (ed.), *Popular Politics, Riot and Labour: Essays in Liverpool History, 1790–1940* (Liverpool,1992).
——, 'Liverpool in the Year of Revolution: The Political and Associational Culture of the Irish Immigrant Community in 1848', in Belchem, J., *Popular Politics, Riot and Labour* (1992), 68–97.
——, 'The Irish in Britain, United States and Australia: Some Comparative Reflections on Labour History', in Buckland, P. and Belchem, J. (eds), *The Irish in British Labour History* (1993), 19–28.
——, 'The Immigrant Alternative: Ethnic and Sectarian Mutuality among the Liverpool Irish during the Nineteenth Century', in Ashton, O., Fyson, R., and Roberts. S. (eds), *The Duty of Discontent: Essays for Dorothy Thompson* (London, 1995), 231–50.
——, 'Class, Creed and Country: The Irish Middle Class in Victorian Liverpool', in Swift, R. and Gilley, S. (eds), *The Irish in Victorian Britain: The Local Dimension* (1999), 190–211.
——, 'The Liverpool-Irish Enclave', in MacRaild, D.M. (ed.), *The Great Famine and Beyond* (2000), 128–46.

Bermant, C., *London's East End: Point of Arrival* (New York, 1975).

Best, G.F.A., 'Popular Protestantism in Victorian Britain', in Robson, R. (ed.), *Ideas and Institutions of Victorian Britain* (London, 1967), 115–42.

Bielenberg, A. (ed.), *The Irish Diaspora* (Harlow, 2000).

Bohstedt, J., 'More than One Working Class: Protestant and Catholic Riots in Edwardian Liverpool', in Belchem, J., *Popular Politics, Riot and Labour* (1992), 173–216.

Bossy, J., *The English Catholic Community, 1570–1850* (London, 1975).

Boyce, D.G., *Englishmen and Irish Troubles* (London, 1972).

Boyce, F., 'From Victorian 'Little Ireland' to Heritage Trail: Catholicism, Community and Change in Liverpool's Docklands', in Swift, R. and Gilley, S. (eds), *The Irish in Victorian Britain: The Local Dimension* (1999), 277–97.

Brady, L.W., *T.P. O'Connor and the Liverpool Irish* (London, 1983).

Brooke, D., *The Railway Navvy* (Newton Abbot, 1983).

Bryson, A., 'Riotous Liverpool, 1815–60', in Belchem, J., *Popular Politics, Riot and Labour* (1992), 98–134.

Buckland, P. and Belchem, J.C. (eds), *The Irish in British Labour History* (Conference Proceedings in Irish Studies, University of Liverpool, 1993).

Busteed, M.A., '"The Most Horrible Spot"?: The Legend of Manchester's Little Ireland', in Briggs, S., Hyland, P. and Sammells, N. (eds), *Reviewing Ireland: Essays and Interviews from Irish Studies Review* (Bath, 1998), 74–89.

——, 'Little Islands of Erin: Irish Settlement and Identity in Mid-Nineteenth Century Manchester', in MacRaild, D.M. (ed.), *The Great Famine and Beyond* (2000), 94–127.

——, Hodgson, R.I., and Kennedy, T.F., 'The Myth and Reality of Irish Migrants in Mid-Nineteenth-Century Manchester: A Preliminary Study', in O'Sullivan, P. (ed.), *The Irish World Wide*, vol. 2, *The Irish in the New Communities* (Leicester, 1992), 26–51.

Butt, J., 'Belfast and Glasgow: Connections and Comparisons, 1790–1850', in Devine, T.M. and Dickson, D. (eds), *Ireland and Scotland, 1600–1850* (Edinburgh, 1983).

Campbell, S., 'Beyond 'Plastic Paddy': A Re-examination of the Second-Generation Irish in England', in MacRaild, D.M. (ed.), *The Great Famine and Beyond* (2000), 266–88.

Canavan, B., 'Story-tellers and Writers: Irish Identity in Emigrant Labourers' Autobiographies, 1870–1970', in O'Sullivan, P. (ed.), *The Irish World Wide*, vol. 3, *The Creative Migrant* (Leicester, 1994), 154–69.

Champ, J., 'The Demographic Impact of Irish Immigration on Birmingham Catholicism, 1800–1850', in Sheils, W.J. and Wood, D. (eds), *The Churches, Ireland and the Irish*, Studies in Church History Series, 25 (Oxford, 1989).

Chase, M., 'The Teeside Irish in the Nineteenth Century', in Buckland, P. and Belchem, J.C. (eds), *The Irish in British Labour History* (1993), 47–58.

Chinn, C., '"Sturdy Catholic Emigrants": The Irish in Early Victorian Birmingham', in Swift, R. and Gilley, S. (eds), *The Irish in Victorian Britain: The Local Dimension* (1999), 52–75.

Coleman, T., *The Railway Navvies* (London, 1965).

——, *Passage to America* (London, 1972).

Collins, B., 'The Irish in Britain, 1780–1921', in Graham, B.J. and Proudfoot, L.J. (eds), *An Historical Geography of Ireland* (London, 1993), 366–98.

——, 'Irish Emigration to Dundee and Paisley during the First Half of the Nineteenth Century', in Goldstrom, J.M. and Clarkson, L.A. (eds), *Irish Population, Economy and Society* (Oxford, 1981).

——, 'The Origins of Irish Immigration to Scotland in the Nineteenth and Twentieth Centuries', in Devine, *Irish Immigrants and Scottish Society* (1991), 1–18.

Connolly, G., 'Irish and Catholic: Myth or Reality ? Another Sort of Irish and the Renewal of the Clerical Profession among Catholics in England, 1791–1918', in Swift, R. and Gilley, S. (eds), *The Irish in the Victorian City* (London, 1985), 225–54.

——, '"Little Brother be at Peace": The Priest as Holy Man in the Nineteenth-Century Ghetto', in Shiels, W.J. (ed.), *Studies in Church History: The Churches and Healing* (Oxford, 1982), 191–205.

Curtin, C., O'Dwyer, R., and O'Tuathaigh, G., 'Emigration and Exile' in Bartlett, T., Curtin, C., O'Dwyer, R., and O'Tuathaigh, G. (eds), *Irish Studies: A General Introduction* (Dublin, 1988), 60–86.

Curtis, L.P., *Anglo-Saxons and Celts* (Bridgeport, Connecticut, 1968).

——, *Apes and Angels: The Irishman in Victorian Caricature* (Newton Abbot,1971; rev. ed., Washington and London, 1997).

Daly, M., *The Famine in Ireland* (Dublin, 1987).

Darragh, J., 'The Catholic Population of Scotland, 1878–1977', in D. McRoberts (ed.), *Modern Scottish Catholicism* (Glasgow, 1979), 211–47.

Davis, G., 'Little Irelands', in Swift, R. and Gilley, S. (eds.), *The Irish in Britain, 1815–1939* (London, 1989), 104–33.

——, *The Irish in Britain, 1815–1914* (Dublin, 1991).

——, 'The Historiography of the Irish Famine', in P. O'Sullivan (ed.), *The Irish World Wide*, vol. 6., *The Meaning of the Famine* (Leicester, 1997), 15–39.

——, 'The Irish in Britain, 1815–1939', in A. Bielenberg (ed.), *The Irish Diaspora* (Harlow, 2000), 19–36.

Delaney, E., '"Almost a Class of Helots in an Alien Land": The British State and Irish Immigration, 1921–45', in MacRaild, D.M. (ed.), *The Great Famine and Beyond* (2000), 240–65.

Devoy, J., *Recollections of an Irish Rebel* (New York, 1929).

Devine, T.M., 'The Welfare State within the Welfare State: The Saint Vincent de Paul Society in Glasgow, 1848–1920', in Shiels, W.J. and Wood, D. (eds), *Voluntary Religion*, Studies in Church History Series, 23 (Oxford, 1986).

—— (ed.), *Irish Immigrants and Scottish Society in the Nineteenth and Twentieth Centuries* (Edinburgh, 1991).

Doyle, P., 'The Catholic Federation, 1906–29', in Shiels, W.J. and Wood, D. (eds), *Voluntary Religion*, Studies in Church History Series, 23 (Oxford, 1986).

Edwards, O.D., 'The Irish in Scotland', in Daiches, D. (ed.), *A Companion to Scottish Culture* (London, 1982), 182–6.

——, 'The Catholic Press in Scotland since the Restoration of the Hierarchy', in McRoberts, D., *Modern Scottish Catholicism 1878–1978* (1979), 156–82.

——, *The Mind of an Activist: James Connolly* (Dublin, 1971).

—— (ed., with Ransom. B.), *James Connolly: Selected Political Writings* (London, 1973).

——, *Burke and Hare* (Edinburgh, 1980).

——, *The Quest for Sherlock Holmes* (Totowa, New Jersey, 1983).

——(with Storey, P.J.), 'The Irish Press in Victorian Britain', in Swift and Gilley, *The Irish in the Victorian City* (1985), 158–78.

Edwards, R. and Williams, T.D. (eds), *The Great Famine: Studies in Irish History, 1845–52* (Dublin, 1956).

Epstein, J., *The Lion of Freedom: Feargus O'Connor and the Chartist Movement, 1832–42* (London, 1982).

Fielding, S.J., 'A Separate Culture? Irish Catholics in Working-Class Manchester and Salford, c. 1890–1939', in Davies, A. and Fielding, S.J. (eds), *Workers' Worlds: Cultures and Communities in Manchester and Salford, 1880–1939* (Manchester, 1992), 23–48.

——, *Class and Ethnicity: Irish Catholics in England, 1880–1939* (Buckingham, 1993).

—— (ed.), *The Church and the People: Catholics and Their Church in Britain, 1880–1939* (Warwick University Working Papers in Social History, 1988).

Finnegan, F., *Poverty and Prejudice: Irish Immigrants in York, 1840–1875* (Cork, 1982).

——, 'The Irish in York', in Swift and Gilley, *The Irish in the Victorian City* (1985), 59–84.

Fitzpatrick, D., *Irish Emigration, 1801–1921* (Dublin, 1984).

——, 'A Curious Middle Place: The Irish in Britain, 1871–1921', in Swift, R. and Gilley, S. (eds), *The Irish in Britain, 1815–1939* (London, 1989), 10–59.

——, '"A Peculiar Tramping People': The Irish in Britain, 1801–70', in W.E. Vaughan (ed.), *A New History of Ireland*, vol. 5, *Ireland Under the Union, I, 1801–70* (Oxford, 1989), 623–60.

——, 'The Irish in Britain: Settlers or Transients?', in Buckland, P. and Belchem, R.J., *The Irish in British Labour History* (1993), 1–10.

——, *Oceans of Consolation: Personal Accounts of Irish Migration to Australia* (Cork, 1994).

——, 'The Irish in Britain, 1871–1921', in W.E. Vaughan (ed.), *A New History of Ireland, vol. 6, Ireland Under the Union, II, 1870–1921* (Oxford, 1996).

Foster, J., *Class Struggle and the Industrial Revolution* (London, 1974).

Foster, R.F., 'Marginal Men and Micks on the Make: The Uses of Irish Exile, c.1840–1922', in Foster, R.F., *Paddy and Mr Punch* (London, 1993).

Gallagher, T., *Paddy's Lament: Ireland 1846–7, Prelude to Hatred* (Dublin,1985).

——, *Glasgow: The Uneasy Peace – Religious Tension in Modern Scotland, 1819–1940* (Manchester, 1987).

——, 'A Tale of Two Cities: Communal Strife in Glasgow and Liverpool before 1914', in Swift, R. and Gilley, S. (eds), *The Irish in the Victorian City* (London, 1985), 106–129.

——, *Edinburgh Divided* (Edinburgh, 1987).

——, 'The Catholic Irish in Scotland: In Search of Identity', in Devine, T.M. (ed.), *Irish Immigrants and Scottish Society* (1991), 19–43.

Garrard, J.A., *The English and Immigration, 1880–1910* (London, 1971).

George, M.D., *London Life in the Eighteenth Century* (London, 1925; rep. 1979).

Gillespie, W., *The Christian Brothers in England* (Bristol, 1975).

Gilley, S., 'Papists, Protestants and the Irish in London', in Cumming, G.J. and Baker, D. (eds), *Popular Belief and Practice*, Studies in Church History Series, 8 (Cambridge, 1972).

Gilley, S., 'The Catholic Faith of the Irish Slums: London, 1840–70', in Dyos, H.J. and Wolff, M. (eds), *The Victorian City: Images and Reality*, 2 vols. (London, 1973), vol. 2, 837–53.

——, 'English Attitudes to the Irish in England, 1780–1900', in Holmes, C. (ed.), *Immigrants and Minorities in British Society* (London, 1978), 81–110.

——, 'Catholics and Socialists in Glasgow, 1906–12', in Lunn, K. (ed.), *Hosts, Immigrants and Minorities: Historical Responses to Newcomers in British Society, 1870–1914* (New York, 1980), 160–200.

——, 'Vulgar Piety and the Brompton Oratory, 1850–1860', in Swift, R. and Gilley, S. (eds), *The Irish in the Victorian City* (London, 1985), 255–66.

——, 'Irish Catholicism in Britain, 1880–1939', in Fielding, S.J. (ed.), *The Church and the People: Catholics and Their Church in Britain 1880–1939* (Warwick University Working Papers in Social History, 1988), 1–28.

——, 'Catholics and Socialists in Scotland, 1900–30', in Swift, R. and Gilley, S. (eds), *The Irish in Britain, 1815–1939* (London, 1989), 212–38.

——, 'Roman Catholicism and the Irish in England', in MacRaild, D.M. (ed.), *The Great Famine and Beyond* (2000), 147–67.

Goodway, D., *London Chartism, 1838–1848* (Cambridge, 1982), 61–67, 'The Irish'.

Greaves, C.D., *The Life and Times of James Connolly* (London, 1961).

Gwynn, D., 'The Irish Immigration' in Beck, G.A. (ed.), *The English Catholics, 1850–1950* (London, 1950), 265–90.

Handley, J.E., *The Irish in Scotland, 1789–1845* (Cork, 1943).

——, *The Irish in Modern Scotland* (Cork, 1947).

——, *The Celtic Story: A History of the Celtic Football Club* (1960).

——, *The Navvy in Scotland* (Cork, 1970).

Hanham, H., 'Religion and Nationality in the Mid–Victorian Army', in Foot, M.R.D. (ed.), *War and Society: Essays in Honour of J.R. Western* (London, 1973).

Hannon, J., *The Life of John Wheatley* (Nottingham, 1988).

Harmon, M. (ed.), *Fenians and Fenianism* (Dublin, 1968).

Harris, R.A., *The Nearest Place that Wasn't Ireland: Early Nineteenth-Century Irish Labour Migration* (Ames, IA, 1994).

Hartigan, M., O'Day, A., and Quinault, R., 'Irish Terrorism in Britain: A Comparison between the Activities of Fenians in the 1860's and those of Republican Groups since 1872', in Alexander, Y. and O'Day, A. (eds), *Ireland's Terrorist Dilemma* (Dordrecht, Netherlands, 1986).

Herson, J., 'Irish Migration and Settlement in Victorian England: A Small-Town Perspective', in Swift, R. and Gilley, S. (eds), *The Irish in Britain, 1815–1939* (London, 1989), 84–103.

——, 'Migration, 'Community' or Integration: Irish Families in Victorian Stafford', in Swift, R. and Gilley, S (eds)., *The Irish in Victorian Britain: The Local Dimension* (Dublin, 1999), 156–89.

Hickey, J.V., *Urban Catholics: Urban Catholicism in England and Wales from 1829 to the Present Day* (London, 1967).

Hickman, M., *Religion, Class and Identity: The State, the Catholic Church and the Education of the Irish in Britain* (Aldershot, 1995).

——, 'Incorporating and Denationalizing the Irish in England: The Role of the Catholic Church', in O'Sullivan, P. (ed.), *The Irish World Wide*, vol. 5, *Religion and Identity* (Leicester, 1996), 196–216.

——, 'Alternative Historiographies of the Irish in Britain: A Critique of the Segregation /Assimilation Model', in Swift, R. and Gilley, S., *The Irish in Victorian Britain: The Local Dimension* (1999), 236–53.

Hickman, M. and Hartigan, M. (eds), *The History of the Irish in Britain: A Bibliography* (London, 1986).

Holmes, C., *Immigrants and Minorities in British Society* (London, 1978), 81–110.

——, *John Bull's Island: Immigration and British Society, 1871–1971* (London, 1988).

Holmes, J.D., *More Roman than Rome: English Catholicism in the Nineteenth Century* (London, 1978).

Hunt, E.H., *British Labour History, 1815–1914* (London, 1981).

Hutchinson, J. and O'Day, A., 'The Gaelic Revival in London, 1900–1922: Limits of

Ethnic Identity', in Swift, R. and Gilley, S. (eds), *The Irish in Victorian Britain: The Local Dimension* (Dublin, 1999), 254–76.

Inglis, K.S., *Churches and the Working Classes in Victorian England* (London, 1963).

Jackson, A., *Ireland, 1798–1998: Politics and War* (Oxford, 1999).

Jackson, J.A., *The Irish in Britain* (London, 1963).

Jeffes, K.T., 'The Irish in Early Victorian Chester: An Outcast Community ?', in Swift, R. (ed.), *Victorian Chester: Essays in Social History, 1830–1900* (Liverpool, 1996), 85–118.

Jones, C., *Immigration and Social Policy in Britain* (London, 1977).

Joyce, P., *Work, Society and Politics: The Culture of the Factory in Later Victorian England* (London, 1980).

Kanya-Forstner, M., 'Defining Womanhood: Irish Women and the Catholic Church in Victorian Liverpool', in MacRaild, D.M. (ed.), *The Great Famine and Beyond* (Dublin, 2000), 168–88.

Kee, R., *The Green Flag* (London, 1972).

Kennedy, R.E., *The Irish: Emigration, Marriage, Fertility* (Berkley, 1973).

Killen, J. (ed.), *The Famine Decade: Contemporary Accounts, 1841–1851* (Belfast, 1995).

Kinealy, C., *This Great Calamity: The Irish Famine 1845–52* (Dublin, 1994)

Kirby, R.J., and Musson, A.E., *The Voice of the People: A Biography of John Doherty, 1798–1854* (Manchester, 1975).

Kirk, N., 'Ethnicity, Class and Popular Toryism, 1850–1870', in Lunn, K. (ed.), *Hosts, Immigrants and Minorities: Historical Responses to Newcomers in British Society, 1870–1914* (Folkestone, 1980), 64–106.

Large, D., 'The Irish in Bristol in 1851: A Census Enumeration', in Swift, R. and Gilley, S. (eds), *The Irish in the Victorian City* (London, 1985), 37–58.

Lavery, F., *Irish Heroes in the War* (London, 1917).

Lees, L.H., 'Patterns of Lower-Class Life: Irish Slum Communities in Nineteenth-Century London', in Thernstrom, S. and Sennett, R. (eds), *Nineteenth-Century Cities* (New Haven, 1969), 359–85.

——, *Exiles of Erin: Irish Migrants in Victorian London* (Manchester, 1979).

Leetham, C., *Luigi Gentili: A Sower for the Second Spring* (London, 1965).

Lesourd, J.A., *Sociologie du Catholicisme Anglais, 1767–1851*, 2 vols (Nancy, 1981).

Letford, L. and Pooley, C., 'Geographies of Migration and Religion: Irish Women in Mid-Nineteenth Century Liverpool', in O'Sullivan, P. (ed.), *The Irish World Wide*, vol. 4, *Irish Women and Irish Migration* (Leicester, 1995), 89–112.

Lowe, W.J., *The Irish in Mid-Victorian Lancashire: The Shaping of a Working Class Community* (New York, 1989).

MacDermott, T.P., 'Irish Workers on Tyneside in the Nineteenth Century', in McCord, N. (ed.), *Essays in Tyneside Labour History* (Newcastle, 1977), 154–77.

Machin, G.I.T., *Politics and the Churches in Great Britain, 1832–1868* (Oxford, 1977).

MacRaild, D.M., 'William Murphy, the Orange Order and Communal Violence: The Irish in West Cumberland, 1871–84', in Panayi, P. (ed.), *Racial Violence in Britain, 1840–1950* (Leicester, 1993), 44–64.

——, '"Principle, Party and Protest": The Language of Victorian Orangeism in the North of England', in West, S. (ed.), *The Victorians and Race* (Aldershot, 1996), 128–40.

——, *Irish Migrants in Modern Britain, 1750–1922* (London, 1999).

——, *Culture, Conflict and Migration: The Irish in Victorian Cumbria* (Liverpool, 1998).

—— (ed.), *The Great Famine and Beyond: Irish Migrants in Britain in the Nineteenth and Twentieth Centuries* (Dublin, 2000).

——, 'Crossing Migrant Frontiers: Comparative Reflections on Irish Migrants in Britain and the United States during the Nineteenth Century', in MacRaild, D.M. (ed.), *The Great Famine and Beyond* (2000), 40–70.

McAuley, J.W., 'Under an Orange Banner: Reflections on the Northern Protestant experiences of Emigration', in O'Sullivan, P. (ed.), *The Irish World Wide,* vol. 5, *Religion and Identity* (Leicester, 1996), 43–69.

McCaffrey, J.F., 'Politics and the Catholic Community since 1878', in McRoberts, *Modern Scottish Catholicism* (1979), 140–55.

——, 'Irish Issues in the Nineteenth and Twentieth Century: Radicalism in a Scottish Context', in Devine, T.M. (ed.), *Irish Immigrants and Scottish Society in the Nineteenth and Twentieth Centuries* (Edinburgh, 1991), 116–37.

McClelland, M., 'Catholic Education in Victorian Hull', in Swift, R. and Gilley, S., *The Irish in Victorian Britain: The Local Dimension* (Dublin, 1999), 101–21.

McClelland, V.A., *Cardinal Manning: His Public Life and Influence, 1865–1892* (London, 1962).

McDonnell, K.G.T., 'Roman Catholics in London, 1850–1865', in Hollaender, A. and Kellaway, W. (eds), *Studies in London History presented to Philip Edmund Jones* (London, 1969), 429–46.

McFarland, E., *Protestants First: Orangeism in Nineteenth-Century Scotland* (Edinburgh, 1990).

McLeod, H., *Class and Religion in the Late Victorian City* (London, 1974).

——, 'Building the "Catholic Ghetto": Catholic Organisations, 1870–1914', in Shiels, W.J. and Wood, D. (eds), *Voluntary Religion* (1986), 411–44.

McRoberts, D. (ed.), *Modern Scottish Catholicism* (Glasgow, 1979).

Messinger, G.S., *Manchester in the Victorian Age: The Half-Known City* (Manchester, 1985).

Milburn, G.E., *Church and Chapel in Sunderland, 1780–1914* (Sunderland Polytechnic Occasional Paper, 4, 1988).

Miller, K., *Emigrants and Exiles: Ireland and the Irish Exodus to North America* (Oxford, 1985).

Millward, P., 'The Stockport Riots of 1852: A Study of Anti-Catholic and Anti-Irish Sentiment', in Swift, R. and Gilley, S. (eds), *The Irish in the Victorian City* (London, 1985), 207–24.

Miskell, L., 'Irish Immigrants in Cornwall: The Camborne Experience, 1861–1882', in Swift, R. and Gilley, S. (eds), *The Irish in Victorian Britain: The Local Dimension* (Dublin, 1999), 31–51.

Mitchell, Martin, *The Irish in the West of Scotland, 1798–1848* (Edinburgh, 1998).

Moore, K., ' "This Whig and Tory Ridden Town": Popular Politics in Liverpool in the Chartist Era', in Belchem, J., *Popular Politics, Riot and Labour* (1992), 38–67.

Mokyr, J., *Why Ireland Starved* (London, 1983).

—— and Ó Gráda, C., 'Across the Briny Ocean: Some Thoughts on Irish Emigration to America, 1800–1850', in Devine, T. and Dickson, D. (eds), *Ireland and Scotland: Essays in Comparative Economic and Social History* (Edinburgh, 1983).

Moran, G., 'Nationalists in Exile: The Brotherhood of St Patrick in Lancashire, 1861–1865', in Swift, R. and Gilley, S. (eds), *The Irish in Victorian Britain: The Local Dimension* (Dublin, 1999), 212–35.

Morgan, D., *Harvesters and Harvesting, 1840–1900* (London, 1982).

Murdoch, N.H., 'From Militancy to Social Mission: The Salvation Army and Street Disturbances in Liverpool, 1879–1887', in Belchem, *Popular Politics, Riot and Labour* (1992), 160–72.

Murray, B., *The Old Firm: Sectarianism, Sport and Society in Scotland* (Edinburgh, 1984).

Neal, F., *Sectarian Violence: The Liverpool Experience, 1819–1914* (Manchester, 1987).

——, English-Irish Conflict in the North-East of England', in Buckland, P. and Belchem, J. (eds), *The Irish in British Labour History* (Liverpool, 1993), 59–85.

——, 'The Famine Irish in England and Wales', in O'Sullivan, P. (ed), *The Irish World Wide,* vol. 6, *The Meaning of the Famine* (Leicester, 1997), 56–80.

——, *Black '47: Britain and the Famine Irish* (London, 1997).

——, 'Irish Settlement in the North-east and North-west of England in the Mid-Nineteenth Century', in Swift, R. and Gilley, S. (eds), *The Irish in Victorian Britain: The Local Dimension* (Dublin, 1999), 76–100.

——, 'The Foundations of the Irish Settlement in Newcastle Upon Tyne: The Evidence in the 1851 Census', in MacRaild, D.M. (ed.), *The Great Famine and Beyond* (2000), 71–93.

Newsinger, J., *Fenianism in Mid-Victorian Britain* (London, 1994).

Norman, E.R., *Anti-Catholicism in Victorian England* (London, 1968).

——, *The English Catholic Church in the Nineteenth Century* (Oxford, 1984).

O'Conor Eccles, C., 'Scottish, Irish and Welsh London', in Sims, G.R. (ed.), *Living London* (London, 1902; reprinted as *Edwardian London* , 4 vols, London, 1990), vol. 3, 98–104.

O'Connor, K., *The Irish in Britain* (London, 1972).

O'Day, A., *The English Face of Irish Nationalism: Parnellite Involvement in British Politics, 1880–1886* (Dublin, 1977).

——, *Parnell and the First Home Rule Episode, 1884–87* (Dublin, 1985).

——, 'Irish Home Rule and Liberalism', in O'Day, A. (ed), *The Edwardian Age:- Conflict and Stability, 1900–1914* (London and Connecticut, 1979), 113–32.

——, 'The Irish Problem', in Gourvish, T.R. and O'Day, A. (eds), *Later Victorian Britain, 1867–1900* (London, 1988), 229–50.

——, 'The Political Organization of the Irish in Britain, 1867–90', in Swift, R. and Gilley, S. (eds), *The Irish in Britain, 1815–1939* (1989), 183–211.

——, 'Varieties of Anti-Irish Behaviour in Britain, 1846–1922', in Panayi, P. (ed.), *Racial Violence in Britain* (1993), 26–43.

——, 'Revising the Diaspora', in Boyce, D.G. and O'Day, A. (eds), *The Making of Modern Irish History: Revisionism and the Revisionist Controversy* (London, 1996),188–215.

——, *Irish Home Rule, 1867–1921* (Manchester, 1998).

——, 'Irish Diaspora Politics in Perspective: The United Irish Leagues of Great Britain and America, 1900–14', in MacRaild, D.M. (ed.), *The Great Famine and Beyond* (2000), 214–39.

O'Day, A. and Stevenson, J. (eds), *Irish Historical Documents Since 1800* (Dublin, 1992).

O'Dowd, A., *Spalpeens and Tattie Hokers: History and Folklore of the Irish Migratory Agricultural Worker in Ireland and Britain* (Dublin, 1991).

Ó Gráda, C., 'Some Aspects of Nineteenth-Century Irish Emigration', in Cullen, L.M. and Smout, T.C. (eds.), *Comparative Aspects of Scottish and Irish Economic and Social History, 1600–1900* (Edinburgh, 1977), 65–73.

O'Leary, P., 'Irish Immigration and the Catholic Welsh District, 1840–50', in Jenkins, H. (ed.), *Politics and Society in Wales, 1840–1922* (Cardiff, 1988).

——, 'A Regional Perspective: The Famine Irish in South Wales', in Swift, R. and Gilley, S., *The Irish in Victorian Britain: The Local Dimension* (1999), 14–30.

——, *Immigration and Integration: The Irish in Wales, 1798–1922* (Cardiff, 2000).

O'Sullivan, P. (ed.), *The Irish World Wide*, 6 vols (London, 1992–97).

——, 'A Literary Difficulty in Explaining Ireland: Tom Moore and Captain Rock, 1824', in Swift, R. and Gilley, S. (eds), *The Irish in Britain, 1815–1939* (1989), 239–74.

Paz, D.G., *Popular Anti-Catholicism in Mid-Victorian England* (Stanford, 1992).

Póirtéir, C. (ed.), *The Great Irish Famine* (Dublin, 1995).

Pooley, C., 'Segregation or Integration? The Residential Experience of the Irish in Mid-Victorian Britain', in Swift, R. and Gilley, S. (eds), *The Irish in Britain, 1815–1939* (London, 1989), 60–83.

——, 'From Londonderry to London: Identity and Sense of Place for a Protestant Northern Irish Woman in the 1930s', in MacRaild, D.M. (ed.), *The Great Famine and Beyond* (2000), 189–213.

Price, R.T., *Little Ireland: Aspects of the Irish and Greenhill, Swansea* (Swansea, 1992).

Proctor, M., *The Irish Community in North West England: a guide to local archive sources* (Liverpool, 1993).

Quinlivan, P., 'Hunting the Fenians: Problems in the Historiography of a Secret Organisation', in O'Sullivan, P. (ed.), *The Irish World Wide*, vol. 3, *The Creative Migrant* (Leicester, 1994), 133–53.

—— and Rose, P., *The Fenians in England, 1865–72: A Sense of Insecurity* (London, 1962).

Read, D., and Glasgow, E., *Feargus O'Connor: Irishman and Chartist* (London, 1961).

Redford, A., *Labour Migration in England, 1800–1850* (London, 1926; rev. ed. Manchester, 1964).

Richter, D., *Riotous Victorians* (London, 1970).

Rose, P., *The Manchester Martyrs* (London, 1970).

Ryan, M.F., *Fenian Memories* (Dublin, 1945).

Samuel, R., 'The Roman Catholic Church and the Irish Poor', in Swift, R. and Gilley, S. (eds), *The Irish in the Victorian City* (London, 1985), 267–300.

——, 'An Irish Religion', in Samuel, R., *Patriotism* (London, 1992), vol. 2, 94–120.

Saville, J., *1848: The British State and the Chartist Movement* (Cambridge, 1987).

Scally, R.J., *The End of Hidden Ireland: Rebellion, Famine and Emigration* (Oxford, 1995).

Senior, H., *Orangeism in Ireland and Britain, 1795–1836* (London, 1966).

Short, K.R.M., *The Dynamite War: Irish-American Bombers in Victorian Britain* (Dublin, 1979).

Skinnider, M., 'Catholic Education in Glasgow, 1818–1918', in Bone, T.R. (ed.), *Studies in Scottish Education 1872–1939* (London, 1967), 13–70.

Sloan, W., 'Religious Affiliation and the Immigrant Experience: Catholic Irish and Protestant Highlanders in Glasgow, 1830–50', in Devine, T.M. (ed.), *Irish Immigrants and Scottish Society* (1991), 67–90.

Spencer, A.E.C.W., 'The Demography and Sociography of the Roman Catholic Church of England and Wales', in Bright, L. and Clements, S. (eds), *The Committed Church* (London, 1966).

Stevenson, J., *Popular Disturbances in England, 1700–1870* (London, 1979).

Strauss, E., *Irish Nationalism and British Democracy* (London, 1951).

Swift, R., 'Crime and the Irish in Nineteenth-Century Britain', in Swift, R. and Gilley, S. (eds), *The Irish in Britain, 1815–1939* (London, 1989), 163–82.

——, *The Irish in Britain 1815–1914: Perspectives and Sources* (Historical Association, London, 1990)

——, 'The Historiography of the Irish in Nineteenth-Century Britain', in O'Sullivan, P. (ed.), *The Irish World Wide*, vol. 2., *The Irish in the New Communities* (1992), 52–81.

——, 'The Historiography of the Irish in Nineteenth-Century Britain: Some Perspectives', in Buckland and Belchem, *The Irish in British Labour History* (1993), 11–18.

——, 'Historians and the Irish: Recent Writings on the Irish in Nineteenth-Century Britain', in MacRaild, D.M. (ed.), *The Great Famine and Beyond* (2000), 14–39.

Swift, R. and Gilley, S. (eds), *The Irish in the Victorian City* (London, 1985).

——, *The Irish in Britain, 1815–1939* (London, 1989).

——, *The Irish in Victorian Britain: The Local Dimension* (Dublin, 1999).

Taplin, E., 'False Dawn of New Unionism? Labour Unrest in Liverpool, 1871–73', in Belchem, J., *Popular Politics, Riot and Labour* (1992), 135–159.

Thompson, D., 'Ireland and the Irish in English Radicalism before 1850', in Epstein, J. and Thompson, D. (eds), *The Chartist Experience: Studies in Working Class Radicalism and Culture, 1830–1860* (London, 1982), 120–51.

Thompson, E.P., *The Making of the English Working Class* (London, 1963).

Treble, J.H., 'The Irish Agitation', in Ward, J.T. (ed.), *Popular Movements, 1830–1850* (London, 1970), 152–82.

——, 'Liverpool Working Class Housing, 1800–51', in Chapman, S. (ed.), *The History of Working Class Housing: A Symposium* (Newton Abbot, 1971), 165–220.

——, 'O'Connor, O'Connell and the Attitudes of Irish Immigrants towards Chartism in the North of England, 1838–48', in Butt, J. and Clarke, I.F. (eds), *The Victorians and Social Protest: A Symposium* (Newton Abbot, 1973).

——, 'The Development of Roman Catholic Education in Scotland, 1878–1978', in McRoberts, D. (ed.), *Modern Scottish Catholicism* (1979), 111–39.

Turton, J., 'Mayhew's Irish: The Irish Poor in Mid-Nineteenth-Century London', in Swift, R. and Gilley, S. (eds), *The Irish in Victorian Britain: The Local Dimension* (Dublin, 1999), 122–55.

Vincent, J.R., *Pollbooks: How Victorians Voted* (London, 1967).

Walker, G., 'The Protestant Irish in Scotland', in Devine, T.M. (ed.), *Irish Immigrants and Scottish Society in the Nineteenth and Twentieth Centuries* (Edinburgh, 1991), 44–66.

Walker, W.A., *Juteopolis: Dundee and its Textile Workers, 1885–1923* (Edinburgh, 1979).

Waller, P.J., *Democracy and Sectarianism: A Political and Social History of Liverpool, 1868–1939* (Liverpool, 1981).

Walton, J., and Wilcox, A. (eds), *Low Life and Moral Improvement in Mid-Victorian England: Liverpool through the Journalism of Hugh Shimmin* (Leicester, 1991).

Walvin, J., *Passage to Britain: Immigration in British History and Politics* (London, 1984).

Williamson, J., 'The Impact of the Irish on British Labour Markets during the Industrial Revolution', in Swift, R. and Gilley, S. (eds), *The Irish in Britain, 1815–1939* (London, 1989), 134–62.

Wolffe, J.R., *The Protestant Crusade in Great Britain, 1829–1860* (Oxford, 1991).

Wood, I.S., 'Irish Immigrants and Scottish Radicalism', in McDougall, I. (ed.), *Essays in Scottish Labour History* (Edinburgh, 1979), 64–89.

——, *John Wheatley* (Manchester, 1990).

Woodham-Smith, C., *The Great Hunger* (London, 1962).

B. JOURNAL ARTICLES

Arnstein, W.L., 'Victorian Prejudice Re-examined', *Victorian Studies*, XI (1968–9), 452–7.

——, 'The Murphy Riots: A Victorian Dilemma', *Victorian Studies*, XIX (1975), 55–71.

Aspinwall, B., 'The Formation of the Catholic Community in the West of Scotland', *Innes Review*, 33 (1982), 44–57.

——, 'Popery in Scotland: Image and Reality, 1820–1920', *Records of the Scottish Church History Society*, 22 (1986), 235–57.

——, 'The Irish Abroad: Michael Condon in Scotland, 1845–78', *Studies in Church History*, 25 (1989), 279–97.

Belchem, J., 'English Working-Class Radicalism and the Irish, 1815–50', *North-West Labour History Society Bulletin*, 8 (1982–3), 5–18.

——, '"Freedom and Friendship to Ireland": Ribbonism in Early Nineteenth-Century Liverpool', *International Review of Social History*, 39 (1994), 33–56.

——, 'Nationalism, Republicanism and Exile: Irish Emigrants and the Revolutions of 1848', *Past and Present*, 146 (1995), 103–35.

——, 'The Liverpool-Irish Enclave', *Immigrants and Minorities*, 18, 2/3 (1999), 128–46.

Best, G.F.A., 'The Protestant Constitution and its Supporters, 1800–1829', *Transactions of the Royal Historical Society*, 8 (1958).

Bhreathnach-Lynch, S., 'Framing the Irish: Victorian Paintings of the Irish Peasant', *Journal of Victorian Culture*, vol. 2, 2 (Autumn 1997), 245–63.

Boyle, J.W., 'Ireland and the First International', *The Journal of British Studies*, XI (May, 1972), 44–62.

Brooke, D., 'Railway Navvies on the Pennines, 1841–71', *Journal of Transport History*, 3 (1975–6), 41–53.

Busteed, M., 'Little Islands of Erin: Irish Settlement and Identity in Mid-Nineteenth Century Manchester', *Immigrants and Minorities*, 18, 22/3 (1999), 94–127.

——, and Hodgson, R., 'Irish Migration and Settlement in Nineteenth-Century Manchester, with Special Reference to the Angel Meadow District', *Irish Geography*, vol. 27, 1 (1994), 1–13.

Cahill, G.A., 'Irish Catholicism and English Toryism', *Review of Politics*, 19 (1957), 62–76.

Chase, M., 'Dangerous People?: The Teeside Irish in the Nineteenth Century', *North-East Labour History Journal*, 28 (1994), 27–41.

Clapham, J.H., 'Irish Immigration into Great Britain in the Nineteenth Century', *Bulletin of the International Committee of Historical Sciences*, V (June, 1933), 596–604.

Collette, C., 'So Utterly Forgotten: Irish Prisoners and the 1924 Labour Government', *North West Labour History Journal*, 16 (1991–2), 73–7.

Collins, B., 'Proto-industrialisation and Pre-Famine Emigration', *Social History*, vol. 7, 2 (1982), 127–46.

Coney, A.P., 'Mid-Nineteenth Century Ormskirk: Disease, Overcrowding and the Irish in a Lancashire Market Town', *Transactions of the Historic Society of Lancashire and Cheshire*, 139 (1990), 33–111.

Connolly, G.P., 'The Transubstantiation of Myth: Towards a New Popular History of Nineteenth-Century Catholicism in England', *Journal of Ecclesiastical History*, 35 (1984), 78–104.

——., 'The Rev. Mr. Peter Kaye: Maverick or Englishman?', *North West Catholic History*, 11 (1984), 8–21.

——, '"With More than Ordinary Devotion to God": The Secular Missioner of the-North in the Evangelical Age of the English Mission', *North West Catholic History*, 10 (1983), 8–31.

——, 'The Catholic Church and the First Manchester and Salford Trade Unions in the Age of the Industrial Revolution', *Transactions of the Lancashire and Cheshire Antiquarian Society*, 135 (1985).

Cooter, R.J., 'Lady Londonderry and the Irish Catholics of Seaham Harbour:"No Popery"Out of Context', *Recusant History*, 13 (1975–6), 288–98.

——, 'On Calculating the Nineteenth Century Catholic Population of Durham and-Newcastle', *Northern Catholic History*, 2 (1975).

Cousens, S.H., 'Emigration and Demographic Change in Ireland, 1851–61', *Economic History Review*, 14 (1961–2), 275–88.

——, 'The Regional Pattern of Emigration during the Great Irish Famine', *Transactions and Papers of the Institute of British Geographers*, 28 (1960), 119–34.

Davis, J., 'From "Rookeries" to "Communities": Race, Poverty and Policing in London, 1850–1985', *History Workshop Journal*, 27 (1989).

Dillon, T., 'The Irish in Leeds, 1851–61', *Thoresby Miscellany*, XVI (1979), 1–29.

Doyle, P., 'The Education and Training of Roman Catholic Priests in the Nineteenth Century', *Journal of Ecclesiastical History*, 35, 2 (1984), 208–19.

——, 'Accommodation or Confrontation: Catholic Responses to the Formation of the Labour Party', *North West Labour History Journal*, 16 (1991–2), 64–72.

Duffy, P., 'Carrying the Hod: Irish Immigrant Labour in the Manchester Building Trades', *North West Labour History Journal*, 16 (1991–2), 36–41.

Dunleavy, J., 'The Manchester Irish National Convention, 1918', *North West Labour History Journal*, 16 (1991–2), 56–60.

Feheney, J.M., 'Delinquency among Irish Catholic Children in Victorian London', *Irish Historical Studies*, XXIII, 92 (1983), 319–29.

Feldman, D., 'There was an Englishman, an Irishman and a Jew . . . Immigrants and Minorities in Britain', *Historical Journal*, 26 (1983).

Fielding, S.J., 'Irish Politics in Manchester, 1890–1914', *International Review of Social History*, 23 (1988), 261–84.

——, 'The Catholic Whit-Walk in Manchester and Salford, 1890–1939', *Manchester-Regional History Review*, 1, 1 (1987), 3–10.

Fitzpatrick, D., 'Irish Emigration in the Later Nineteenth Century', *Irish Historical Studies*, XXII, 86 (1980), 126–43.

Frow, R., and E., 'Biographies of Irish Chartists', *North West Labour History Journal*, 16 (1991–2), 86–93.

Gilley, S., 'The Roman Catholic Mission to the Irish in London, 1840–60', *Recusant History*, 10 (1969–70), 123–45.

——, 'Protestant London, No Popery and the Irish Poor, 1830–70', *Recusant History*, vol. 10 (1969–70), 210–30; 11 (1971), 21–46.

——, 'Heretic London, Holy Poverty and the Irish Poor, 1830–70', *Downside Review*, 89 (1971), 64–89.

——, 'The Garibaldi Riots of 1862', *Historical Journal*, 16, 4 (1973), 697–732.

——, 'The Roman Catholic Church and the Nineteenth-Century Irish Diaspora', *Journal of Ecclesiastical History*, 35 (1984), 188–207.

——, 'Roman Catholicism and the Irish in England', *Immigrants and Minorities*, 18, 2/3 (1999), 147–167.

Glynn, S., 'Irish Immigration to Britain, 1911–51: Patterns and Policy', *Irish Economic and Social History*, 8 (1981).

Hamer, D.A., 'The Irish Question and Liberal Politics, 1886–1894', *Historical Journal,* 12 (1969).

Harris, R., 'The Failure of Republicanism among Irish Migrants to Britain, 1800–40', *Eire-Ireland,* 21 (1986), 122–36.

Haslett, J. and Lowe, W.J., 'Household Structure and Overcrowding among the Lancashire Irish, 1851–71', *Histoire Sociale,* 10 (1977).

Hunter, J., 'The Gaelic Connection: The Highlands, Ireland and Nationalism 1873–1922', *Scottish Historical Review,* 54 (1975), 179–204.

Hyland, B., 'Eva Gore-Booth: An Irishwoman in Manchester', *North West Labour History Journal,* 16 (1991–2), 52–5.

Jackson, J., 'The Irish in East London', *East London Papers,* 6 (1963).

Kanya-Forstner, M., 'Defining Womanhood: Irish Women and the Catholic Church in Victorian Liverpool', *Immigrants and Minorities,* 18, 2/3 (1999), 168–88.

Kemnitz, T.M., 'Approaches to the Chartist Movement: Feargus O'Connor and Chartist Strategy', *Albion,* 5 (1973), 67–73.

Kerr, B.M., 'Irish Seasonal Migration to Great Britain, 1800–1838', *Irish Historical Studies,* II (1942–3), 365–80.

Koseki, T., 'Patrick O'Higgins and Irish Chartism', *Ireland-Japan Papers,* 2 [Hosei University] (1988)

——, 'The Liverpool Irish and the Threat of Physical Force', *Ireland-Japan Papers,* 3 [Hosei University] (1989).

Larkin, E., 'The Devotional Revolution in Ireland, 1850–75', *American Historical Review,* 77 (1972), 625–52.

Lawton, R., 'Irish Immigration to England and Wales in the Mid-Nineteenth Century', *Irish Geography,* IV (1959–63), 35–54.

Lees, L.H., 'Mid-Victorian Migration and the Irish Family Economy', *Victorian Studies,* XX (1976), 25–43.

Lewis, C.R., 'The Irish in Cardiff in the Mid-Nineteenth Century', *Cambria,* VII (1980), 13–41.

Lobban, R.D., 'The Irish Community in Greenock in the Nineteenth Century', *Irish Geography,* VI (1971), 270–81.

Lovell, J., 'The Irish and the London Dockers', *Bulletin of the Society for the Study of Labour History,* II (1975), 63–5.

Lowe, W.J., 'The Irish in Lancashire, 1846–71: A Social History', *Irish Economic and Social History,* II (1975).

——, 'The Lancashire Irish and the Catholic Church, 1846–71', *Irish Historical Studies,* XX (1976), 129–55.

——, 'Social Agencies among the Irish in Lancashire during the Mid-Nineteenth-Century', *Saothar,* 3 (1977), 15–20.

——, 'Lancashire Fenianism, 1846–71', *Transactions of the Historic Society of Lancashire and Cheshire,* 126 (1977), 156–85.

——, 'The Chartists and the Irish Confederates: Lancashire, 1848', *Irish Historical Studies,* XXIV, 94 (1984), 172–96.

MacRaild, D.M., 'Irish Immigration and the "Condition of England" Question: The Roots of an Historiographical Tradition', *Immigrants and Minorities,* 14, 1 (March 1995), 67–85.

——, 'A Case of Undercutting Wages?: Sectarian Tension and the Barrow Anti-Irish Riot of 1864', *Transactions of the Cumberland and Westmorland Antiquarian and Archaeological Society,* XCVI (1996), 215–22.

——, 'Culture, Conflict and Labour Migration: Victorian Cumbria's Ulster Dimension', *Saothar*, 21 (1996), 23–38.

——, 'Crossing Migrant Frontiers: Comparative Reflections on Irish Migrants in Britain and the United States during the Nineteenth Century', *Immigrants and Minorities*, 18, 2/3 (1999), 40–70.

Mason, F.M., 'The Newer Eve: The Catholic Women's Suffrage Society in England, 1911–23', *Catholic Historical Review*, 52 (1986).

McCaffrey, J.F., 'The Irish Vote in Glasgow in the Later Nineteenth Century', *Innes Review*, 21 (1970), 30–36.

——, 'Roman Catholics in Scotland in the 19th and 20th centuries', *Records of the Scottish Church History Society*, 21 (1983).

——, 'The Stewardship of Resources: Financial Strategies of Roman Catholics in the Glasgow District, 1800–70', *Studies in Church History*, 24 (1987), 359–70.

——, 'Irish Immigrants and Radical Movements in the West of Scotland in the Early Nineteenth Century', *Innes Review*, vol. 29, 1 (1988), 52–4.

McGill, J., and Redmond, T., 'The Story of the Manchester Martyrs', *North West Labour History Journal*, 16 (1991–2), 42–51.

Miller, D., 'Irish Catholicism and the Great Famine', *Journal of Social History*, IX (1975–6), 81–98.

Mokyr, J., and O'Grada, C., 'Emigration and Poverty in Pre-Famine Ireland', *Explorations in Economic History*, 19 (1982), 360–384.

Moody, T.W., 'Michael Davitt and the British Labour Movement, 1882–1906', *Transactions of the Royal Historical Society*, 4 (1953), 53–76.

Morris, K.L., 'John Bull and the Scarlet Woman: Charles Kingsley and Anti-Catholicism in Victorian Literature', *Recusant History*, 23, 2 (Oct. 1996), 190–218.

Mulkern, P., 'Irish Immigrants and Public Disorder in Coventry, 1845–1875', *Midland History*, 21 (1996), 119–35.

Murphy, P., 'Irish Settlement in Nottingham in the Early Nineteenth Century', *Transactions of The Thornton Society*, 98 (1994), 82–91.

Neal, F., 'The Birkenhead Garibaldi Riots of 1862', *Transactions of the Historic Society of Lancashire and Cheshire*, 131 (1982), 87–111.

——, 'Liverpool, the Famine Irish and the Steamship Companies', *Immigrants and Minorities*, 5, 1 (1985), 28–61.

——, 'Manchester Origins of the English Orange Order', *Manchester Region History Review* (Autumn 1990), 12–24.

——, 'A Criminal Profile of the Liverpool Irish', *Transactions of the Historic Society of Lancashire and Cheshire*, 140 (1991), 161–99.

——, 'English-Irish Conflict in the North West of England: Economics, Racism, Anti-Catholicism or Simple Xenophobia ?', *North West Labour History Journal*, 16 (1991–2), 14–25.

——, 'Lancashire, the Famine Crisis and the Poor Law: A Study in Crisis Management', *Irish Economic and Social History*, 22 (1995), 26–46.

——, 'The Foundations of the Irish Settlement in Newcastle upon Tyne: The Evidence in the 1851 Census', *Immigrants and Minorities*, 18, 2/3 (1999), 71–93.

O'Connell, B., 'Irish Nationalism in Liverpool, 1873–1923', *Eire-Ireland*, 10 (1975), 24–37.

O'Day, A., 'Irish Diaspora Politics in Perspective: The United Irish Leagues of Great Britain and America, 1900–14', *Immigrants and Minorities*, 18, 2/3 (1999), 214–239.

Ó Gráda, C., 'A Note on Nineteenth-Century Irish Emigration Statistics', *Population Studies*, 29 (1975), 145–48.

O'Higgins, R., 'The Irish Influence in the Chartist Movement', *Past and Present*, 20 (1961), 83–96.

O'Leary, P., 'Anti-Irish Riots in Wales, 1826–82', *Llafur,* V, 4 (1991–2), 27–36.

Ó Tuathaigh, M.A.G., 'The Irish in Nineteenth-Century Britain: Problems of Integration', *Transactions of the Royal Historical Society*, 31 (1981), 149–74.

Parry, J., 'The Tredegar Anti-Irish Riots of 1882', *Llafur*, III (1983), 20–3.

Paz, D.G., 'Popular Anti-Catholicism in England, 1850–1851', *Albion*, 11 (1979), 331–59.

Pooley, C.G., 'The Residential Segregation of Migrant Communities in Mid-Victorian Liverpool', *Transactions of the Institute of British Geographers*, II, 3 (1977), 369–72.

——, 'Irish Settlement in North West England in the Mid-Nineteenth Century: A Geographical Critique', *North West Labour History Journal*, 16 (1991–2), 26–35.

Reid, T.D.W., and N., 'The 1842 "Plug Plot" in Stockport', *International Review of Social History*, XXIV (1979).

Richardson, C., 'Irish Settlement in Mid-Nineteenth Century Bradford', *Yorkshire Bulletin of Economic and Social Research*, XX (1975), 40–57.

——, 'The Irish in Victorian Bradford', *The Bradford Antiquary*, 9 (1976), 294–316.

Shallice, A., 'Orange and Green and Militancy: Sectarianism and Working-Class Politics in Liverpool, 1910–14', *North West Labour History Journal*, 6 (1979–80), 15–22.

Smith, A.W., 'Irish Rebels and English Radicals, 1798–1829', *Past and Present,* 7 (1955), 78–85.

Smith, J., 'Labour Tradition in Glasgow and Liverpool', *History Workshop*, 17 (Spring, 1974).

Stack, J.A., 'The Catholics, the Irish Delinquent and the origins of Reformatory Schools in Nineteenth-Century England and Scotland', *Recusant History*, 23, 3 (May 1997), 372–88.

Steele, E.D., 'The Irish Presence in the North of England, 1850–1914', *Northern History*, XII (1976), 220–41.

Swift, R., 'Crime and Ethnicity: The Irish in Early Victorian Wolverhampton', *West Midlands Studies*, 13 (1980), 1–5.

——, 'Anti-Catholicism and Irish Disturbances: Public Order in Mid-Victorian-Wolverhampton', *Midland History*, IX (1984), 87–108.

——, '"Another Stafford Street Row": Law, Order and the Irish Presence in Mid-Victorian Wolverhampton', *Immigrants and Minorities*, 3 (1984), 5–29.

——, 'The Outcast Irish in the British Victorian City: Problems and Perspectives', *Irish Historical Studies*, XXV (1987), 264–76.

——, 'Anti-Irish Violence in Victorian England: Some Perspectives', *Criminal Justice History*, 15 (1994), 127–40.

——, 'Heroes or Villains?: The Irish, Crime and Disorder in Victorian England', *Albion*, 29, 3 (1998), 399–421.

——, 'Historians and the Irish: Recent Writings on the Irish in Nineteenth-Century Britain', *Immigrants and Minorities*, 18, 2/3 (1999), 14–39.

Treble, J.H., 'The Attitude of the Roman Catholic Church towards Trade Unionism in the North of England, 1833–42', *Northern History*, 5 (1970), 93–113.

——, 'The Navvies', *Scottish Labour History Society Journal,* V (1972).

——, 'Irish Navvies in the North of England, 1833–42', *Transport History*, 6 (1973), 227–47.

——, 'The Development of Roman Catholic Education in Scotland, 1878–1978', *Innes Review*, 29, 2 (1978).

Turley, F., 'Centenary of the Fenian Raid', *The Cheshire Sheaf* (October 1967), 45–6.

Walker, R.B., 'Religious Changes in Liverpool in the Nineteenth Century', *Journal of Ecclesiastical History*, 19, 2 (Oct. 1968), 195–211.

Walker, W.M., 'Irish Immigrants in Scotland: Their Priests, Politics and Parochial Life', *Historical Journal*, 15 (1972), 649–67.

Werly, J.M., 'The Irish in Manchester, 1832–49', *Irish Historical Studies*, XVIII (1973), 345–58.

Williams, A.M., 'Migration and Residential Patterns in Mid-Nineteenth Century Cardiff', *Cambria*, vi, 2 (1979), 1–27.

Williams, F.J., 'The Irish in the East Cheshire Silk Industry, 1851–61', *Transactions of the Historic Society of Lancashire and Cheshire*, 136 (1986), 99–126.

Williamson, J.G., 'The Impact of the Irish on British Labour Markets during the Industrial Revolution', *Journal of Economic History*, XLVI (September 1986), 693–721.

Wood, I.S., 'John Wheatley, the Irish and the Labour Movement in Scotland', *Innes Review*, XXXI (1980), 71–85.

Yeo, E., 'Christianity in Chartist Struggle, 1838–42', *Past and Present*, 91 (1981), 83–94.

C. THESES

Bartlett, A., 'The Churches in Bermondsey, 1880–1939' (University of Birmingham PhD thesis, 1987).

Benjamin, H.W., 'The London Irish: A Study in Political Activism, 1870–1910' (University of London PhD thesis, 1971).

Betney, N.R., 'An Irish Tale? Emigration or Immigration: A Study of Irish Migration' (University of York MA thesis, 1987).

Bryson, A., 'Riot and its control in Liverpool, 1815–60' (Open University MPhil thesis, 1990).

Cassirer, R., 'The Irish Influence on the Liberal Movement in England, 1798–1832' (University of London PhD thesis, 1940).

Champ, J., 'Assimilation and Separation: The Catholic Revival in Birmingham, 1650–1850' (University of Birmingham PhD thesis, 1989).

Collins, B., 'Aspects of Irish Immigration into Two Scottish Towns (Dundee and Paisley) in the Mid-Nineteenth Century' (University of Edinburgh MPhil thesis, 1978).

Connolly, G.P., 'Catholicism in Manchester and Salford' (University of Manchester PhD thesis, 1980).

Cooter, R.J., 'The Irish in County Durham and Newcastle, 1840–1880' (University of Durham MA thesis, 1973).

Danaher, N., 'The Irish in Leicester, 1841–1891' (University of North London PhD thesis, 1999).

Fielding, S.J., 'The Irish Catholics of Manchester and Salford: Aspects of their Religious and Political History 1890–1939' (University of Warwick PhD thesis, 1988).

Gilbert, P.J., 'In the midst of a Protestant people: the development of the Catholic community in Bristol in the nineteenth century' (Brunel University PhD thesis, 1996).

Hall, R., 'Irish music and dance in London, 1890–1970: a socio-cultural history' (University of Sussex PhD thesis, 1994).

Herson, J., 'Why the Irish went to Stafford: A Case Study of Irish Settlement in England, 1830–1871' (London School of Economics MSc thesis, 1986).

Hickey, J.V., 'The Origin and Growth of the Irish Community in Cardiff' (University of Wales MA thesis, 1959).

Horgan, D.T., 'The Irish Catholic Whigs in Parliament 1847–74' (University of Minnesota PhD thesis, 1975).

Hutchinson, I.G.C., 'Politics and Society in Mid-Victorian Glasgow, 1846–86' (University of Edinburgh PhD thesis, 1974).

Ingram, P., 'Sectarianism in the North West of England, with special reference to class relationships in the City of Liverpool, 1846–1914' (Lancashire Polytechnic PhD thesis, 1988).

Ives, E.J., 'The Irish in Liverpool. A Study of Ethnic Identification and Social Participation' (University of Liverpool MPhil thesis, 1988).

Jackson, J.A., 'The Irish in London: A Study of Migration and Settlement in the past hundred years' (University of London MA thesis, 1958).

Kanya-Forstner, M., 'Irish women in Victorian Liverpool' (University of Liverpool PhD thesis, 1997).

Koseki, T., 'Chartism and Irish Nationalism, 1829–48: Bronterre O'Brien, the London Irish and Attempts at a Chartist-Irish Alliance' (University of Birmingham MPhil thesis, 1988).

Lees, L.H., 'Social Change and Social Stability among the London Irish' (University of Harvard PhD thesis, 1969).

Lowe, W.J., 'The Irish in Lancashire, 1846–71' (Trinity College Dublin MA thesis, 1975).

MacDermott, M., 'Irish Catholics and the British Labour Movement: a study with special reference to London, 1918–1970' (University of Kent MA thesis, 1979).

MacRaild, D.M., 'The Irish in North Lancashire and West Cumberland, 1850–1906: Aspects of the social history of Barrow-in-Furness and Cleator Moor and their hinterlands' (University of Sheffield PhD thesis, 1993).

Maguire, M.G.P., 'A Community at War: the Irish in Britain and the War of Independence' (University of Surrey PhD thesis, 1983).

Masson, U., 'The Development of the Irish and Roman Catholic Communities of Merthyr Tydfil and Dowlais in the Nineteenth Century' (University of Keele MA thesis, 1975).

McClelland, M., 'Early Educational Endeavour: A Study of the Work of the Hull Mercy Nuns, 1855–1930' (University of Hull MPhil thesis, 1993).

McFarland, E., 'The Loyal Orange Institution in Scotland, 1799–1900' (University of Glasgow PhD thesis, 1986).

Miskell, L., 'Custom, conflict and community: a study of the Irish in South Wales and Cornwall, 1861–91' (University of Wales PhD thesis, 1996).

Moore, K., '"This Whig and Tory-Ridden Town": Popular Politics in Liverpool, 1815–50' (University of Liverpool MPhil thesis, 1988).

O'Connor, B.J., 'The Irish Nationalist Party in Liverpool, 1873–1922' (University of Liverpool MA thesis, 1971).

O'Day, A., 'The Irish Parliamentary Party in British Politics, 1880–86' (University of London PhD thesis, 1971).

O'Leary, P., 'Immigration and Integration. A Study of the Irish in Wales, 1798–1922' (University of Wales PhD thesis, 1989).

Papworth, J.D., 'The Irish in Liverpool, 1835–71: Family Structure and Residential Mobility' (University of Liverpool PhD thesis, 1982).

Peavitt, H., 'The Irish, Crime and Disorder in Chester, 1841–1871' (University of Liverpool PhD thesis, 2000).

Pooley, C.G., 'Migration, mobility and residential areas in nineteenth-century Liver-
     pool' (University of Liverpool PhD thesis, 1978).
Quinn, J., 'The Mission of the Churches to the Irish in Dundee, 1846–86' (University
     of Stirling MLitt thesis, 1994).
Quirke, J., 'The Development of the Roman Catholic Community in Wolverhamp-
     ton, 1828–67' (Wolverhampton Polytechnic MA thesis, 1983).
Rafferty, O.P., 'The Church, the State, and the Fenian Threat, 1861–75' (University of
     Oxford PhD thesis, 1996).
Reid, C.A.N., 'The Chartist Movement in Stockport' (University of Hull MA thesis,
     1974).
Schofield, R.A., 'A Peculiar Tramping People ? Irish and long-distance British
     migrants in a northern English manufacturing town: Keighley, 1841–81' (Open
     University PhD thesis, 1990).
Scott, C. L., 'A Comparative Re-examination of Anglo-Irish Relations in Nineteenth-
     Century Manchester, Liverpool and Newcastle-Upon-Tyne' (University of
     Durham PhD thesis, 1998).
Sharpe, J., 'Reapers of the Harvest: the Redemptionists in the United Kingdom,
     1843–1898' (University of London PhD thesis, 1986).
Sloan, W., 'Aspects of the Assimilation of Highland and Irish Migrants in Glasgow,
     1830–70' (University of Strathclyde MPhil thesis, 1987).
Tebbutt, M.J., 'The Evolution of Ethnic Stereotypes: An examination of stereotyping,
     with particular reference to the Irish in Manchester during the late nineteenth
     century' (University of Manchester MPhil thesis, 1982).
Tennant, L.M., 'Ulster Emigration, 1851–1914' (University of Ulster MPhil thesis,
     1989).
Treble, J.H., 'The place of the Irish Catholics in the social life of the North of England,
     1829–51' (University of Leeds PhD thesis, 1969).
Savage, D.C., 'The General Election of 1886 in Great Britain and Ireland' (University
     of London PhD thesis, 1958).
Summers, V.M., 'Irish Life and Criminality in Perspective: A Study of Cardiff,
     c.1840–1920' (Open University MA thesis, 1999).
Wolffe, J., 'Protestant Societies and Anti-Catholic Agitation in Great Britain,
     1829–1860' (University of Oxford PhD thesis, 1985).
Woolaston, E.P.M., 'The Irish Nationalist Movement in Great Britain, 1886–1908'
     (University of London MA thesis, 1958).
Ziesler, K.I., 'The Irish in Birmingham, 1830–1970' (University of Birmingham PhD
     thesis, 1989).

Index